IMAGES
of America

HOLLYWOODLAND

I0806141

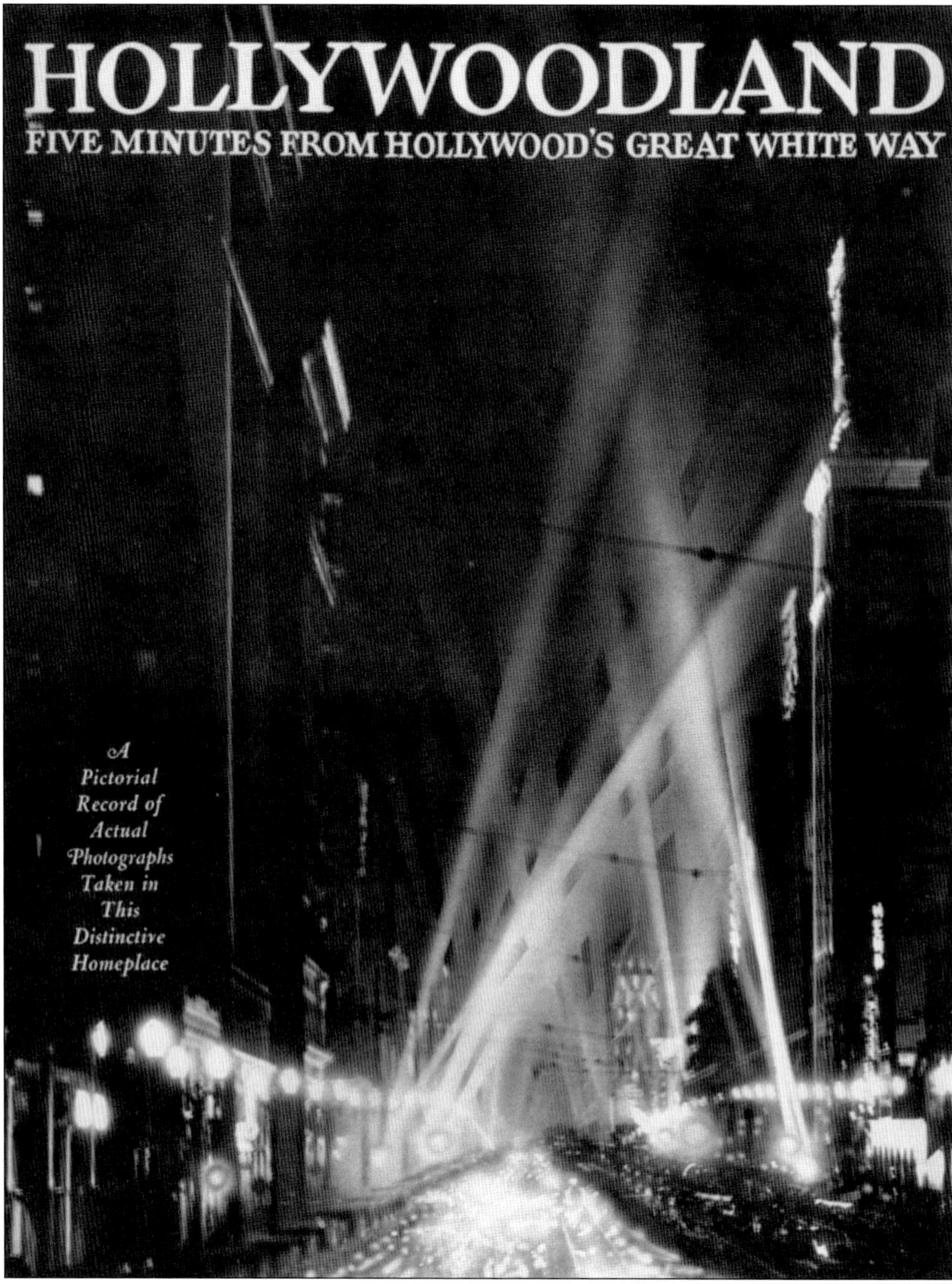

The Hollywoodland advertising department wrote the elaborate 16-page rotogravure brochure *Hollywoodland: Five Minutes from Hollywood's Great White Way* in 1925, releasing it under the name of Hollywoodland's lead developer, S.H. Woodruff. It contained letters and quotes from residents speaking to its benefits, as well as a smorgasbord of photographs documenting the homes, amenities, and views offered in the division. (Allison Francis.)

ON THE COVER: Surveyors perched on the top of Bronson Canyon measure the iconic Hollywoodland sign located at the top of Beachwood Canyon, Hollywood, California. (Bison Archives.)

IMAGES of America

HOLLYWOODLAND

Mary Mallory
and Hollywood Heritage, Inc.

ARCADIA PUBLISHING

Copyright © 2011 by Mary Mallory and Hollywood Heritage, Inc.
ISBN 978-0-7385-7478-3

Published by Arcadia Publishing
Charleston, South Carolina

Printed in the United States of America

Library of Congress Control Number: 2010941639

For all general information, please contact Arcadia Publishing:
Telephone 843-853-2070
Fax 843-853-0044
E-mail sales@arcadiapublishing.com
For customer service and orders:
Toll-Free 1-888-313-2665

Visit us on the Internet at www.arcadiapublishing.com

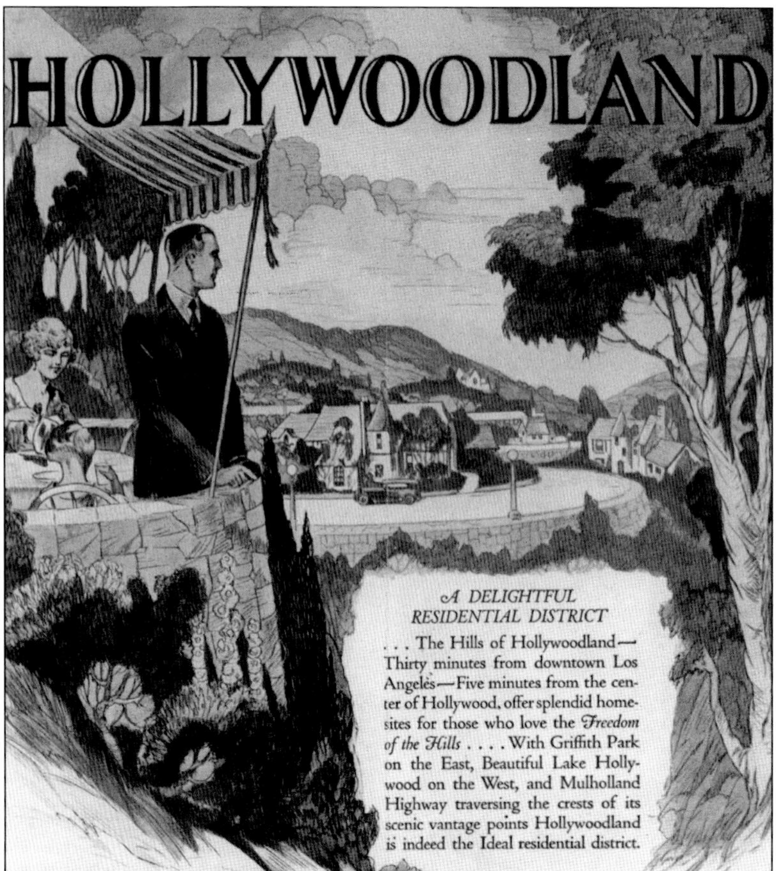

This early Hollywoodland brochure spoke to the discerning homebuyer looking to find a quality home in a superb environment. It promoted the fairy tale nature of the project, as it stated that every home controlled its own domain and also featured unparalleled views over much of the Southland. The homes blended harmoniously with nature. (Hollywood Heritage, Inc.)

Contents

Acknowledgments

This volume is based upon photographs in Hollywood Heritage's S.H. Woodruff, Hollywood Homeowners Association, and Edward Cohan Collections, as well as photographs from Bison Archives (Bison), the Margaret Herrick Library of the Academy of Motion Picture Arts and Sciences (AMPAS), the author's collection (MM), Jim Dawson, Tommy Lamey, Richard Adkins, and Allison Francis. Unless otherwise noted, all images appear courtesy of Hollywood Heritage, Inc.

I would like to thank the Board of Hollywood Heritage for their support and assistance during this project: Richard Adkins, Robert S. Birchard, Bob B. Blue, Claire Bradford, Amy Condit, Bryan Cooper, Brian Curran Jr., Margot Gerber, Laurie Goldman, George Kiel, Christy McAvoy, Alan Simon, Jeff Stutts, Stan Taffel, Hillsman Wright, and Valerie Yaros. The staff at the Margaret Herrick Library has been most helpful, especially Matt Severson, Faye Thompson, Sue Guldin, Allison Francis, Michael Tyler, Libby Wertin, Kristine Krueger, Jenny Romero, Barbara Hall, and Susan Oka. Marc Wanamaker has been very generous with his help and support for this project. Other people who have provided support, help, and information include Karie Bible, Joan Myers, Donna Hill, Mark Vieira, Mike Hawks, Eve Golden, Susan Pinsky, David Starkman, Jim Dawson, James Zeruk Jr., Christine O'Brien, Gaelyn Whitley Keith, and Fran Offenhauser. I would like to add a thank-you to all the early stillsmen who took the magnificent photographs that appear in this volume. Without them, this history would be incomplete. I especially would like to thank my parents, Gene and Lou Mallory, for their love, guidance, and support.

Introduction

This is the story of a real estate subdivision more famous for its giant advertising sign than for its elegant architecture. Hollywoodland, the first themed hillside home development in the United States, built at the top of Beachwood Canyon in Hollywood, California, contains one of the world's most famous icons, the Hollywood sign. Tracy E. Shoults and S.H. Woodruff, the developers, envisioned Hollywoodland as an elegant throwback to old California.

The two men joined a partnership led by transportation moguls E.P. Clark and M.H. Sherman and the *Los Angeles Times* publisher Harry Chandler to subdivide and develop property in Beachwood Canyon in the spring of 1923. Shoults died suddenly of a heart attack in July 1923, and Woodruff was promoted to head developer.

In April 1923, Shoults and Sherman hired architect John L. DeLario to head the Hollywoodland design team. DeLario also favored the look and feel of Spanish and Mediterranean homes in Southern California but updated for more modern sensibilities. He called this type of home California Renaissance. Architectural styles were limited to only four: English Tudor, French Normandy, Mediterranean, and Spanish.

Style was important; developers painted Hollywoodland as an elegant, exclusive enclave affordable to the middle classes. Details mattered as well; granite retaining walls, terraces, and stairs created a peaceful fairy tale ambiance, as did the storybook homes built into the area's dramatic hills.

Special amenities catered to a more upscale buyer looking for a lifestyle package: recreational and sports opportunities, landscaping and gardens, and a small local shopping center.

The Hollywoodland sales team was one of the first to recognize the value and importance of new media in promoting the project. They invited newsreel cameramen to record demolition and construction, formed radio bands to gain free advertising opportunities, invited equestrian groups to ride through the neighborhood, and created elegant rotogravure brochures.

The developers also understood the importance of creating a unique brand and quickly established one with their enormous calling card, a 480-foot-long series of letters spelling out the word "Hollywoodland" day and night, visible for miles.

All these unique qualities attracted artists, bohemians, and successful businessmen to buy, build, and live in the restricted neighborhood.

In 1927, Woodruff formed a new real estate syndicate to buy and develop property at Dana Point, California, a small town bordering the Pacific Ocean south of Laguna Beach. He and most of his major staff focused their attention on Dana Point, while also continuing selling in Hollywoodland. The stock market crash ultimately doomed the Dana Point development and Hollywoodland, forcing Woodruff to turn the undeveloped property in Hollywoodland back to M.H. Sherman in the mid-1930s.

The press continued to refer to the neighborhood as Hollywoodland into the 1940s, in advertisements for apartments and stories about residents, but began referring to it as Beachwood Canyon in more serious news stories. New homes arose in barren spots on the hillsides, creating a more densely packed neighborhood. While the name Beachwood did not possess the cachet of Hollywoodland, the area became even more visible and well known.

More celebrities moved into the neighborhood while maintaining their privacy, thanks to its very hillside location. Others seemed to go out of their way to court publicity. Many also frequented the Beachwood Village coffee shop and market.

The ultimate representative of the neighborhood is the Hollywood sign, an international icon that denotes Hollywood and its filmmaking machine. Seldom photographed until nearly destroyed in the 1940s from lack of maintenance, the sign soon gained popularity before regularly appearing in print, television, and film. Filming became a regular part of life in the canyon by the 1970s, popularizing the area. Swarms of tourists clog the streets daily looking for access to the sign.

While the name Hollywoodland seems almost forgotten and seldom used today, its storied past lives on in the architecture and history of the current Beachwood Canyon, connoting the quiet charm and beauty of Hollywood's premiere 1920s hillside housing development.

One

The Magnificent Hills of Hollywoodland

Hollywood, California, was booming in the 1920s. Once a dusty little farming community, Hollywood was growing into a powerful economic force for Los Angeles County. Film studios of all shapes and sizes dotted the landscape, with more coming every day. Hotels and businesses thrived along Hollywood Boulevard. Employees of these organizations required homes nearby, and real estate development skyrocketed.

Transportation czars and real estate moguls E.P. Clark and M.H. Sherman decided to move ahead with subdividing their real estate tract at the top of Beachwood Canyon and sell plots to the public. Along with investors Harry Chandler, publisher of the *Los Angeles Times*; developer Tracy E. Shoults; and architect S.H. Woodruff, they announced in late March 1923 that their new development, called Hollywoodland, was open for business.

Clark and Sherman, early transplants from Arizona, had virtually cornered the Los Angeles trolley and streetcar business by the 1890s. They acquired large parcels of land adjacent to their planned routes for later subdividing into residential lots.

Chandler had led the *Los Angeles Times* since 1917, after joining the paper as a clerk in 1883. He acted as Southern California's largest press agent, employing the *Times* as the greatest booster of projects with which he was affiliated.

Shoults, a Southern California native, began selling real estate in Los Angeles in the late 1890s, rising to become one of the city's top real estate subdividers. In 1920, he began developing Marlborough Square, Windsor Heights, and Windsor Square near Larchmont and Wilshire Boulevards.

Shoults hired architect S.H. Woodruff as head designer for the real estate tracts after a career designing buildings in New York, San Francisco, and Los Angeles. Woodruff had a checkered legal career before he began working with the developer.

When Shoults dropped dead of a heart attack in July 1923, Woodruff was named the lead developer for the Hollywoodland project.

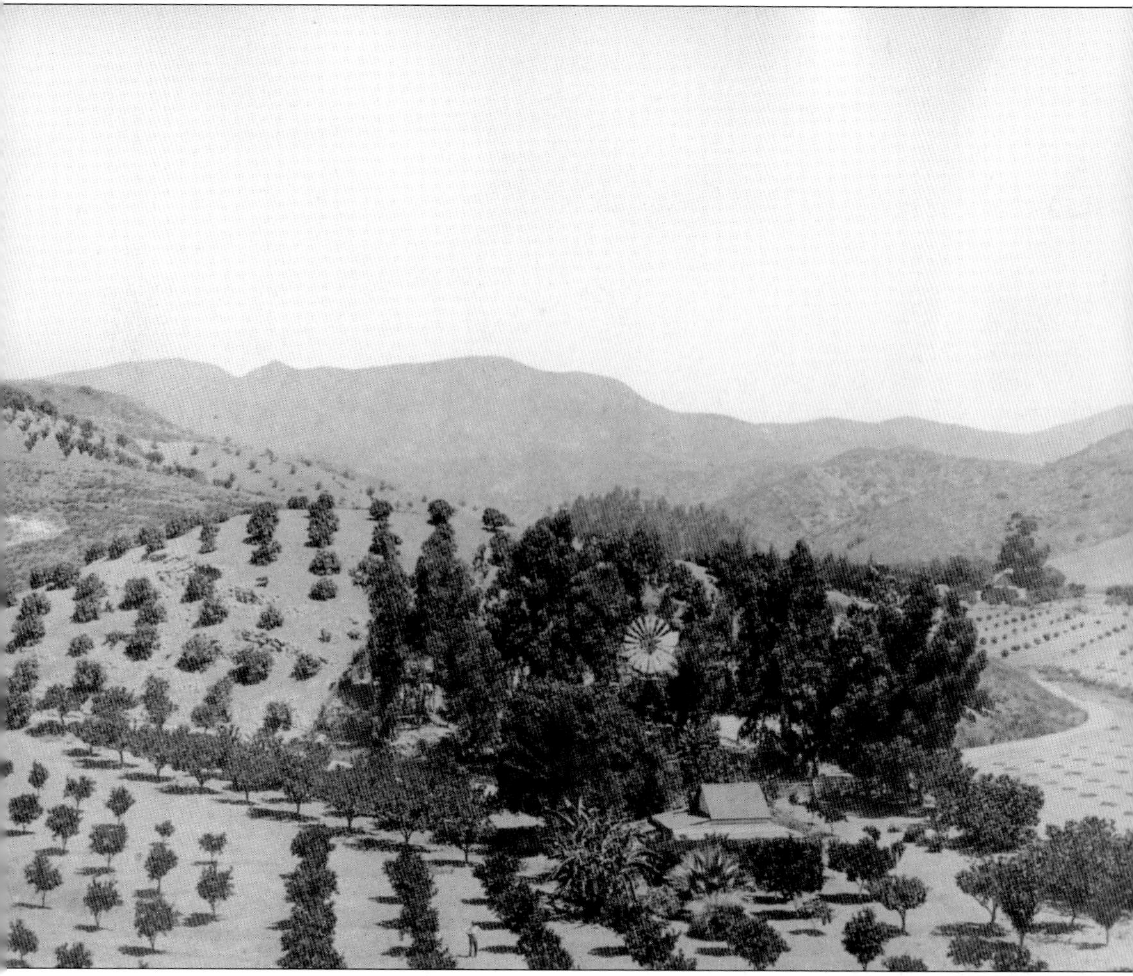

In early days, the area of Beachwood Canyon was either empty land or used for farming, as seen in the photograph, and did not exist on maps. The eastern half of what became Hollywoodland first appeared in records when the federal government issued a patent to the Southern Pacific Railroad on February 9, 1884. On September 26, 1890, the Railroad sold the land to Julia E. Lord for an undetermined amount, and four days later she leased it to Quong Yuen Chung "for the right to cut wood." Deeds for mining interests first appeared on December 12, 1893, but were terminated by court action in 1896. On February 8, 1900, Lord bought the western half of the Hollywoodland site from the federal government. As noted in a *Los Angeles Times* article dated December 22, 1968, she sold the entire 640 acres on July 8, 1905, to E.P. Clark and M.H. Sherman. (Bison.)

In 1880, Henry Claussen built a farmhouse, pictured center, on a hill overlooking a dirt road later named Beachwood Drive. It was located in an unnamed canyon later called Beachwood Canyon in honor of developer Albert Beach. The Claussen home still exists, in the 6100 block of Winans Drive, between Gower Street and Beachwood Drive. Formerly facing south, it was moved north on the property and rotated to face east. (Bison.)

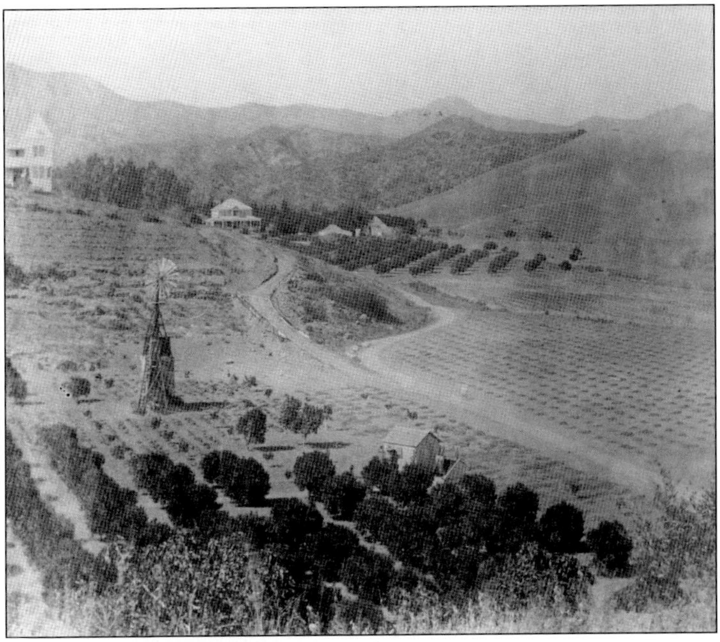

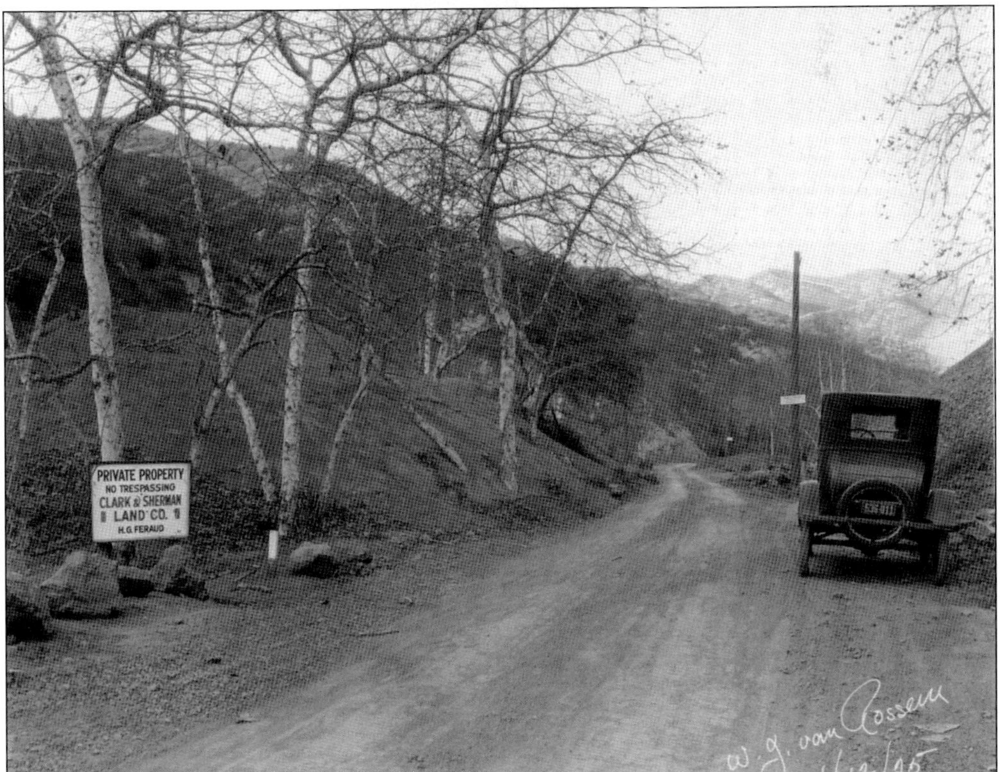

E.P. Clark and M.H. Sherman, brothers-in-law originally from Arizona, controlled the streetcar business in Los Angeles County and bought up land near their transportation lines for later redevelopment. From 1905 to 1923, they operated a rock and granite quarry on the future Hollywoodland site, pictured above, before beginning construction.

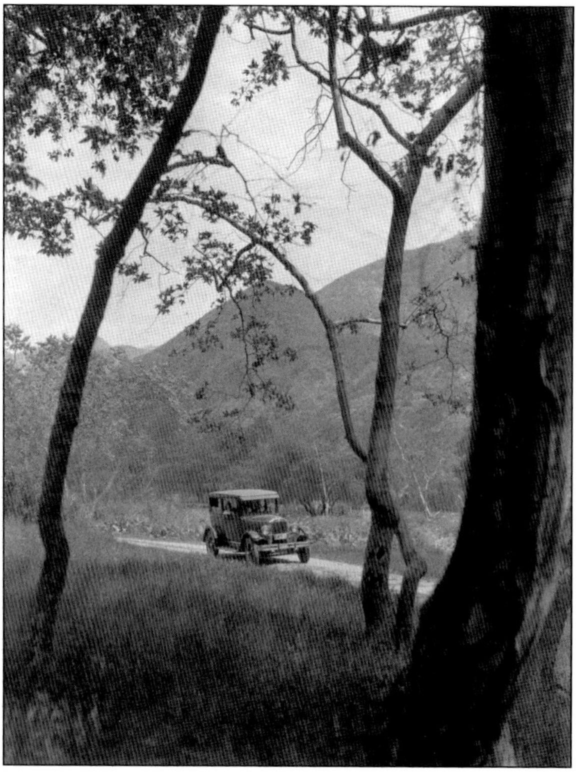

Unknown persons drive up Beachwood Canyon. Hollywood citizens used an almost natural amphitheater at the head of Beachwood Canyon to perform William Shakespeare's play *Julius Caesar* in honor of his 300th birthday in May 1916. A cast of hundreds, including Theodore Roberts, Tully Marshall, Tyrone Power, and Douglas Fairbanks, performed the play to an audience of thousands.

Two unidentified men pose in a car on a road near the top of the Hollywoodland property. Before development, the bucolic landscape was filled with oak trees, sage, ferns, wildflowers, poppies, and springs. The only inhabitants were such wild animals as foxes, coyotes, deer, rabbits, skunks, squirrels, raccoons, possums, snakes, and lizards.

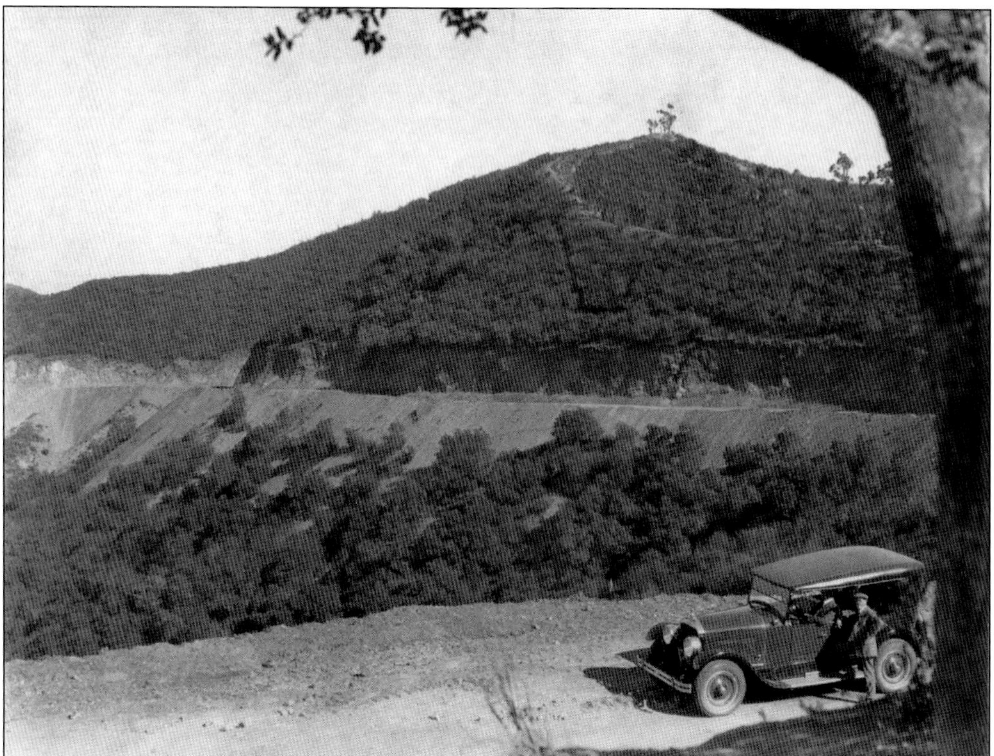

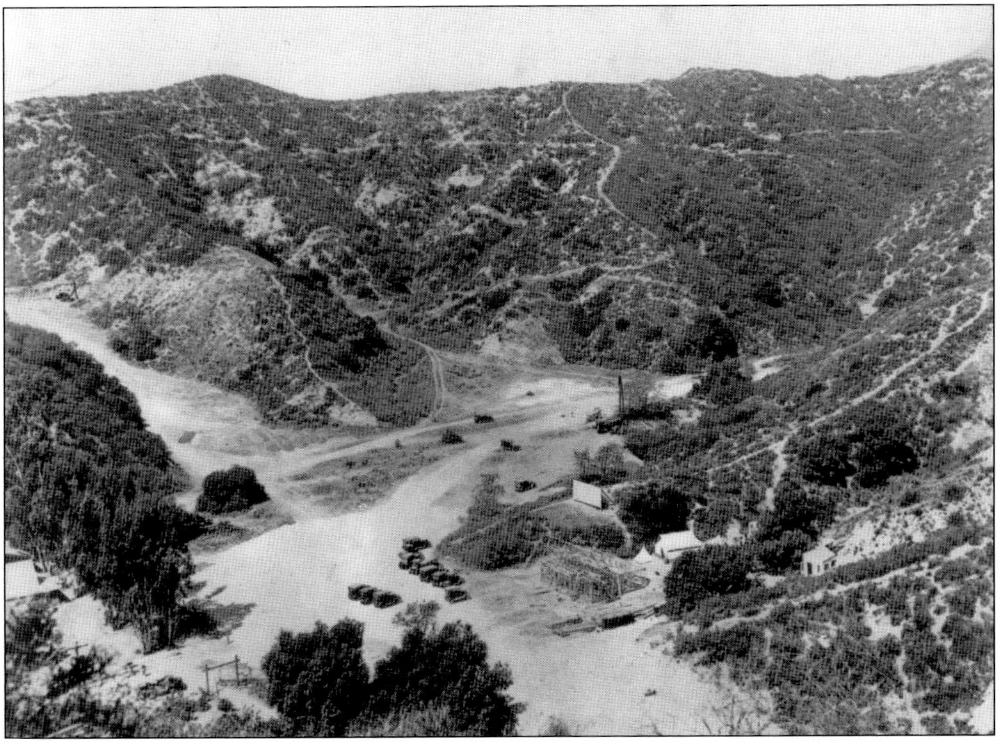

The Clark and Sherman Real Estate Company, and partners E.P. Clark, M.H. Sherman, Harry Chandler, Tracy E. Shoults, and S.H. Woodruff, announced on March 31, 1923, they would open the land for development. The sales office at 2700 North Beachwood Drive is halfway constructed in the right center of the photograph. The present-day Beachwood Village occupies the land where the eucalyptus grove stands in the lower left.

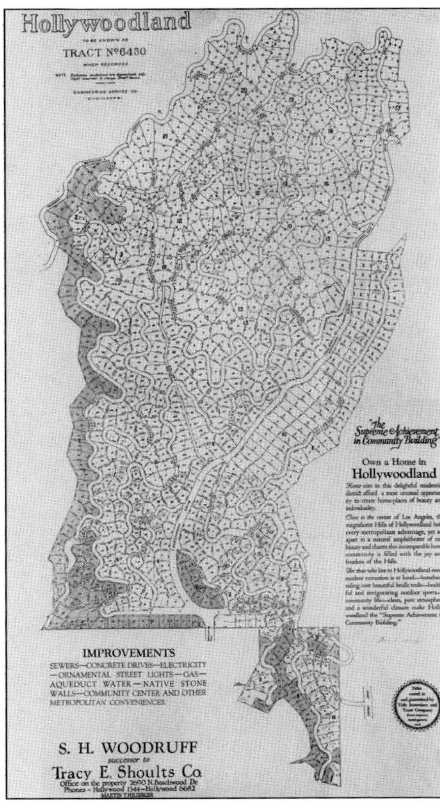

The tract map stated Hollywoodland was to be known as Tract No. 6450. S.H. Woodruff employed it as an advertisement to promote the size, scope, and uniqueness of the division. It listed the infrastructure improvements included in the development for potential residents, as well as the natural, health, and scenic benefits.

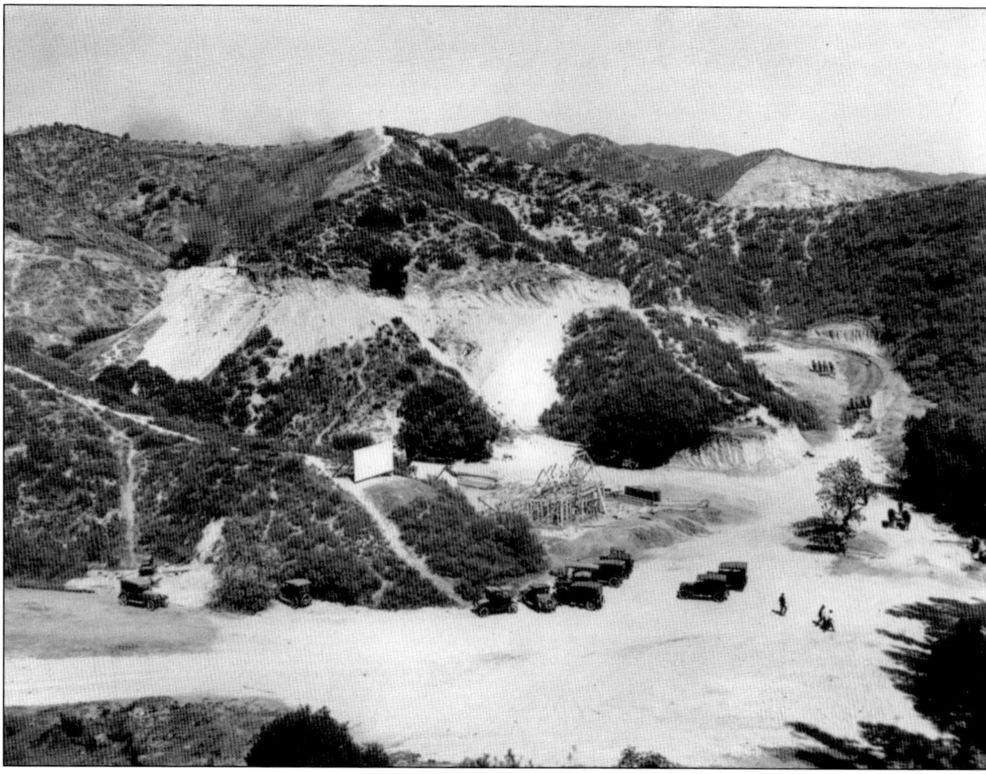

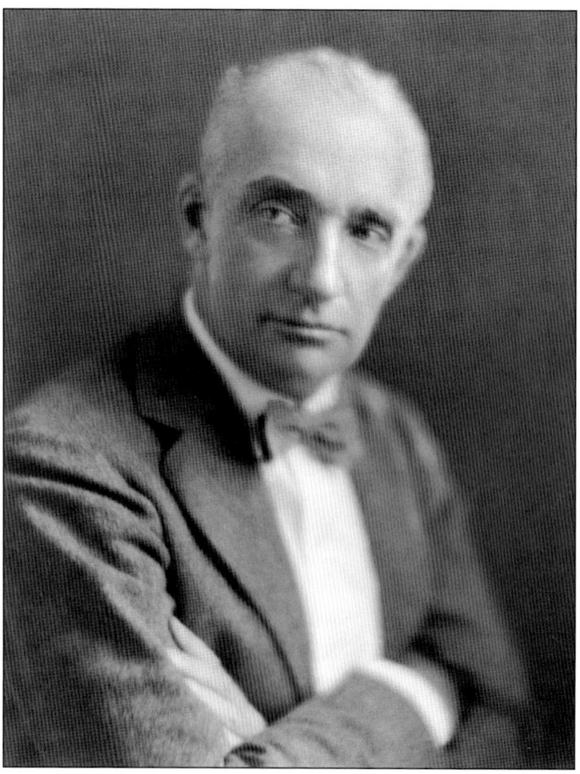

E.P. Clark and M.H. Sherman turned development over to Tracy E. Shoults and S.H. Woodruff because they had successfully sold and promoted Windsor Heights, Windsor Square, Marlborough Square, and West Hollywood Tract to upper middle class Angelenos. Construction continues on the sales office at 2700 North Beachwood Drive along with the smoothing of roads.

S.H. Woodruff was also a tinkerer working on inventions in his spare time. In 1917, he applied for a patent on an aerial torpedo with his working partner Lloyd Giles. Woodruff designed a portable radio in 1924 to entertain the equestrian Hollywoodland rangers. Weighing 40 pounds, it fit into saddlebags and was capable of picking up stations as far away as Chicago, Detroit, and Pittsburgh on a clear day.

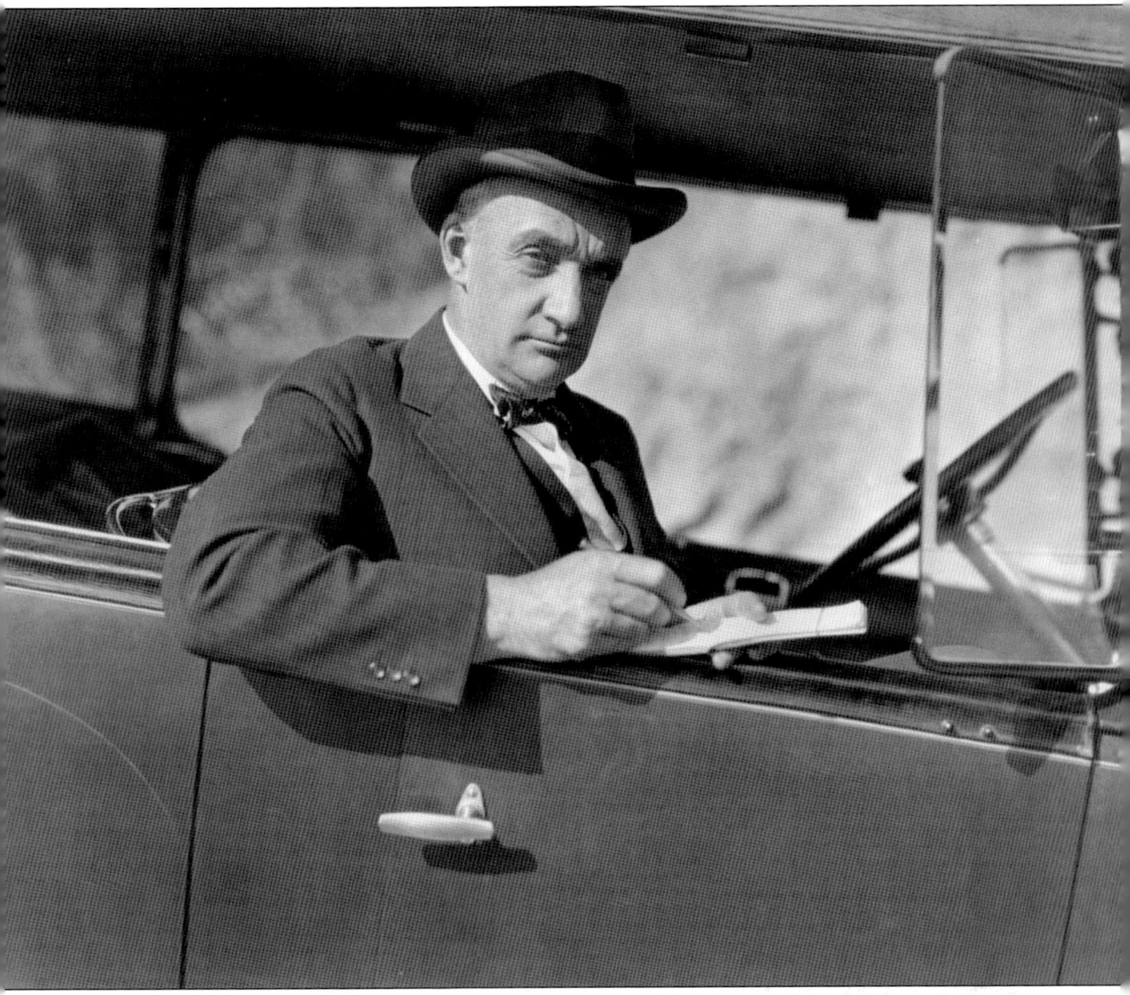

S.H. Woodruff's past was littered with complaints, criminal charges, and civil charges before he began working with Tracy E. Shoults at Windsor Square in 1920. Woodruff had worked successfully in drafting and as an architect around the country while also experiencing personal difficulties. He had been sued for back rent by a landlord in New York in 1909. A financier and building owner sued Woodruff in San Francisco for overstating his experience and for cost overruns on a hotel project near Union Square, a case that went to the California Supreme Court in 1912. He had also endured protests over a stone quarry in the Mission District of San Francisco. In 1919, Woodruff was arrested in Brentwood, California, on a federal charge of defrauding through the US Mail. He and a partner had sold land in Arizona to a buyer who had been promised notes at the post office after purchase, only to discover these notes were worthless. Charges were later dropped.

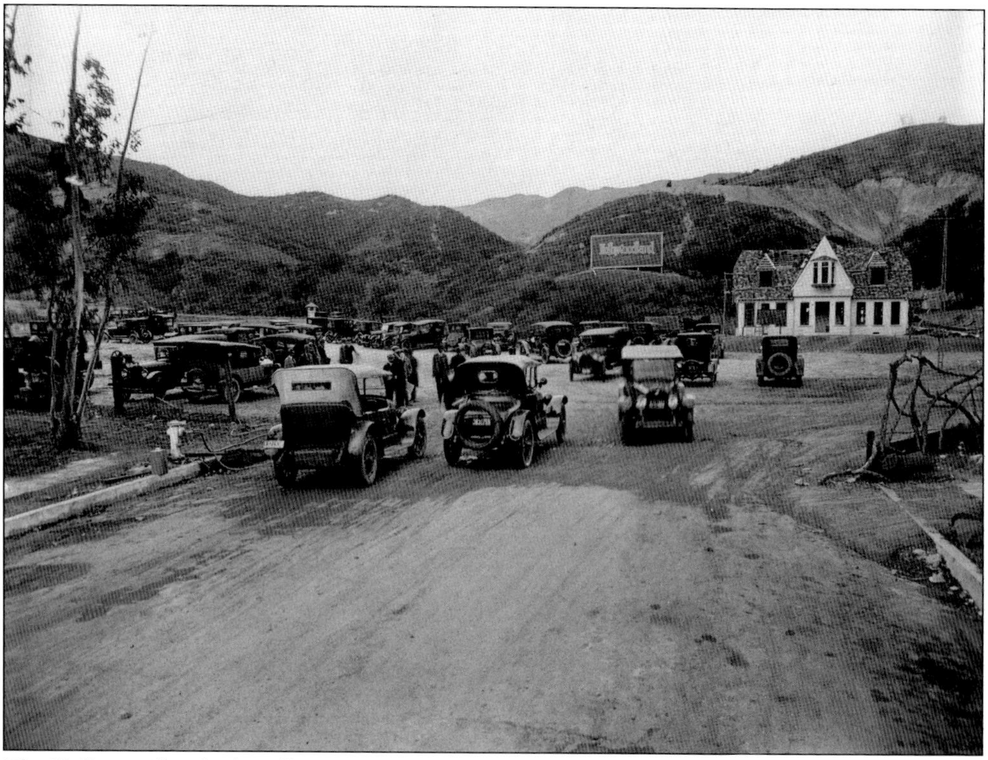

The Hollywoodland sales office at 2700 North Beachwood Drive is pictured as it nears completion. The first Hollywoodland sign is the billboard to the left of the building. Early construction work required horse- and mule-pulled wagons and men picking and shoveling their way through the steep and rocky hillside.

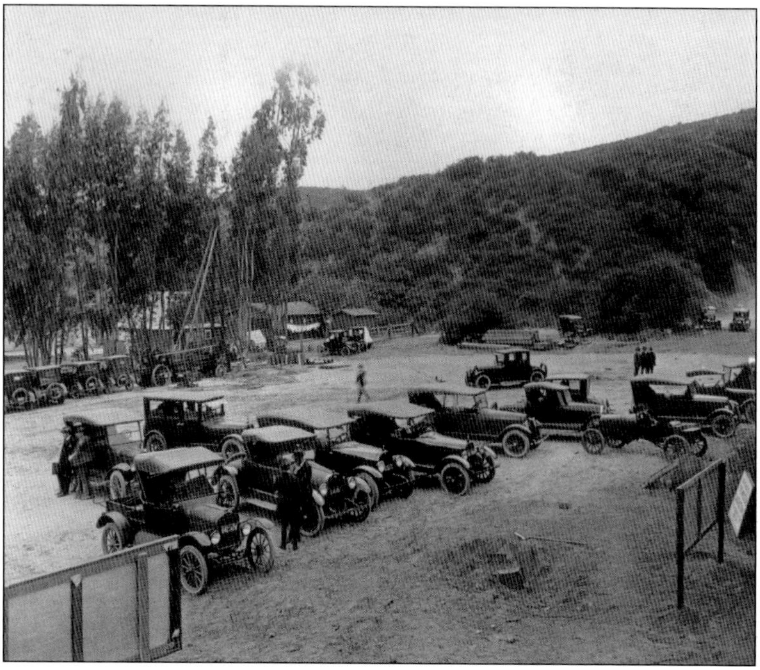

Construction crews parked their cars in front of the real estate office at 2700 North Beachwood Drive before going about their jobs in the subdivision. This area also became the parking location for visitors coming to view the construction process. The Hollywoodland development team continually found great promotional hooks to bring in visitors.

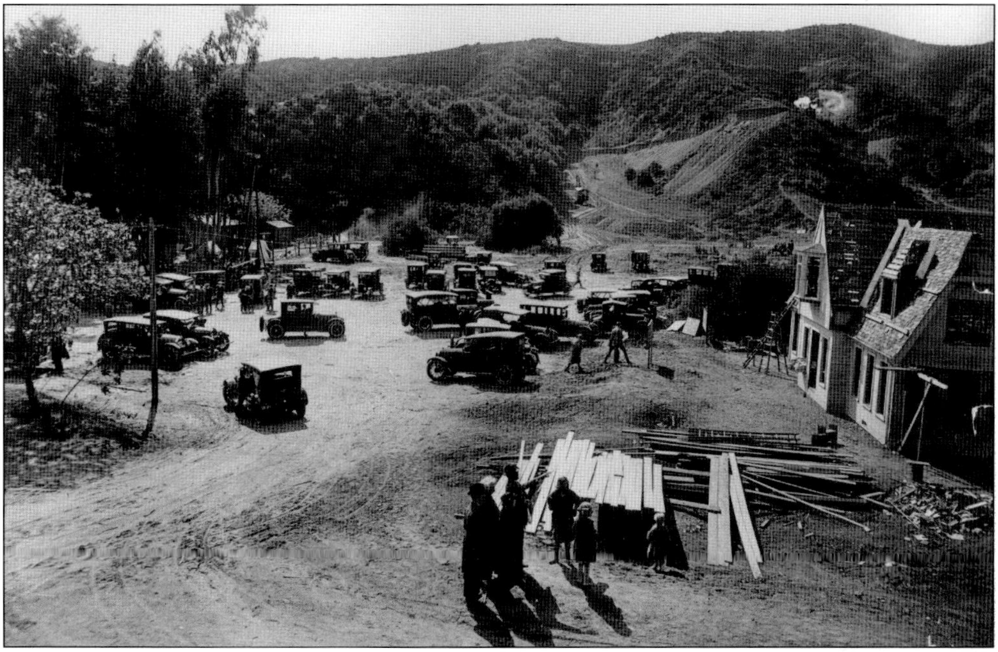

Western Construction Company, located at 127 North Larchmont Boulevard, built and designed homes throughout the West. They began constructing at Windsor and Marlborough Squares in 1920. The company was reorganized in 1923 with S.H. Woodruff as president, M.H. Sherman as vice president, and P.J. Lechner as general manager, later moving locations to 2690 North Beachwood Drive.

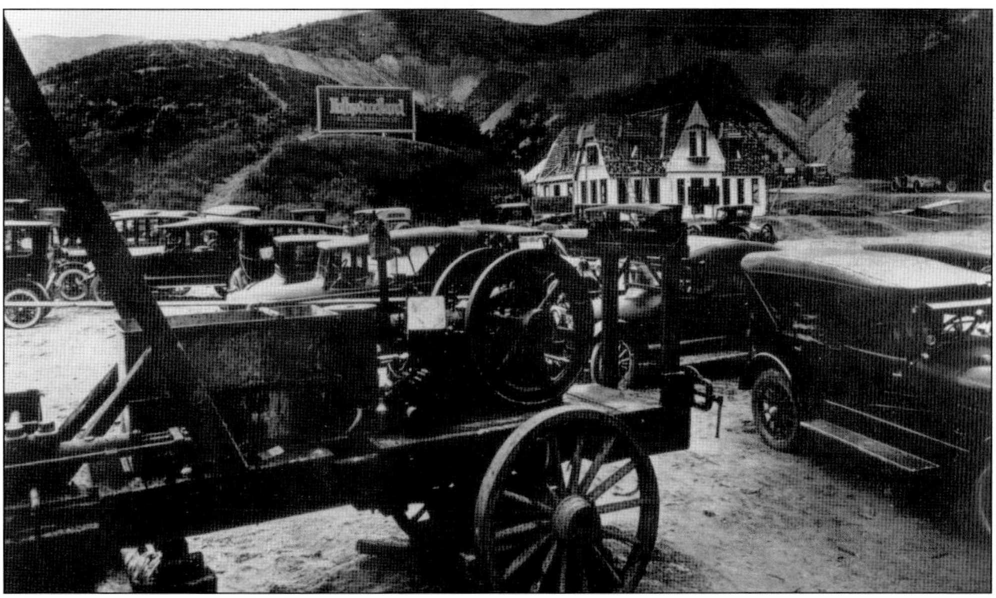

Western Construction Company successfully managed all elements of the construction process. They used rocks and granite from the nearby Clark and Sherman quarry as construction materials for walls, terraces, and homes. They employed their own crews from the other Tracy E. Shoults and S.H. Woodruff developments. The Hollywoodland sales office at 2700 North Beachwood Drive is at the right.

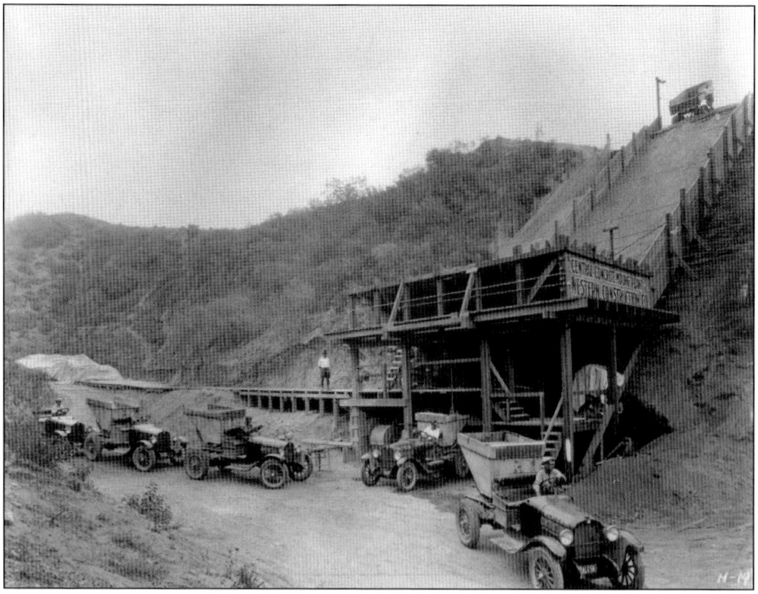

To speed the construction process, Tracy E. Shoults and S.H. Woodruff established their own concrete plant on Hollyridge Drive. Woodruff considered it more time effective and cost conscious to create concrete at the plant and then send small trucks up the hills to deliver slurry to the construction sites.

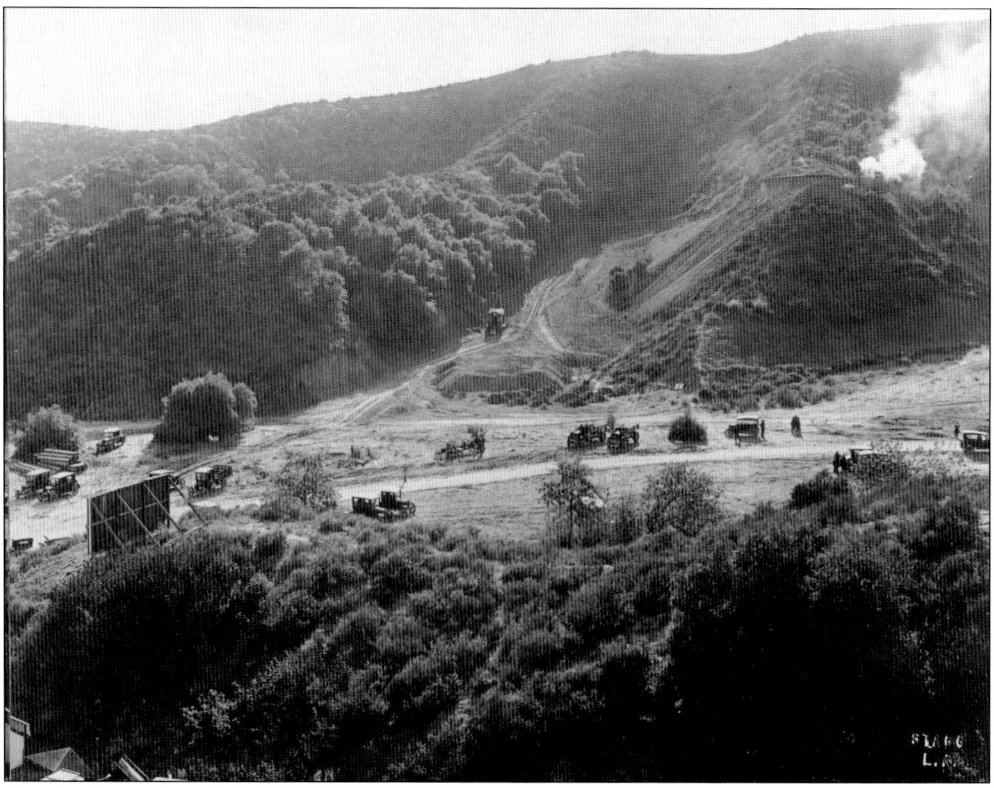

The Hollywoodland development team employed a fleet of five Dodge trucks from Graham Brothers to carry the concrete mixture up the hills to construction sites. These trucks were powerful enough to climb the steep grades but small enough to move quickly. The steep slope of Belden Drive can be seen as it is being constructed.

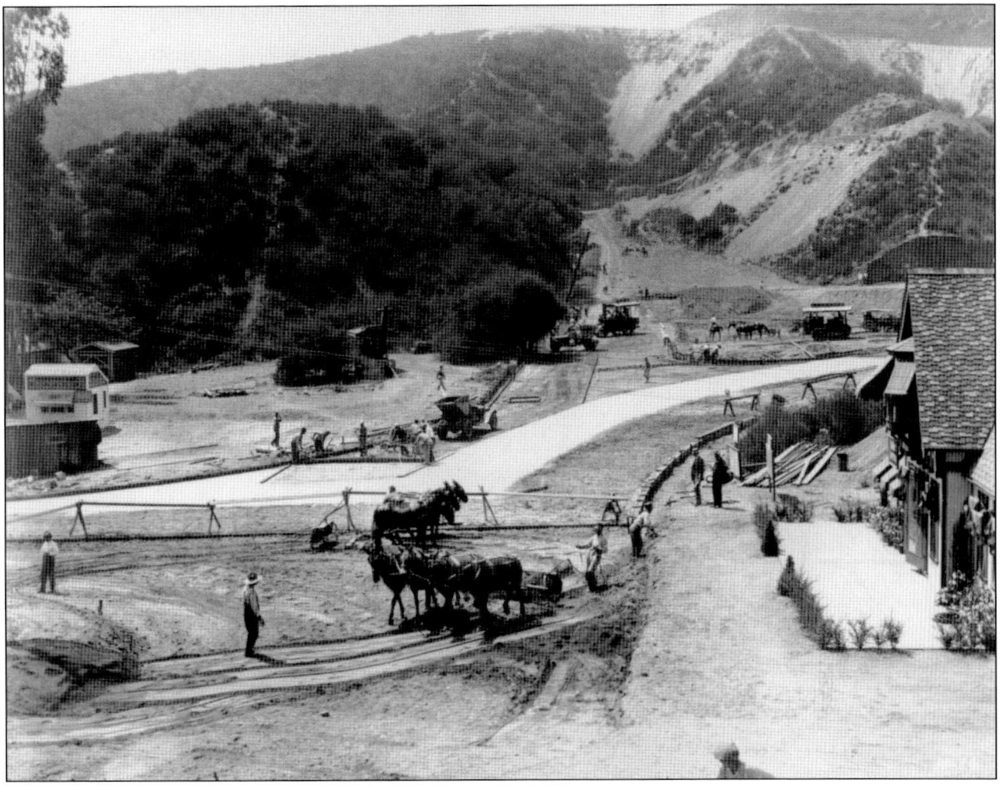

Initial work in building the roads often required demolition in the hills before men with pick axes and shovels dug up stones and granite. Steam shovels cut up large chunks of earth to create gentle grades. Men with pack animals smoothed out and packed the dirt before crews could lay the cement, as evidenced in this photograph outside the sales office at 2700 North Beachwood Drive.

After pack animals smoothed out the dirt, trucks brought in the concrete mixture. Near the intersection of Beachwood Drive and Belden Drive, the crew creates curbs and molds before pouring the concrete and working it in with shovels and tools. A large roller evened out the surface before a man checked to make sure the top was entirely level.

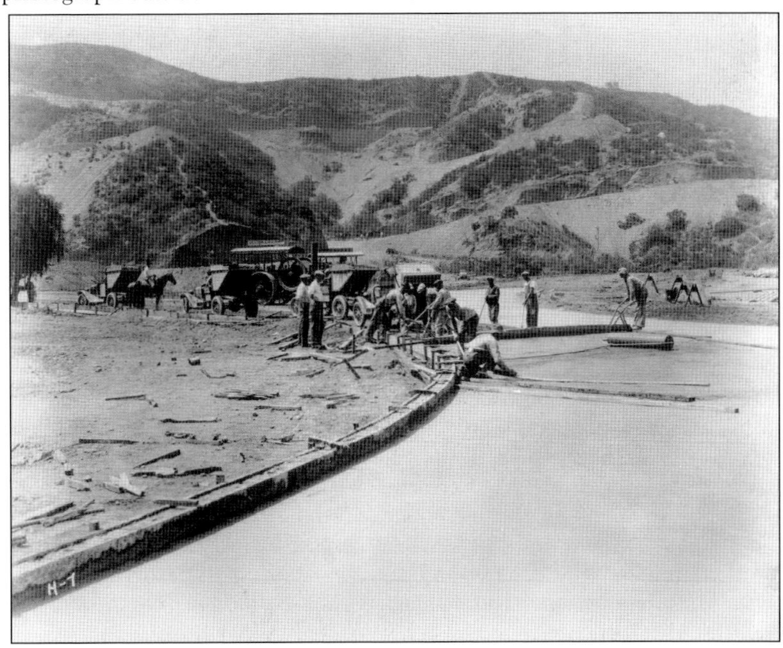

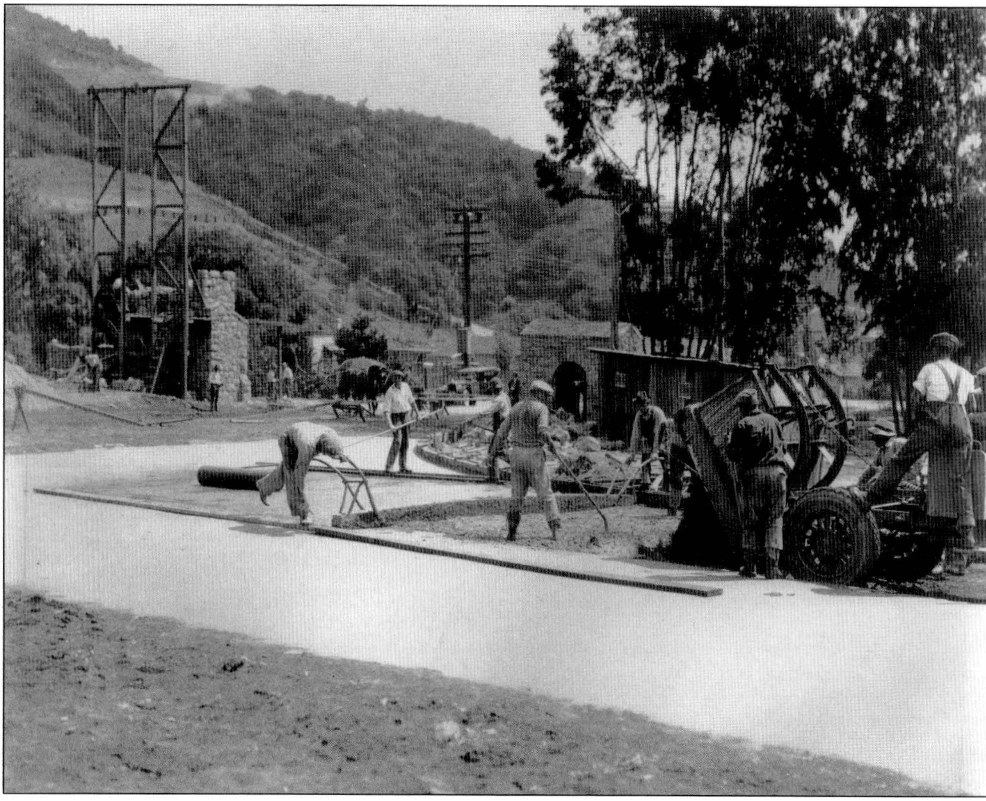

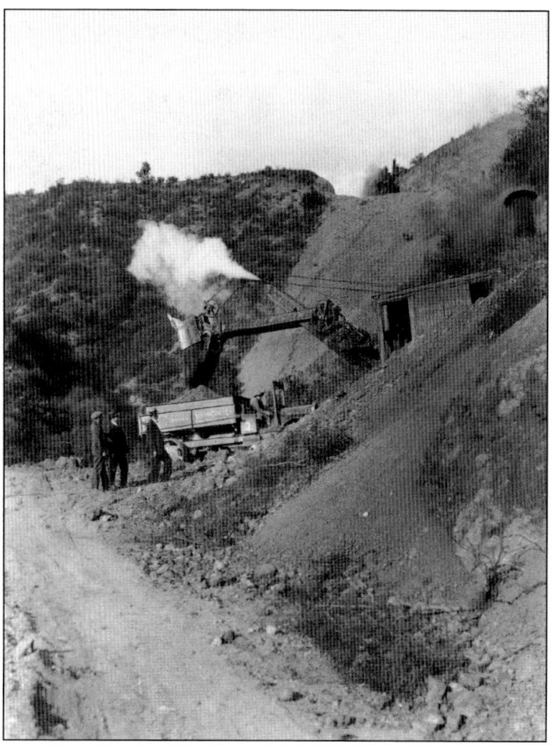

One crew lays and smoothes concrete as it builds Beachwood Drive north into the canyon. The crew in the background can be seen around the building platform as it constructs the stone entrance gate on the eastern side of Beachwood Drive. The rocks came from the onsite quarry as well as from demolition blasts.

Pictured from left to right, an unidentified man, L.J. Burrud, and S.H. Woodruff watch one of the Western Construction Company steam shovels chew up land as it completes an intersection of two Hollywoodland roads in 1923. After demolition of steep slopes, the shovels would create gentle, winding roads up the canyon to allow easier access by cars. (AMPAS.)

One of the steam shovels slowly works its way up Westshire Drive above the construction office. On the opposite side of the canyon, another shovel labors its way up Belden Drive. The gentle grades allowed easy access and construction but also created a more graceful appearance to the tract's streets.

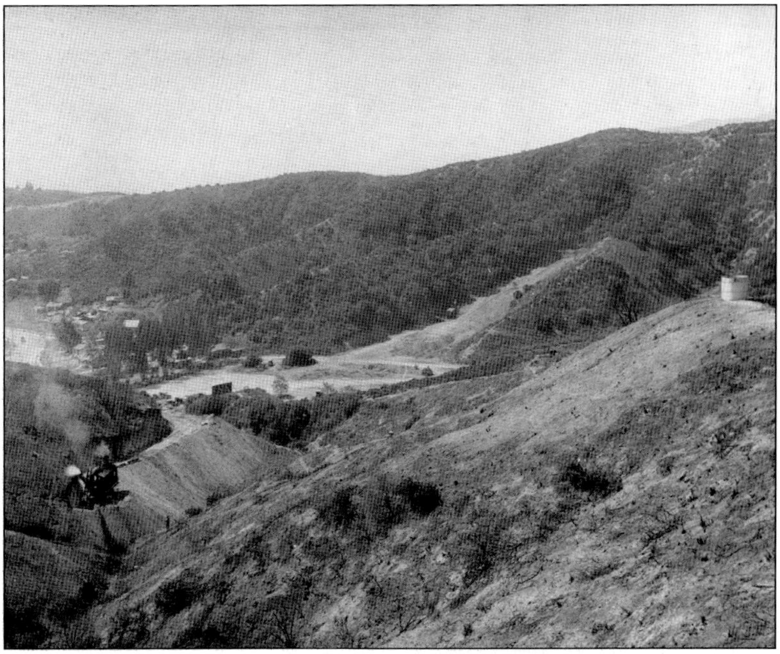

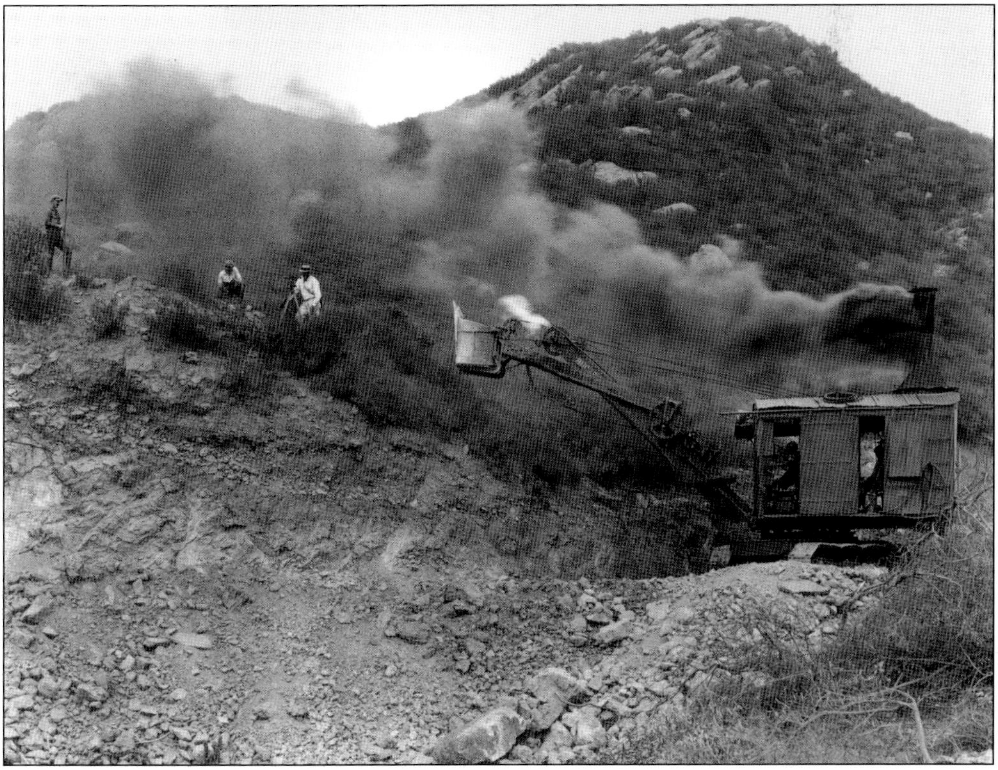

The Hollywoodland surveying team is pictured in action as they measure land to prepare maps and plans for the construction and development of the neighborhood's streets. Workers carefully examined the topography to ensure that the roads followed the natural contour of the land, which allowed for quicker and easier construction. (AMPAS.)

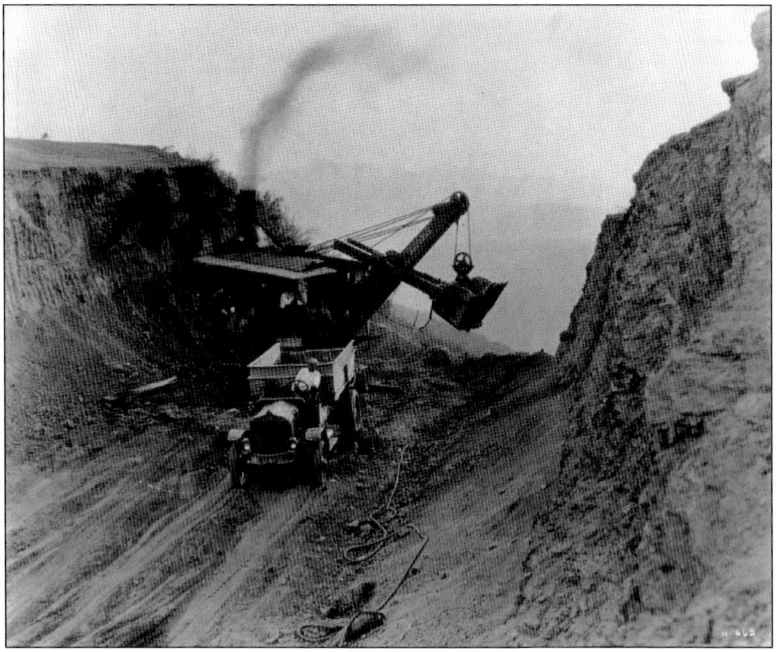

A steam shovel chews away the landscape as it helps prepare a road near the top of one of the hills. Roadwork was laborious, as crews found natural passes in the environment before blasting through the hill. Once that was completed and the men removed rocks and granite, the shovels ate their way through the hill.

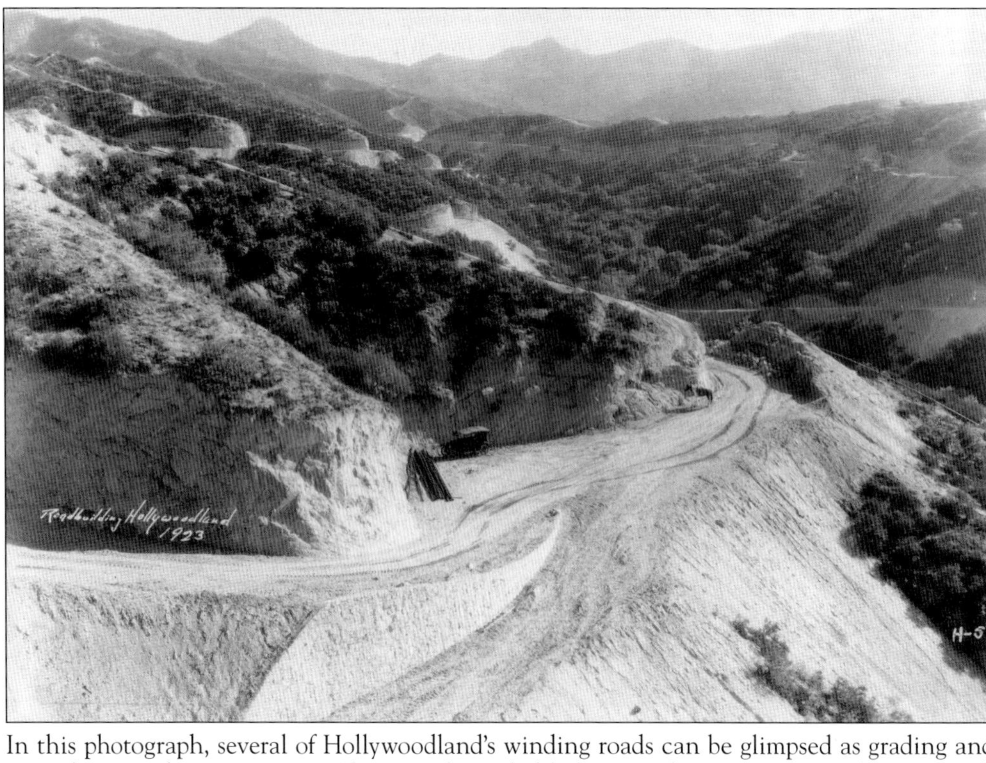

In this photograph, several of Hollywoodland's winding roads can be glimpsed as grading and smoothing work commences. Where roads circled ledges or wherever upper and lower roads converged, granite retaining walls were constructed to prevent landslides and maintain the integrity and strength of the construction work. Roads were built 26 feet wide.

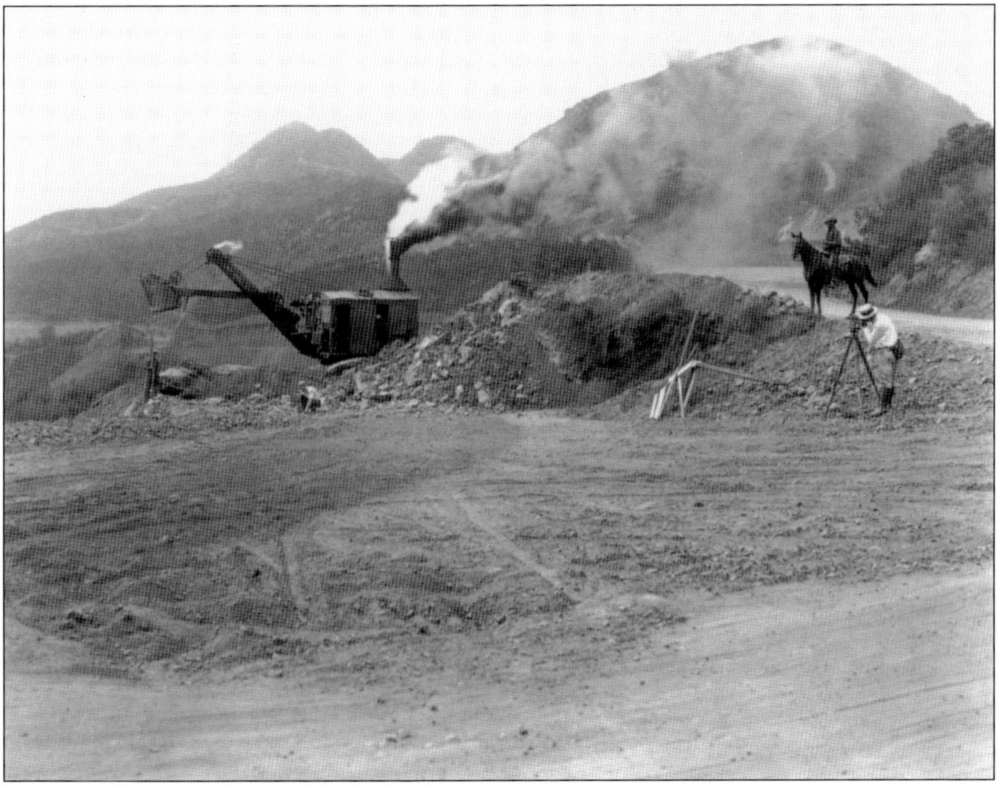

The unidentified surveyor and crew measure the grade of several converged roads high in the hills above Hollywoodland. Most streets possessed English names like Heather Drive, Ledgewood Drive, Rockcliff Drive, Westshire Drive, Rodgerton Drive, Woodshire Drive, Deronda Drive, Durand Drive, Flagmoor Place, Pelham Place, and Hollyridge Drive. Belden Drive and Lechner Place were respectfully named after a homeowner and the manager of Western Construction Company. (AMPAS.)

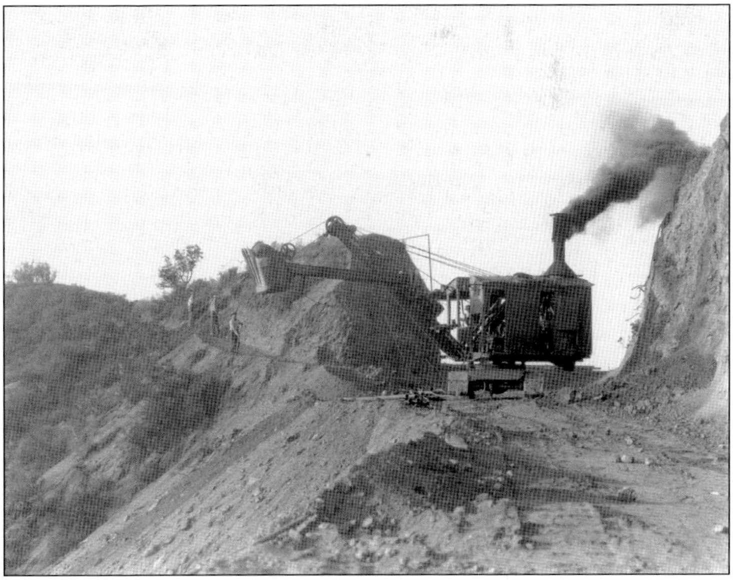

One of the steam shovels completes its work eating through one of the hills. Much of the dirt dug up was employed as filler to help smooth out and create road surfaces. The men pictured are taking the dirt dropped by the shovel and smoothing it out to create a pathway. (AMPAS.)

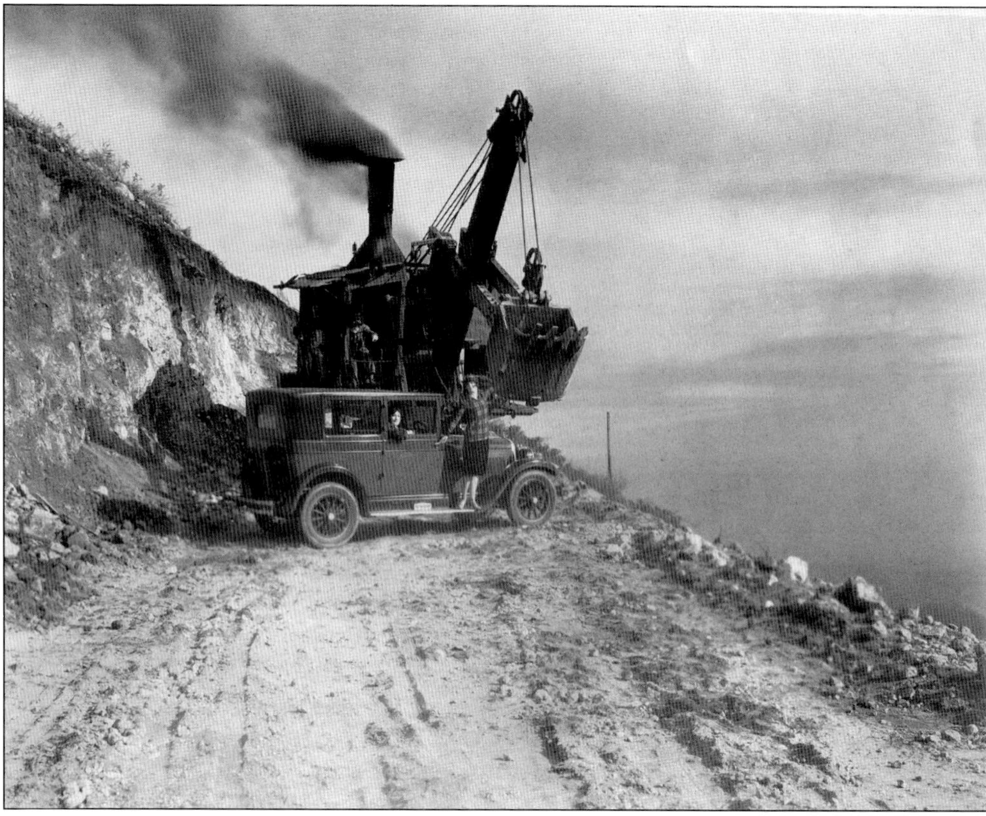

Two unidentified Mack Sennett starlets pose in front of one of the Hollywoodland steam shovels near the top of Beachwood Canyon. The Sennett stillsmen took a series of photographs throughout the development that were sent across the country to magazines and newspapers, promoting both the film company and the new real estate tract. (Bison.)

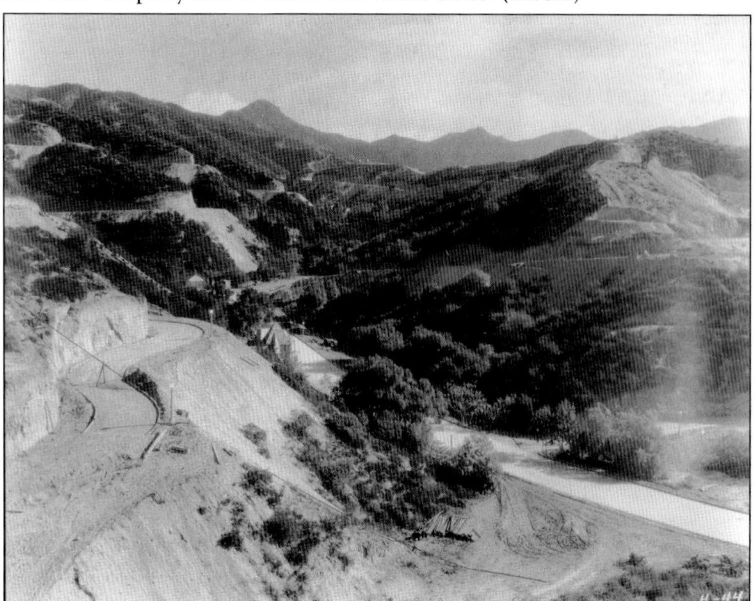

The first part of Beachwood Drive in the middle of the photograph is finished and ready. Other roads are in various stages of completion. Some have been cut, others have been graded, and some are smoothed out in preparation for concrete to be laid. Ornamental light posts also dot the landscape on lower roads.

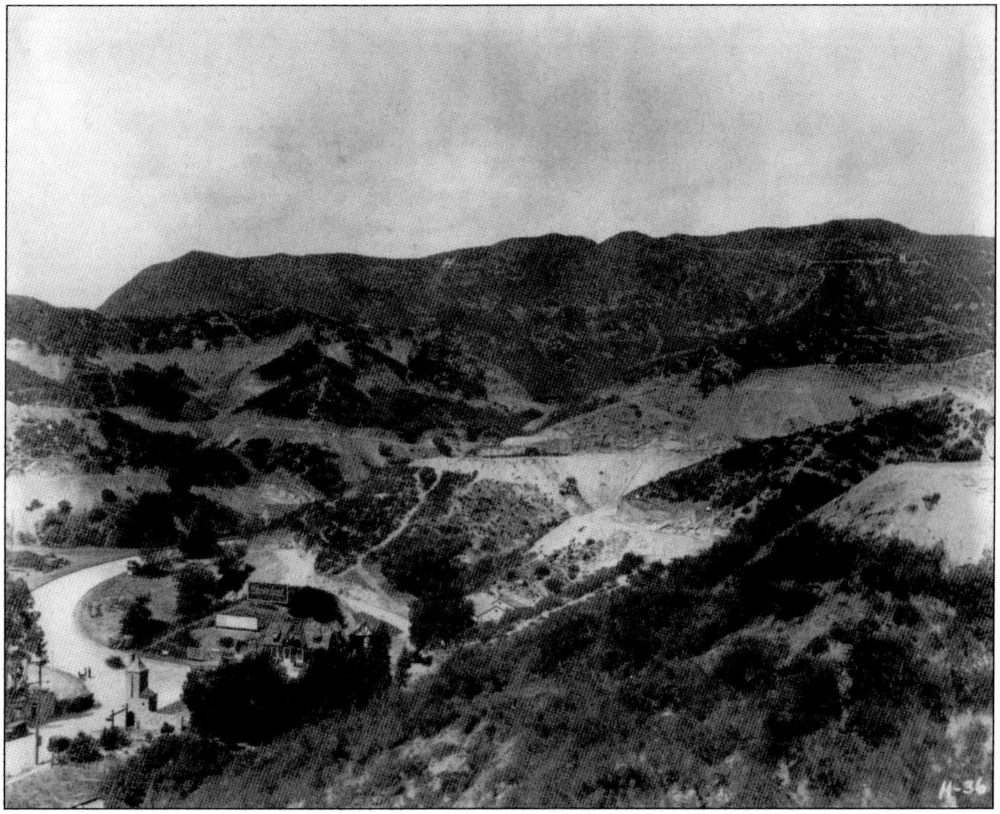

Looking north from a hillside below the Hollywoodland entrance, a temporary "H" at the right rests where the Hollywoodland sign will be constructed on the hill. The peak at the far left is Mount Cahuenga. The large "H" in the center represents the city of Hollywood and has no connection to the development.

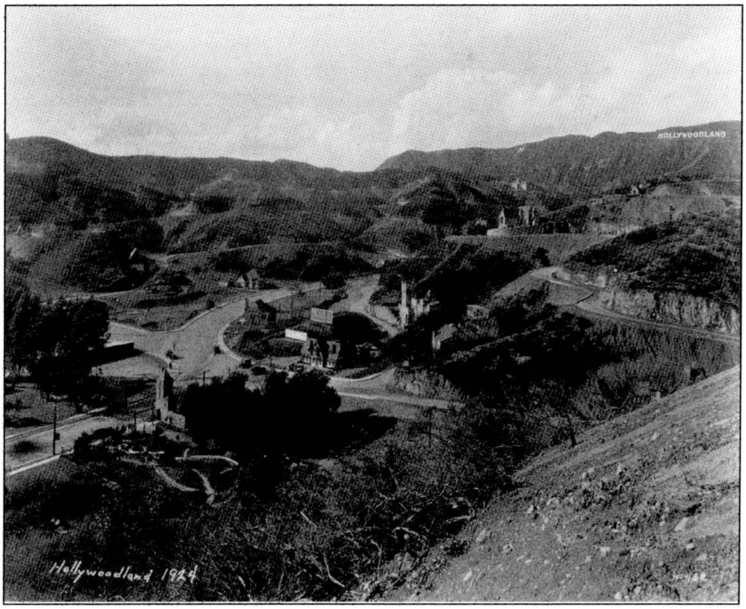

Looking north from a vantage point just off Pelham Place south of the entrance, part of the Hollywoodland tract can be seen. In the middle of the photograph is the completed real estate office with the Hollywoodland billboard beside it. The western gate of the entrance portal has yet to be completed.

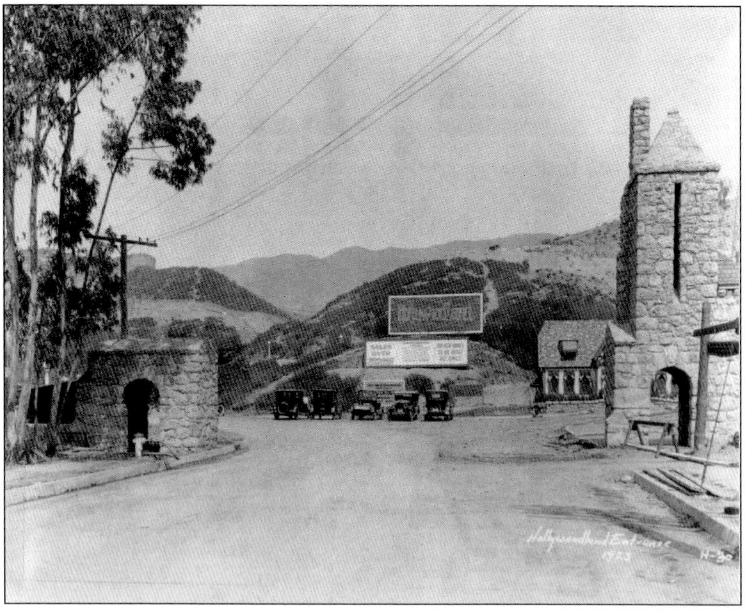

The Hollywoodland gates appear near completion at the subdivision's entrance in 1923. Just above them in the photograph is the Hollywoodland billboard and sales tally billboard, with the sales and construction office to the right. Developers originally intended for the gates to be guarded from 6:30 p.m. to 6:30 a.m. year round, but finances scuttled that idea.

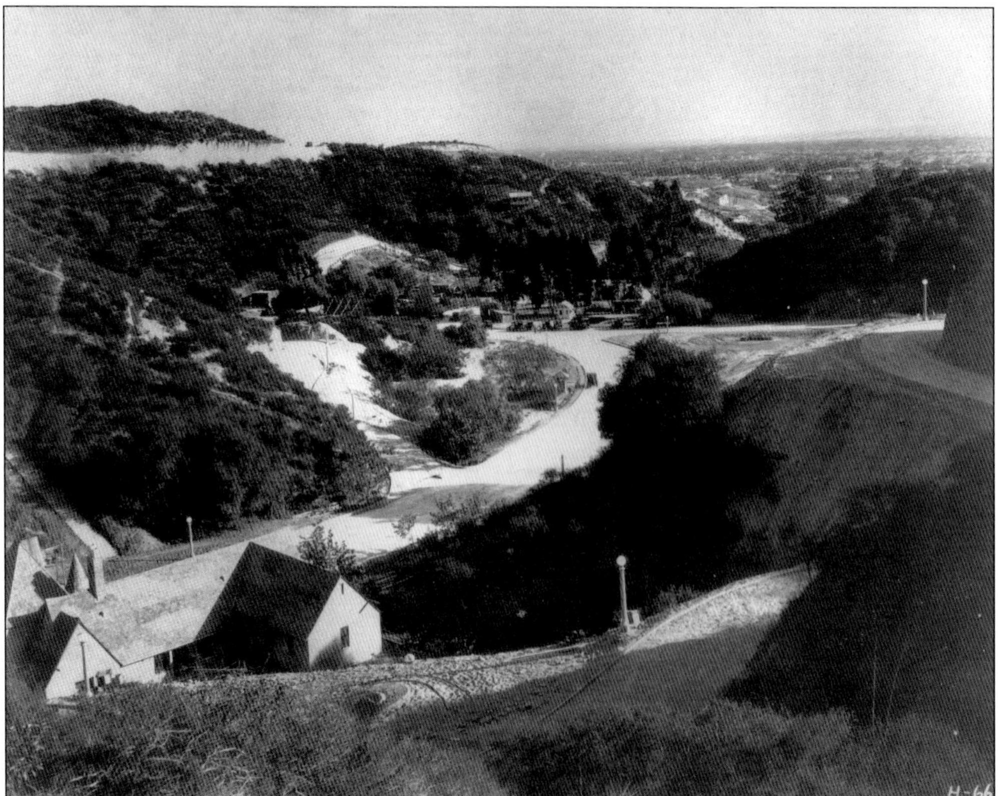

Here is a view of the Hollywoodland tract looking southwest from above Beachwood Drive and Rodgerton Drive. One of the neighborhood's stone staircases can be viewed in the bottom left of the photograph. Some of the small farmhouses in lower Beachwood Canyon can be viewed south of the Hollywoodland entrance.

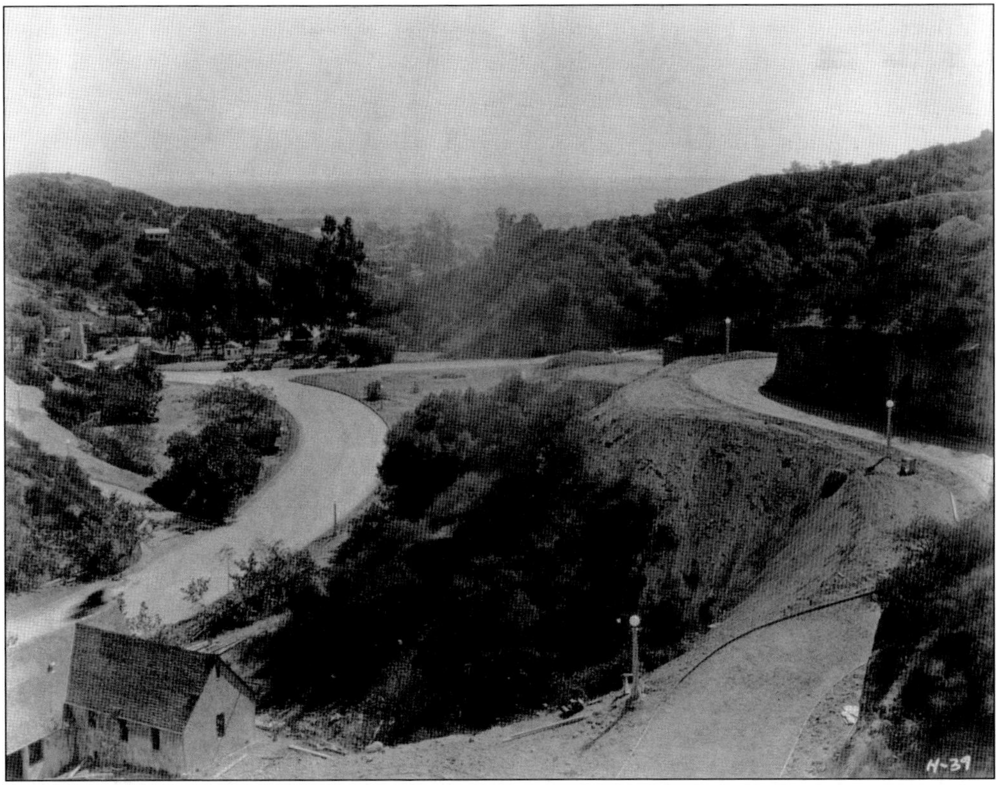

Looking south toward the farmhouses at the mouth of Beachwood Canyon and the city of Hollywood, the gates at the Hollywoodland entrance can be glimpsed along with part of the tract's billboard. Ornamental light posts dot Westshire Drive, Beachwood Drive in the center of the photograph, Belden Drive, and Rodgerton Drive.

Houses at Durand Drive, Heather Drive, Ledgewood Drive, Rodgerton Drive, and Rockcliff Drive are in the process of being constructed. The house at top left is the Felix Adler residence. Each home looms over the landscape with views in many directions. Brochures touted Hollywoodland as a "superb environment without excessive cost."

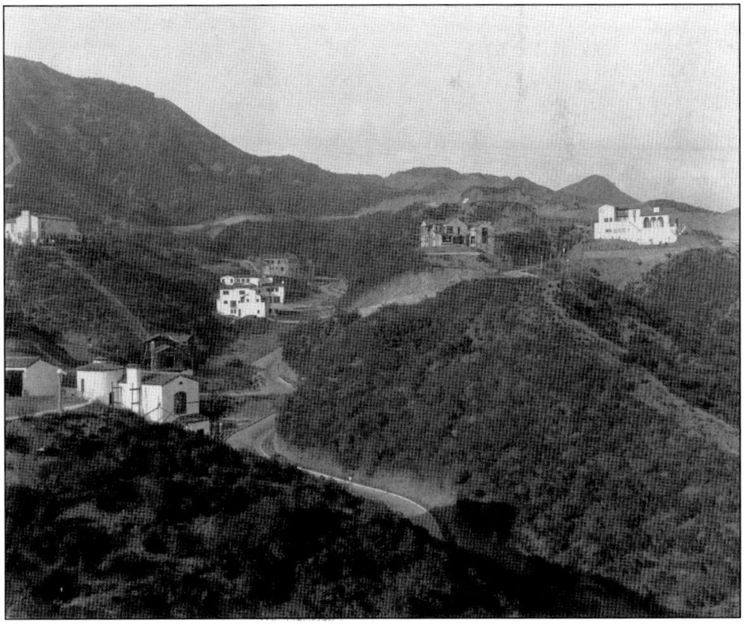

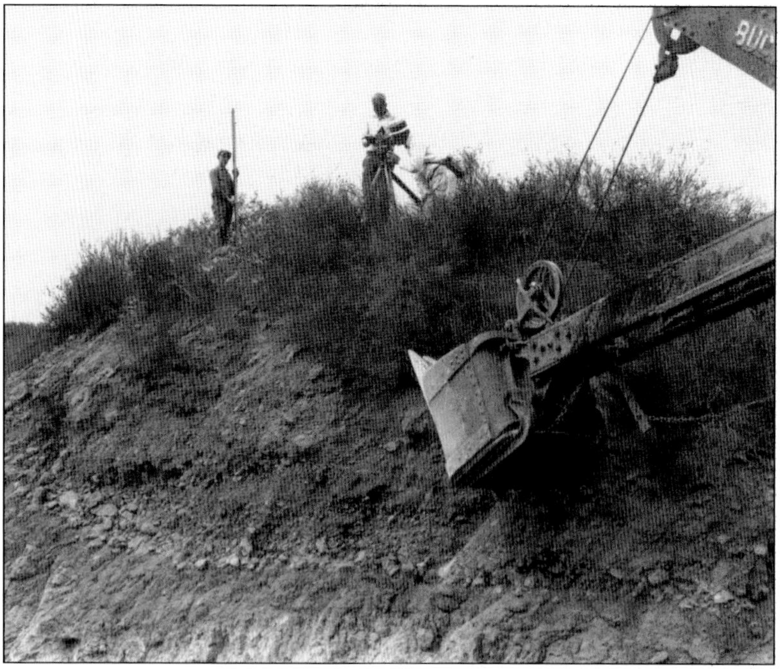

The engineering team prepares the way for construction on the road to the proposed Mack Sennett house in 1925. The Sennett house was scheduled to be built at the very top of the development on the promontory directly above the Hollywoodland sign, visible to both the San Fernando Valley and Hollywood sides. (AMPAS.)

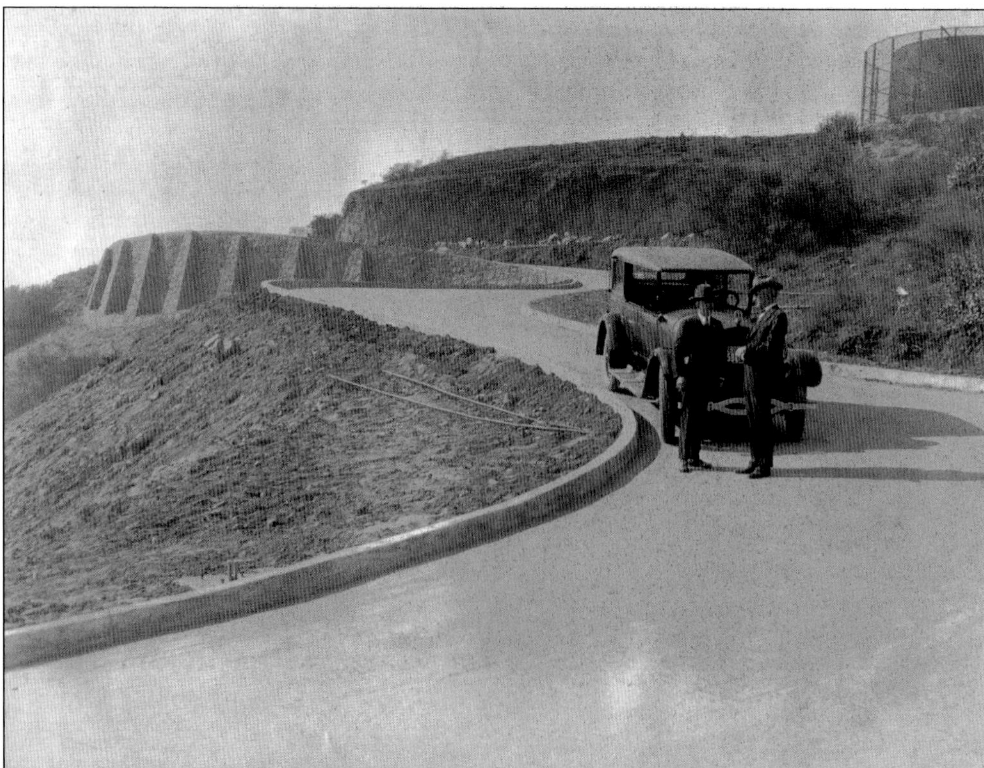

L.J. Burrud and S.H. Woodruff view one of the completed roads. One of the giant granite retaining walls holding up parts of the road can be glimpsed behind them. The stones came from the original giant demolition as well as from the Clark and Sherman quarry on the property.

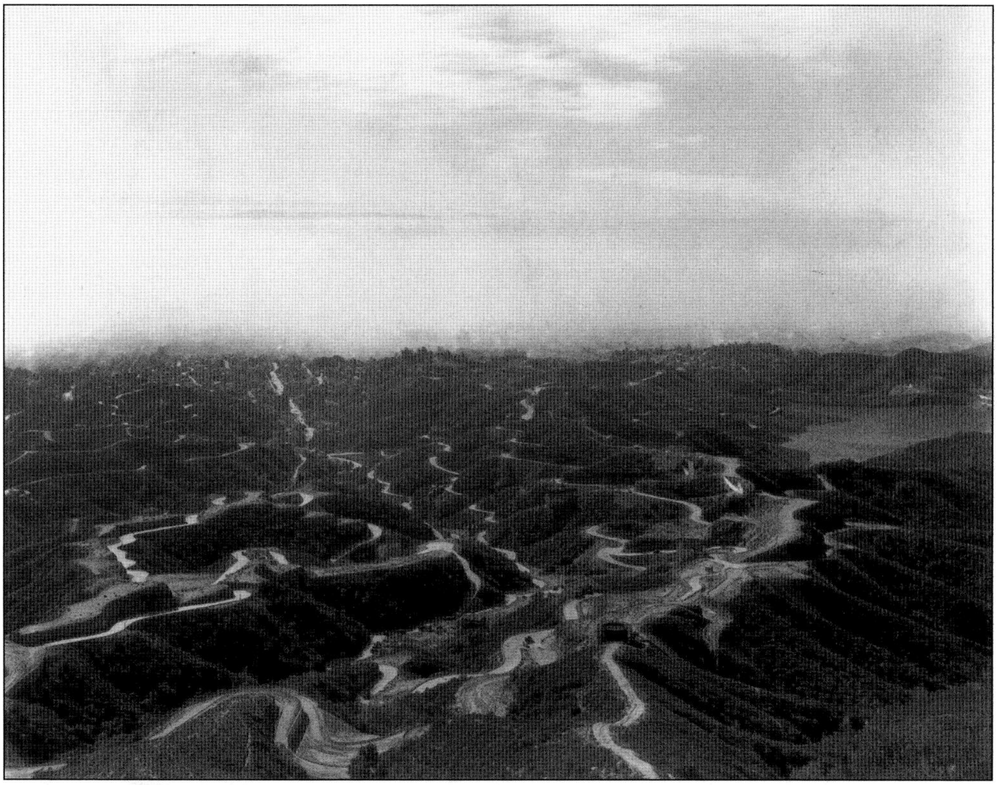

This is a view from the top of Hollywoodland's summit looking down on the roads and development below it in 1925. Lake Hollywood can be glimpsed to the right in the photograph. Advertising claimed that, on a clear day, viewers could see the Los Angeles basin, the Hollywood hills to the west, Hollywood, downtown Los Angeles, and even the coastline 16 miles away.

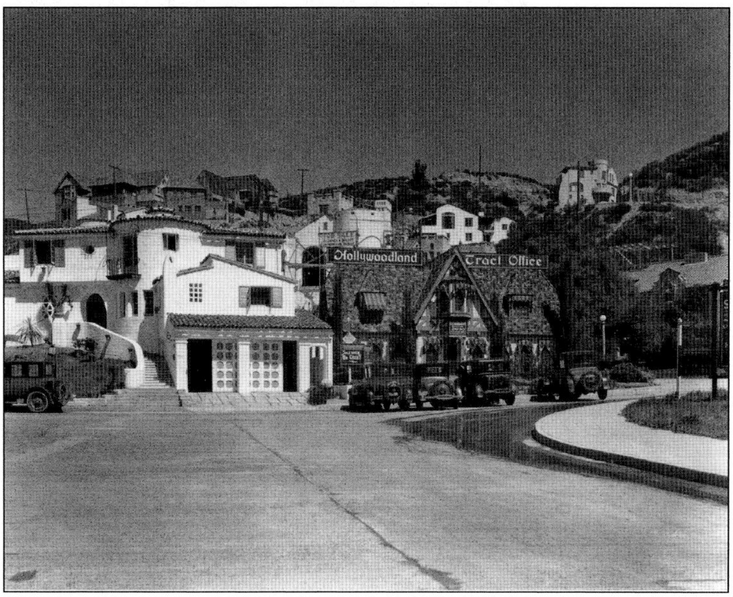

The Hollywoodland sales office can be seen at 2700 North Beachwood Drive, with the Einar Petersen house to its left in this 1927 photograph. Most of the homes in Hollywoodland were constructed for specific owners or builders, with special architecture, design, and landscaping, rather than the mass-produced lot of homes typical to most subdivisions.

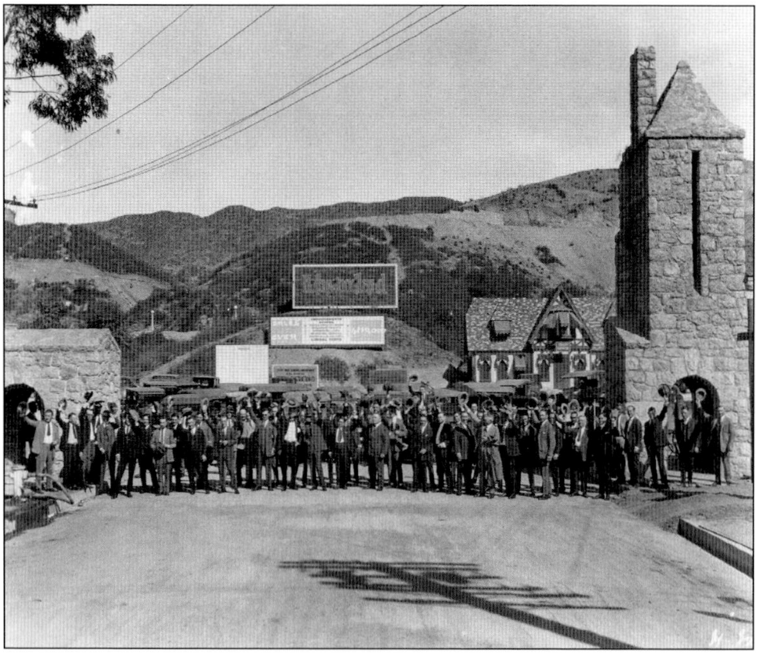

The Hollywoodland advertising and sales team stands at the Hollywoodland entrance gates in front of the tract's sales office in 1923. Tracy E. Shoults and S.H. Woodruff valued loyalty and experience, employing many of the same people who had previously worked at the Windsor Square, Marlborough Square, and West Hollywood tracts. (Bison.)

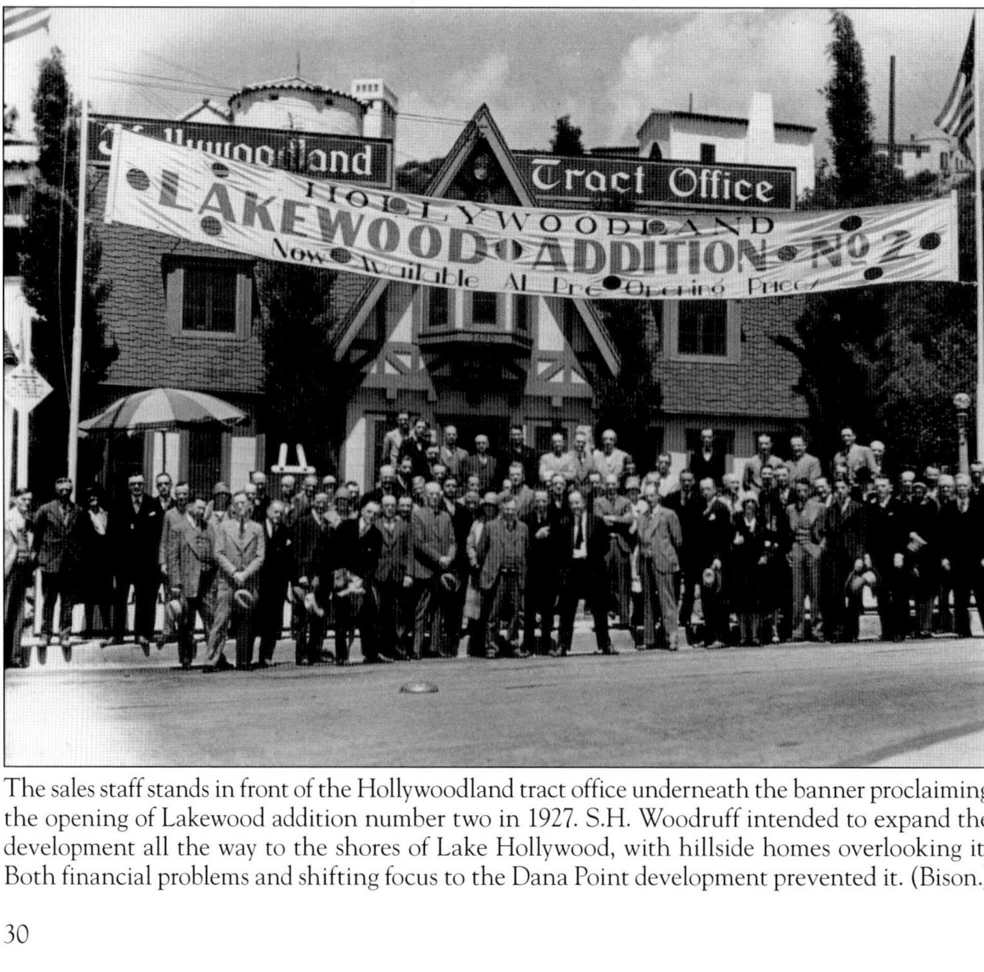

The sales staff stands in front of the Hollywoodland tract office underneath the banner proclaiming the opening of Lakewood addition number two in 1927. S.H. Woodruff intended to expand the development all the way to the shores of Lake Hollywood, with hillside homes overlooking it. Both financial problems and shifting focus to the Dana Point development prevented it. (Bison.)

Two

Conveniences of Metropolitan Living

When Tracy E. Shoults and S.H. Woodruff opened the Hollywoodland real estate tract in 1923, they were determined to make it a unique hillside community. Resident R.W. Richardson called it "the Utopia of residential sites." To entice buyers, they promoted how fine their amenities were, even such basic ones as electricity, gas, water, sewers, telephone service, paved streets, ornamental street lights, trees, mail service, garbage collection, views, and parking. The developers particularly noted how Hollywoodland offered health-enhancing benefits like calmness, clean air, exercise, and the natural environment. Woodruff and his sales staff embraced Mulholland Highway, which would offer a scenic drive and more entrances to the community. They also highlighted Lake Hollywood, created when Mulholland Dam was constructed nearby.

Developers promised scores of special features. The developers boasted of many desirable future possibilities, such as tennis courts, swimming pool, community center, clubhouse with auditorium, locker rooms, children's wading pool, tea court, putting green, and horse stables. Out of these, however, only the tennis courts, putting green, and stables were constructed. Woodruff did hire locally renowned landscape architect Theodore Payne to plant a wide variety of wildflowers throughout the neighborhood.

For those more interested in shopping, Woodruff commissioned architect John L. DeLario to design a small business district in the Spanish style with grocery store, drugstore, and other shops. To help those commuting to work, the developers provided free coach service to the Hollywoodland entrance gates, where the Pacific Electric bus picked up passengers for travel into Hollywood and Los Angeles. One unusual bonus came their way when art dealer J.F. Kanst moved his gallery into his home on Mulholland Highway, bringing artists into the area.

Woodruff also employed music to promote the development. In 1924, he established the Hollywoodland Community Orchestra, which played on KFI radio through 1925. Al Wesson, a student at the University of Southern California and the leader of the ensemble, had written the song "All Hail" in 1923, which later became the school's alma mater. Woodruff also formed the Hollywoodland–Dana Point Marimba Symphony Orchestra in 1929, which played pioneer songs on radio station KMTR.

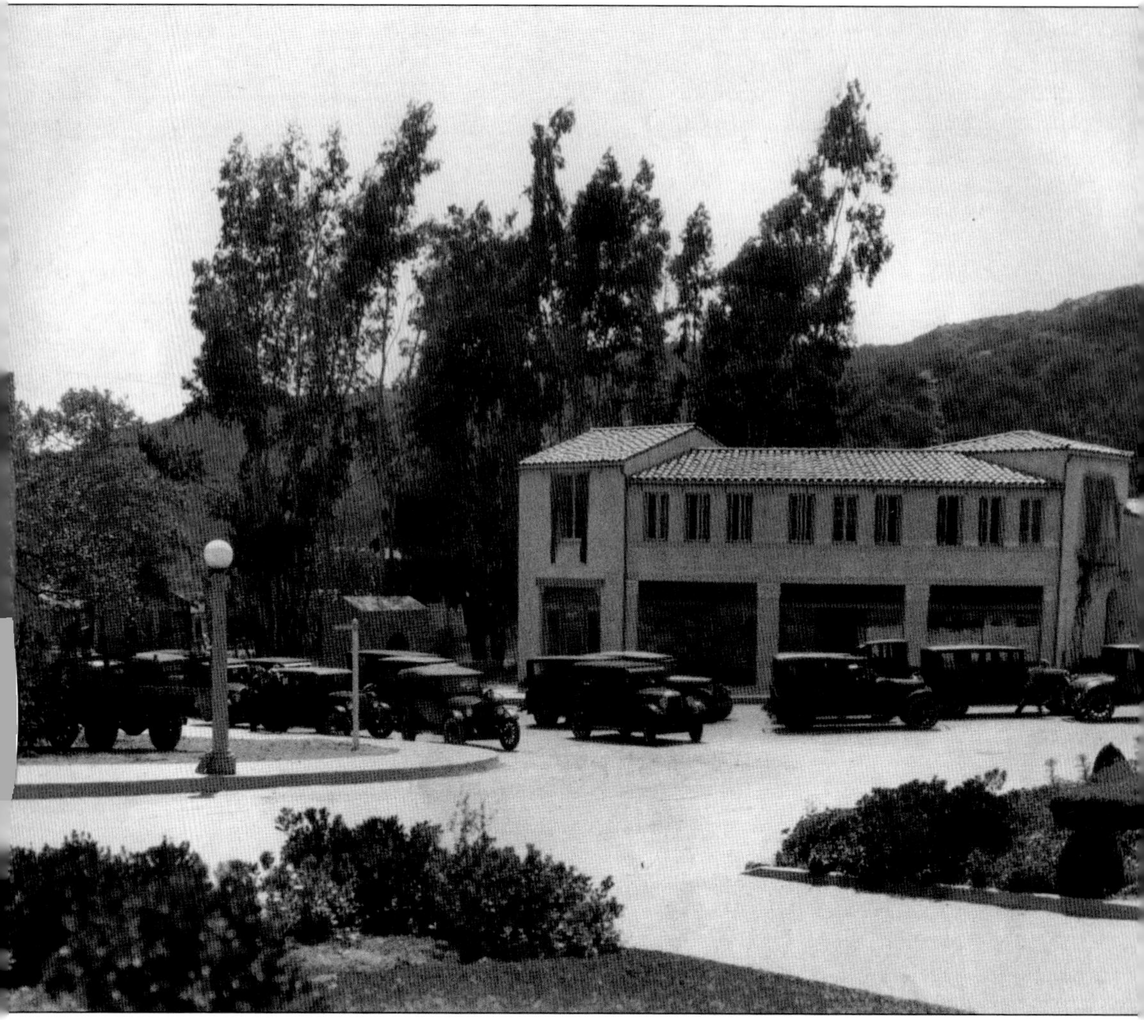

Automobiles hurry past part of the Beachwood Village complex of markets and stores located at the intersection of Beachwood and Belden Drives and designed in the Spanish style by architect John L. DeLario. Hollywoodland possessed many amenities atypical of most subdivisions. Developers claimed in promotional material that this small complex was the first of its type for hillside housing developments. So that residents did not have to travel into Hollywood for basic goods, S.H. Woodruff built a grocery store, meat market, vegetable market, a drugstore, and other businesses. Among the newspaper clippings in Hollywood Heritage's Woodruff Collection was one providing background information on shop owners and managers. "Bill" Coad, formerly manager of Sun Drug Company, managed the Beachwood Drug Store; Betty Sinclair ran the beauty parlor; "Jack" Gregg managed the Deluxe Markets 1-2-3; Joe Castendyke ran the cleaners and dyers for the neighborhood; and Jonathan Williams operated the Barber shop.

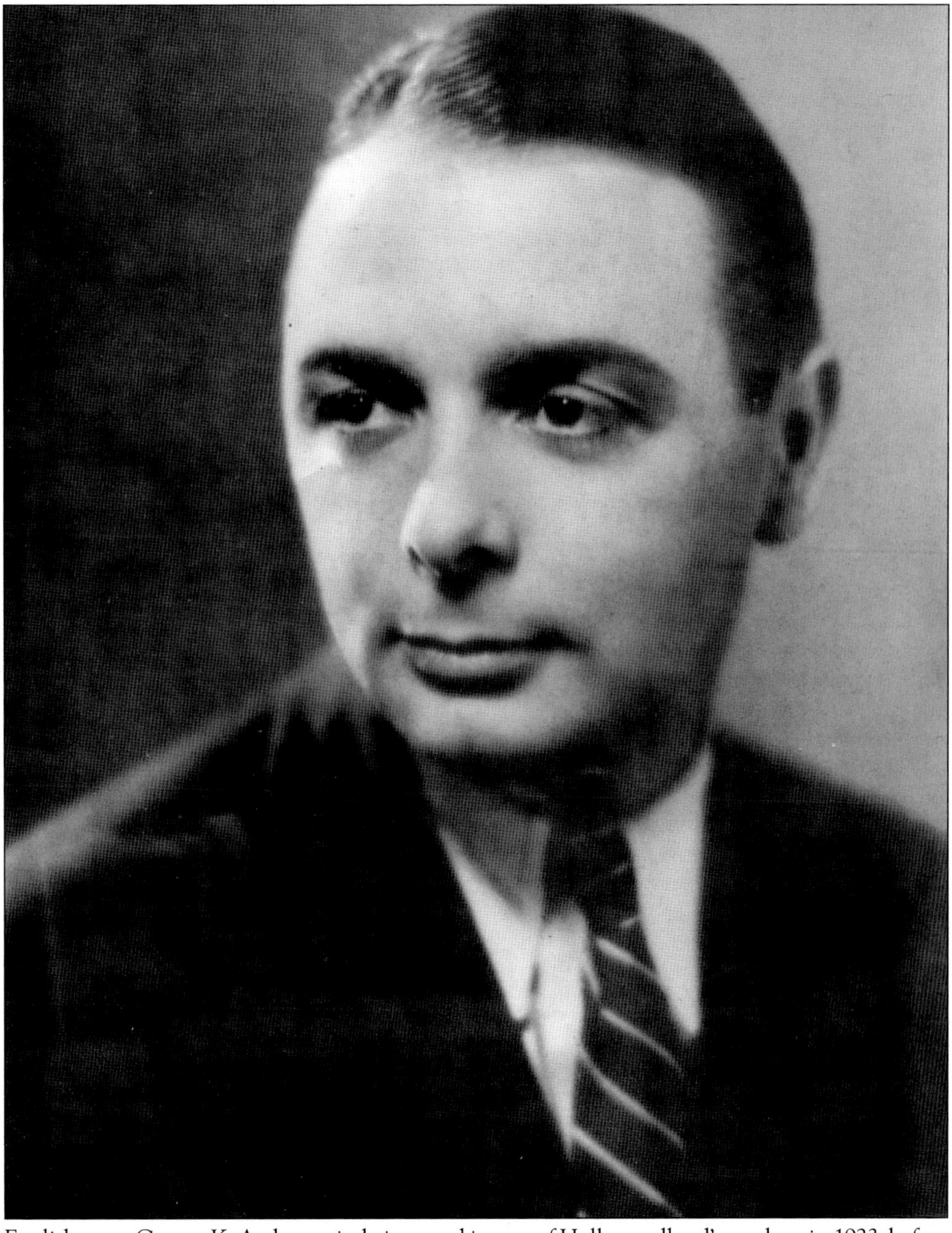

English actor George K. Arthur quietly invested in one of Hollywoodland's markets in 1923, before selling his interest in 1925, according to the *Los Angeles Times*. The son of a traveling salesman and a department store merchandise demonstrator, Arthur began working as a child to help make ends meet. After serving in the bugle corps for Britain during World War I, he studied acting and took small parts in Shakespearean plays. Arthur landed his first film role starring in *Kipps* in 1922, which became a big success. He came to America in 1923 and starred in the film *Hollywood* before financing and starring in the 1925 film *Salvation Hunters*, Josef Von Sternberg's first directorial effort. Arthur would later star in films for MGM and Paramount, many with the Swedish Karl Dane, before eventually becoming a producer and distributor of films for television. (MM.)

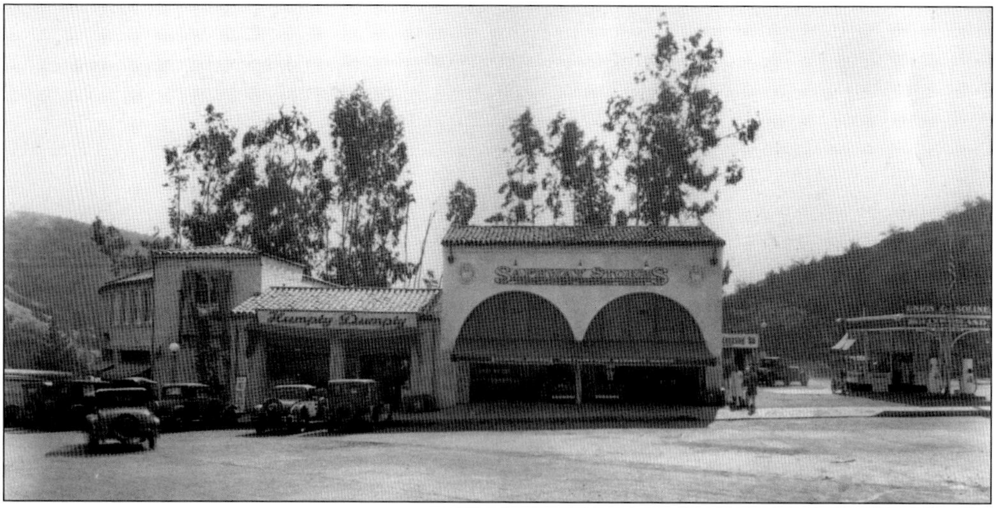

The Belden Drive view of the Hollywoodland business district reveals most of the businesses composing Beachwood Village. The drugstore is the first building with the curved window, the Humpty Dumpty market is in the middle of the photograph, the Safeway Store on its right, and the local gasoline station at the far right. (Bison.)

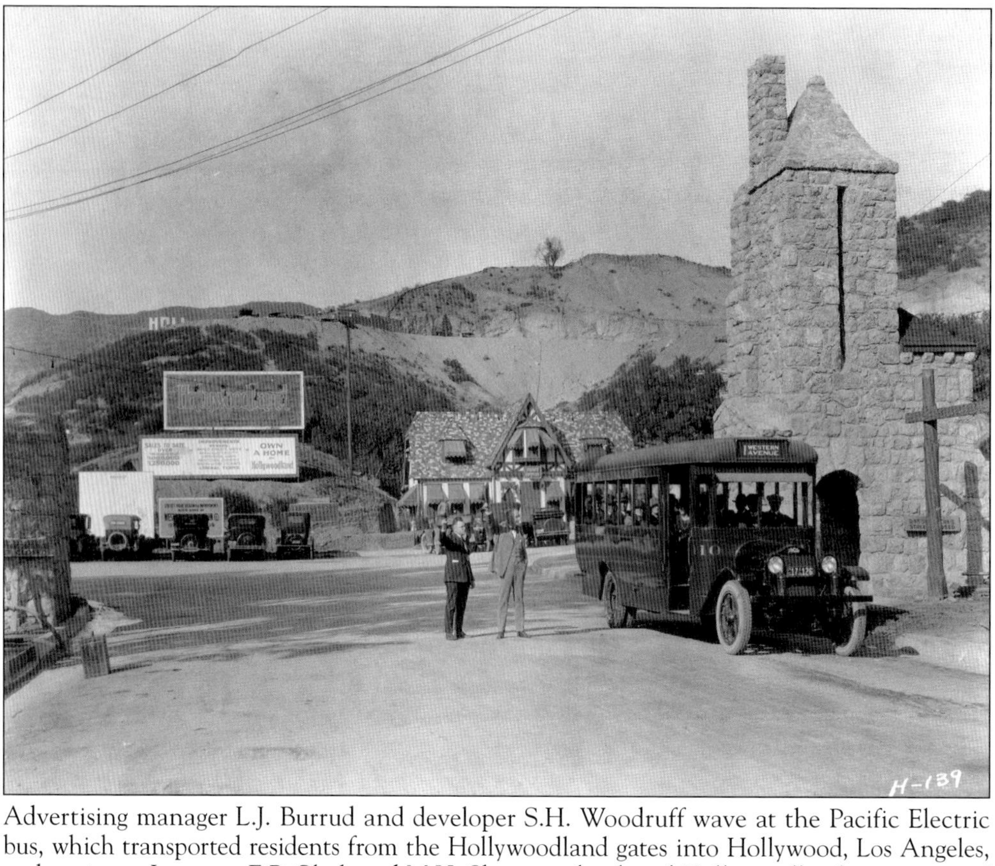

Advertising manager L.J. Burrud and developer S.H. Woodruff wave at the Pacific Electric bus, which transported residents from the Hollywoodland gates into Hollywood, Los Angeles, and environs. Investors E.P. Clark and M.H. Sherman developed Hollywoodland as a means of increasing ridership on their trolley and streetcar lines.

S.H. Woodruff provided a special Hollywoodland shuttle service as a bonus amenity for local homeowners. These special eight passenger jitneys transported neighborhood residents from their homes to the granite entrance gates, where they caught the Pacific Electric buses that ferried people into Hollywood. (Bison.)

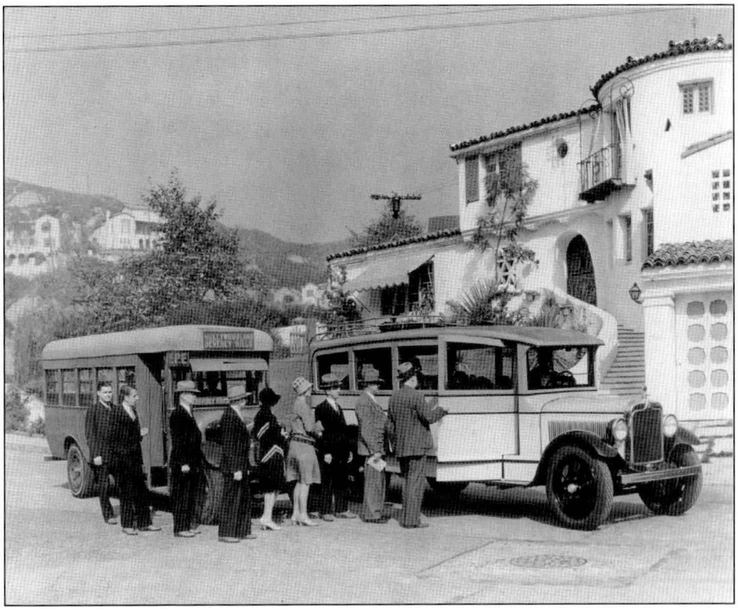

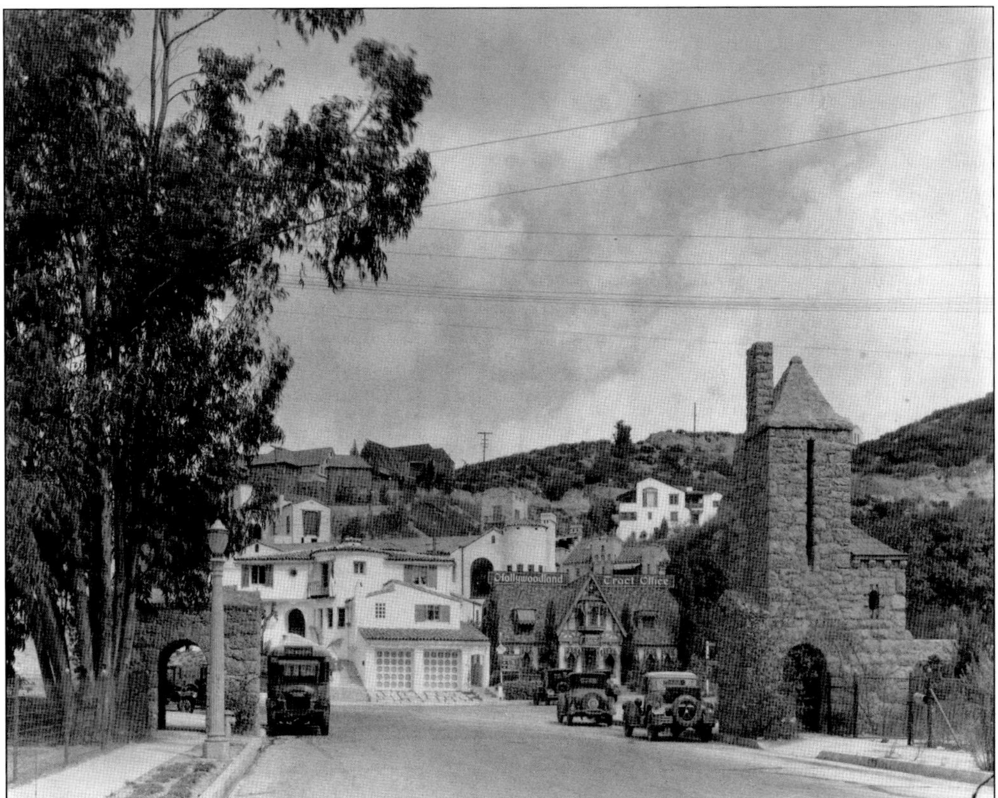

The Pacific Electric bus that served Hollywoodland is parked at the tract's granite entrance gates in 1927. European stonemasons, who lived in tents on the property, built the elegant gates for the development using rock and granite from the nearby quarry. The City of Los Angeles named them Historic-Cultural Landmark No. 20 on May 24, 1963.

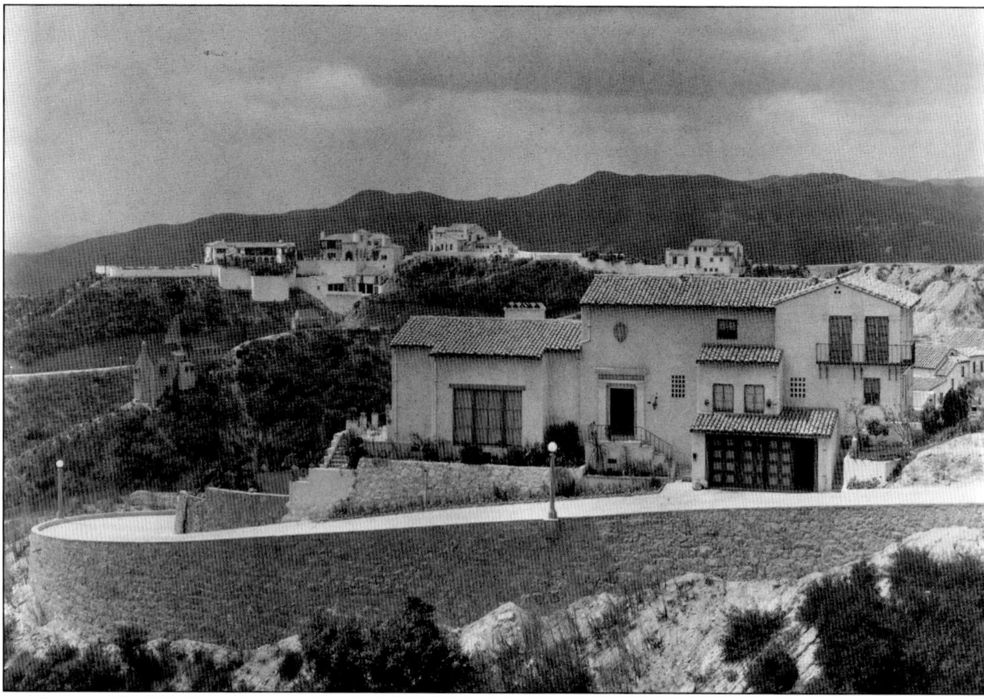

Looking at two different views of Rockcliff Place from Deronda Drive, one of the granite retaining walls found in Hollywoodland can be seen in the center of the photograph. Built with stone quarried on the premises or discovered during the demolition process, these walls were employed to strengthen and maintain homes, hillsides, and roads. The granite provided structural support that kept construction from collapsing and falling down the hills. The stones also provided a special fairy tale look that helped give Hollywoodland an elegant boost over other real estate developments. Masons built decorative fireplaces, terraces, fountains, and patios using the granite, as well as stone stairways to connect various streets. The City of Los Angeles named the retaining walls and six granite stairways Historic-Cultural Landmarks No. 535 on June 11, 1991.

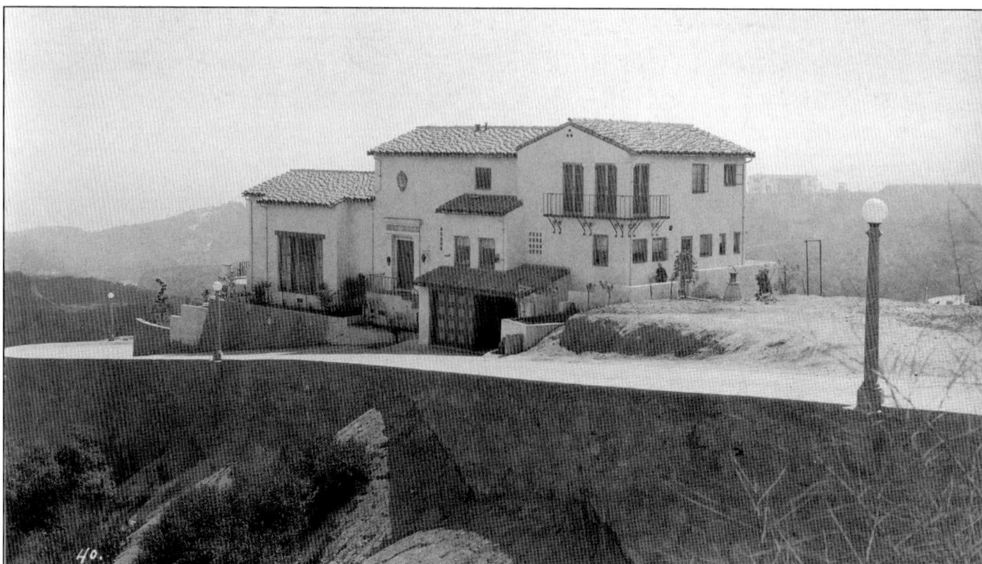

Stonemasons constructed stairways throughout the Hollywoodland tract to connect upper and lower roadways. The stairways were composed of granite and stone mined from the area. Some included the giant stone planters down the center. Two unidentified young women stand on one of these planter-lined stairways. (Bison.)

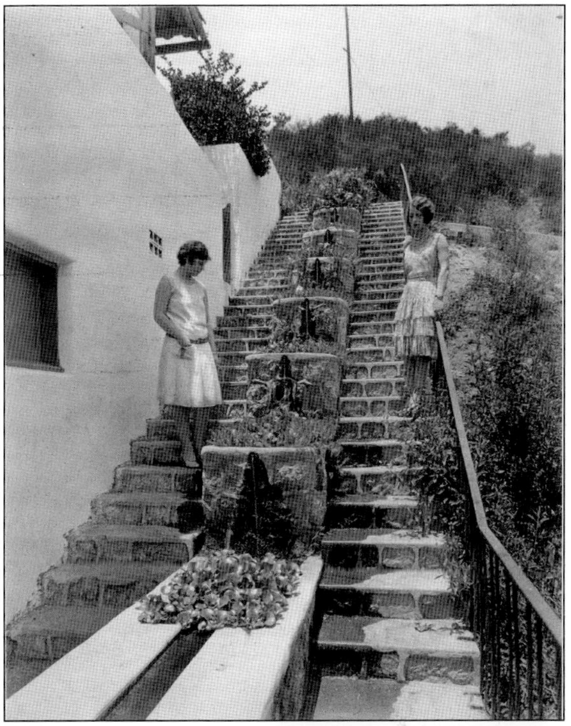

The hillside can be glimpsed in this view from the Roderick Burnham estate across the canyon and toward Griffith Park. S.H. Woodruff and his sales staff widely promoted the views available from homesites. Woodruff claimed the beauty visible out of homeowners' windows as "an everchanging panorama which fits your moods is the master painting that you may frame."

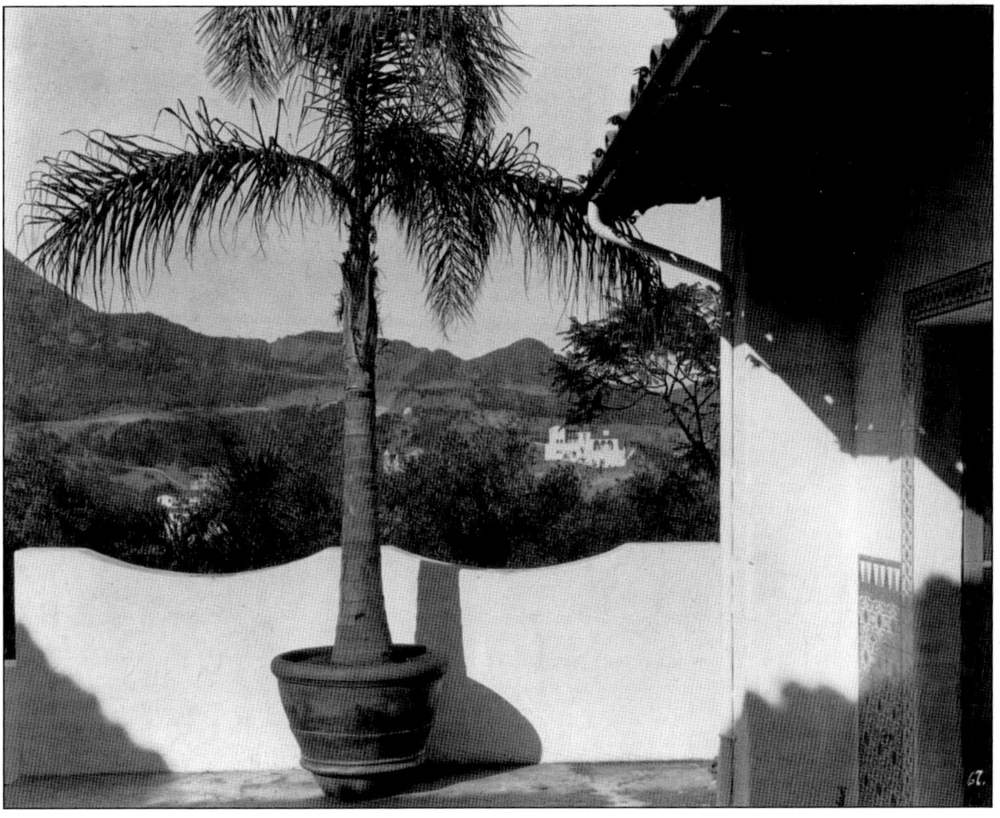

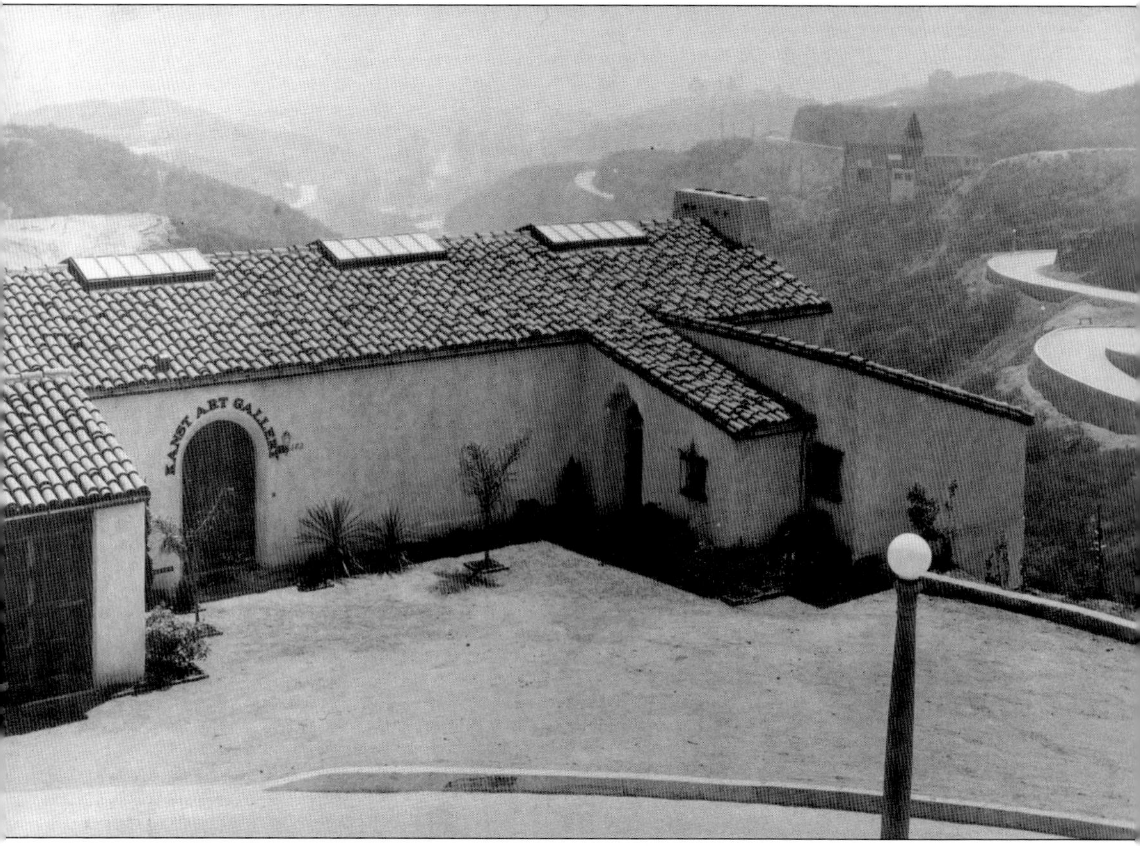

Hollywoodland was probably one of the only subdivisions that could boast that it possessed an art gallery in its midst. J.F. Kanst, a longtime Los Angeles art dealer, built a home at 6182 Mulholland Highway in 1923, using part of it as a gallery. Kanst had operated a business in Los Angeles since 1895, when he opened an exhibit space downtown. He held exhibits of various artists, hosted auctions and lectures, and sponsored occasional appearances by authors, celebrities, and the like. One of the artists he exhibited in 1925, Chicago native Joseph Birren, was a famous landscape painter. During his stay in Hollywoodland, Birren produced three paintings saluting the development: *Hollywoodland*, *Lake Hollywood*, and *Mulholland Dam*. While Kanst presented exhibits filled with beautiful things, he considered the view out of one of his large windows the best piece of art in the place.

Two unidentified Mack Sennett starlets pose with their car at the top of Beachwood Canyon. Community advertising played up the gorgeous views from the Hollywoodland hills in an attempt to lure local visitors as well as tourists. The developers promoted "that it was high above the city with a commanding view in every direction."

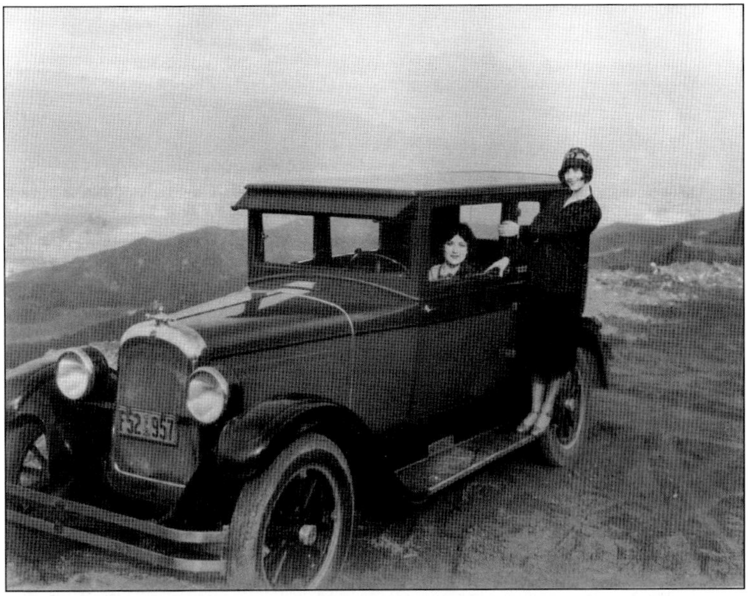

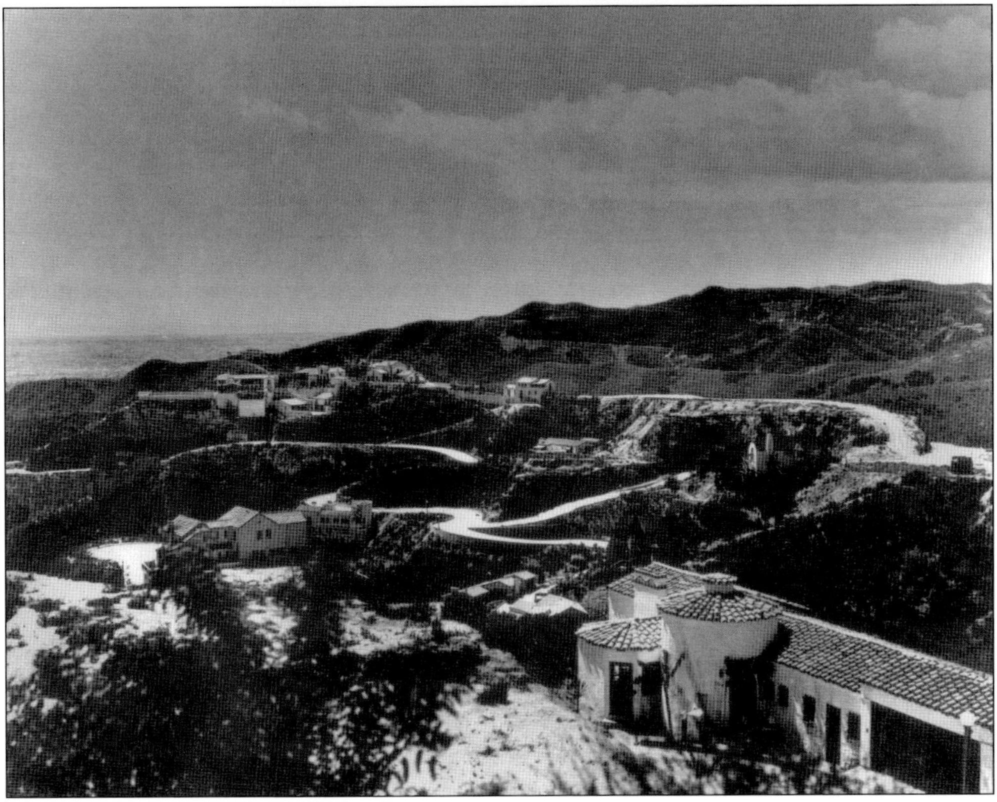

Here is a view over part of the western side of Hollywoodland with the unfinished Mulholland Highway visible at the right center. Because Hollywoodland builders constructed homes to fit the contours of the hills, no owner experienced blocked views. Every home, whether modest or luxurious, possessed its own special panorama. Mount Cahuenga is located in the center of the photograph.

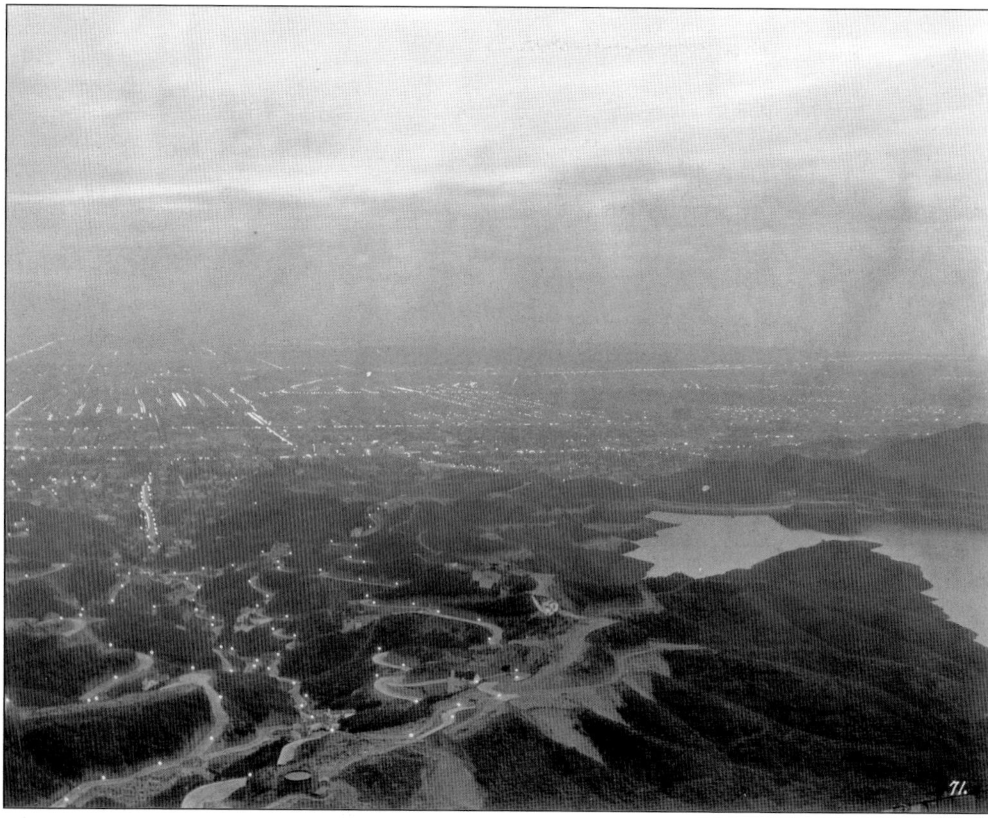

The street and city lights twinkle below Hollywoodland in this twilight photograph. Beachwood Drive is visible center left with Lake Hollywood to the right. In a letter the developers printed in one of their brochures, J.F. Kanst stated, "Our landscape is full of color by day and stretches before us like a jeweled carpet at night."

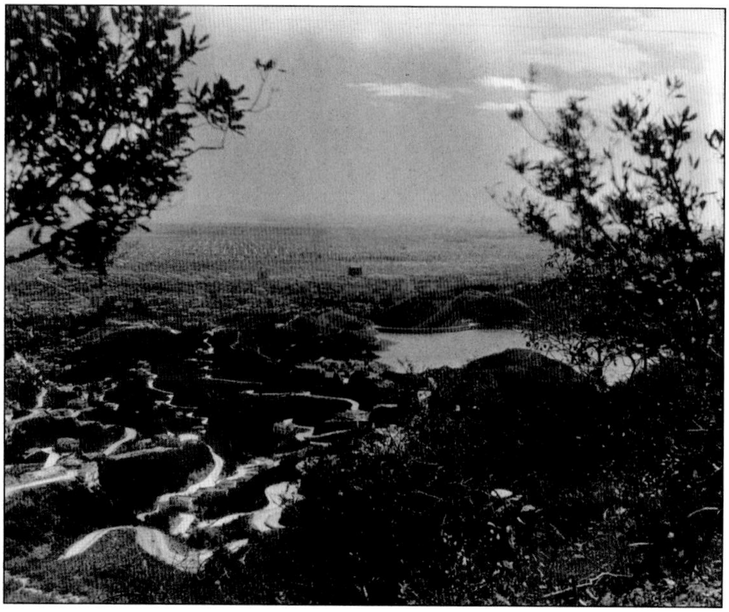

In daylight, much of the southland is visible from the top of Hollywoodland. Hollywood, downtown Los Angeles, and the ocean could be glimpsed from the summit of the development. Lake Hollywood is pictured on the right. S.H. Woodruff intended to build homes overlooking the lake and perched on its east banks, but finances prevented it.

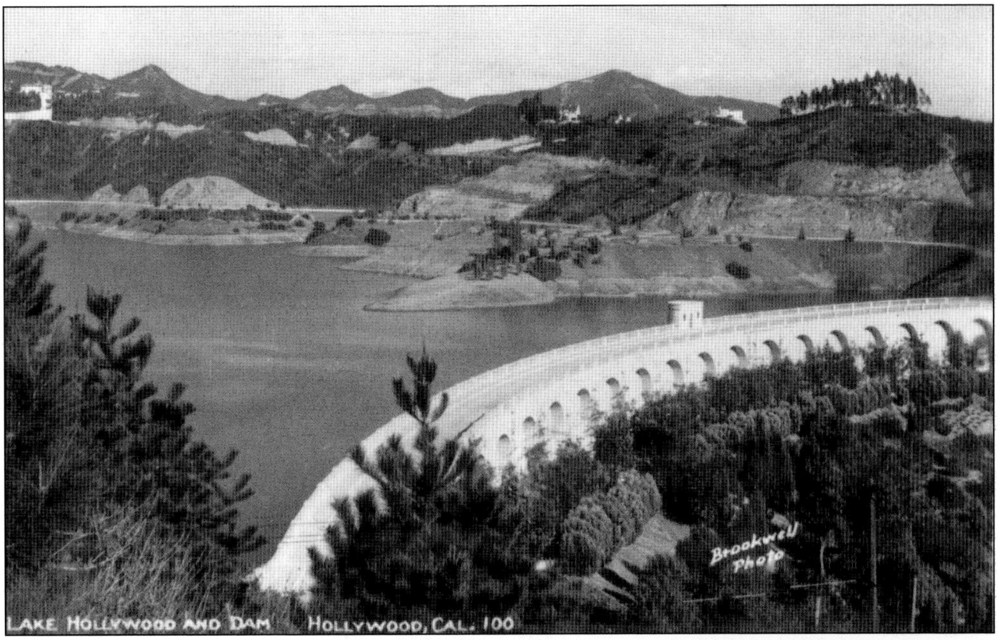

Even though Lake Hollywood was not part of Hollywoodland, the developers quickly capitalized on its location. They promoted the lakeside views of homes on the hills surrounding it. In this photograph, homes in Hollywoodland look down on the lake, with Castillo del Lago the home on the far left.

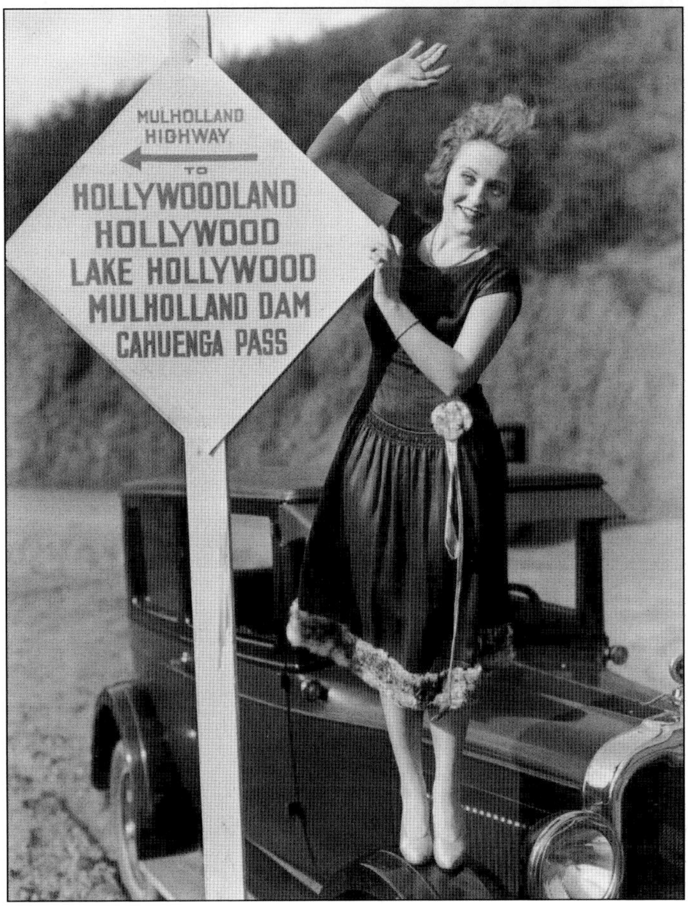

An unidentified starlet poses with one of the street signs on Mulholland Highway near the entrance to Griffith Park. S.H. Woodruff and his staff heavily promoted the road, mentioning that it would provide extra entrances to the development for residents. The salesmen also promoted the scenic views the road provided. (AMPAS.)

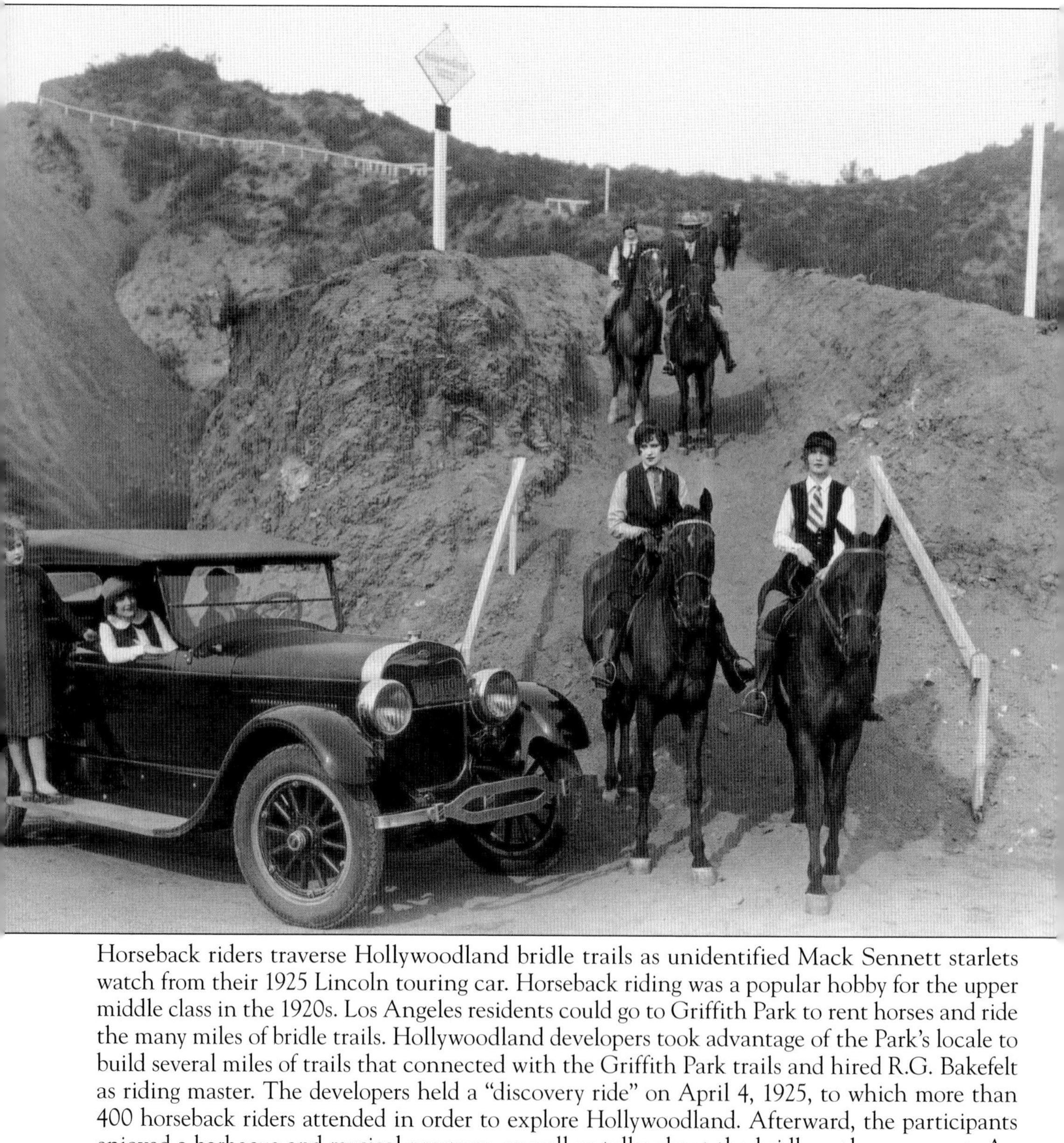

Horseback riders traverse Hollywoodland bridle trails as unidentified Mack Sennett starlets watch from their 1925 Lincoln touring car. Horseback riding was a popular hobby for the upper middle class in the 1920s. Los Angeles residents could go to Griffith Park to rent horses and ride the many miles of bridle trails. Hollywoodland developers took advantage of the Park's locale to build several miles of trails that connected with the Griffith Park trails and hired R.G. Bakefelt as riding master. The developers held a "discovery ride" on April 4, 1925, to which more than 400 horseback riders attended in order to explore Hollywoodland. Afterward, the participants enjoyed a barbecue and musical program, as well as talks about the bridle-path movement. An article in the May 31, 1925, *Los Angeles Times* by Charles H. Owens even claimed that there were 65 miles of bridle trails between the Park and Hollywoodland, which cost around $50,000 to build. (AMPAS.)

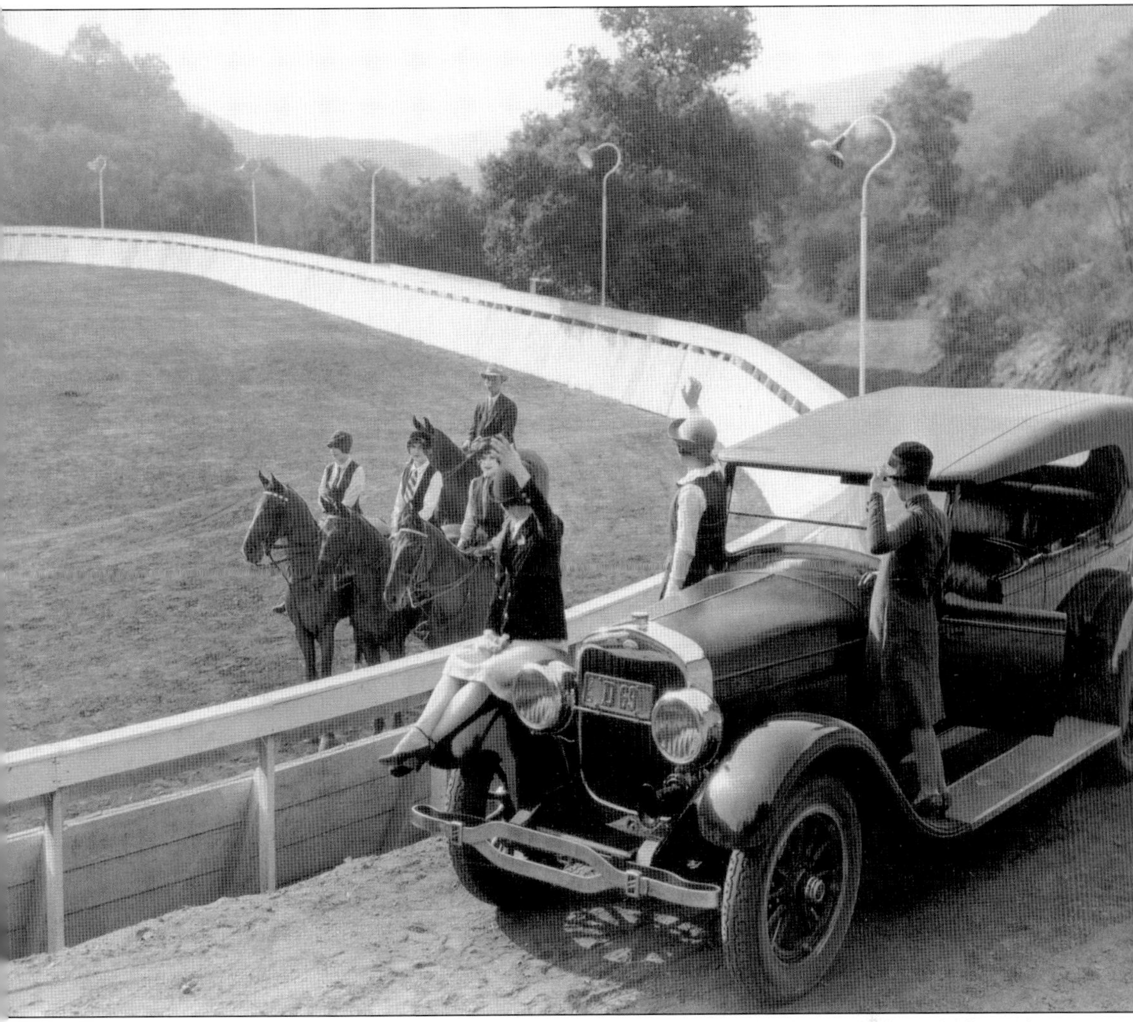

The horseback riding ring provide by Hollywoodland to its residents has unidentified Mack Sennett beauties waving at participants from their 1925 Lincoln touring car. The ring provided exercise and training for those learning English-style riding, as well as a practice area for those participating in jumping exercises. Residents could board their horses at Hollywoodland Riding Stables or hire horses at Hollywoodland Riding School. In newspaper articles, Hollywoodland advertising manager L.J. Burrud claimed that the Hollywoodland trails were the first to be built in any Southern California housing development. S.H. Woodruff took out newspaper advertisements and sent out press releases promoting how tired, harried businessmen could take a morning canter for inspiration before heading to work, or to just take part in health-giving exercise. The stable later changed hands and now runs under the name Sunset Ranch Hollywood Stables at the top of Beachwood Drive. (AMPAS.)

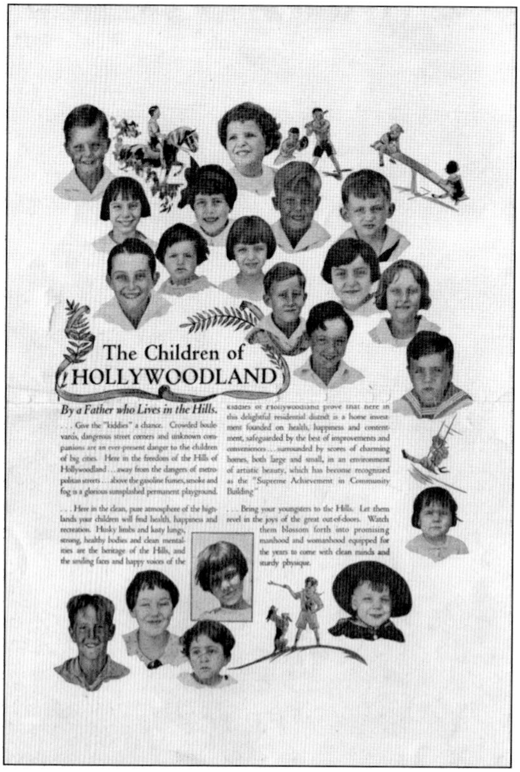

S.H. Woodruff and his sales staff heavily promoted the health benefits of living at Hollywoodland to potential buyers, especially those with children. This advertisement stressed that the tract provided children freedom, clean sky and atmosphere, beautiful views, access to nature, and plenty of physical activities to promote healthy bodies and minds.

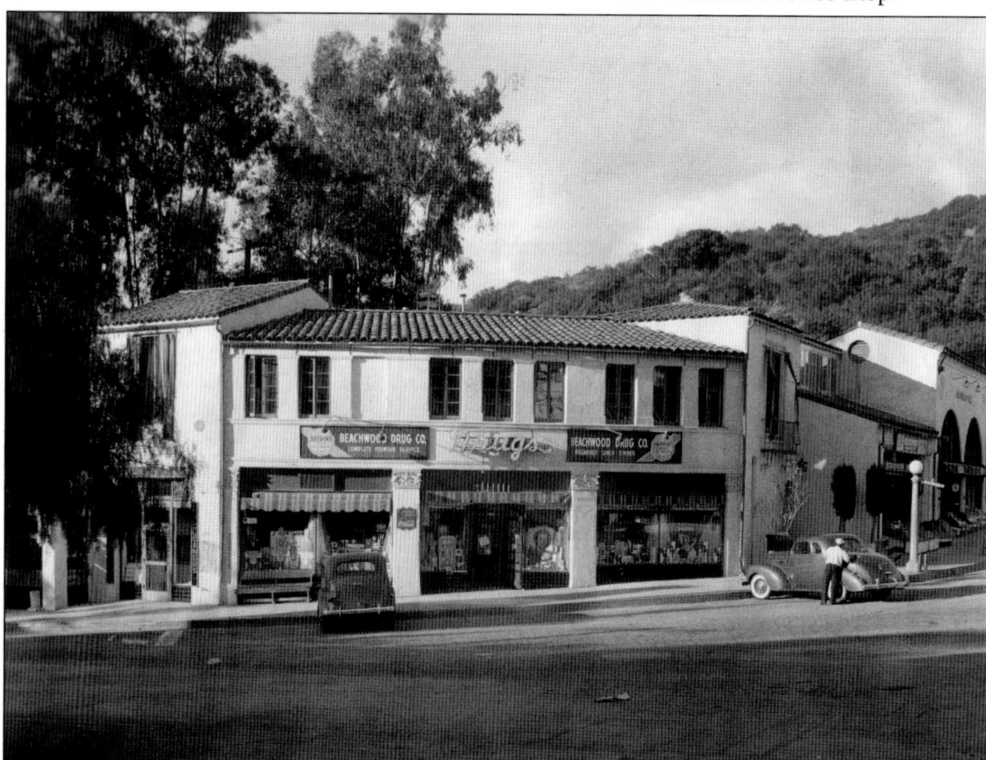

By the early 1940s, several of the businesses in Beachwood Village experienced new ownership. The Beachwood Drug Company had slightly altered the exterior of the building; a dry cleaners had opened next door, and markets continued along Belden Drive. In the 1950s, architect John Lautner renovated the drugstore exterior, which later became a coffee shop.

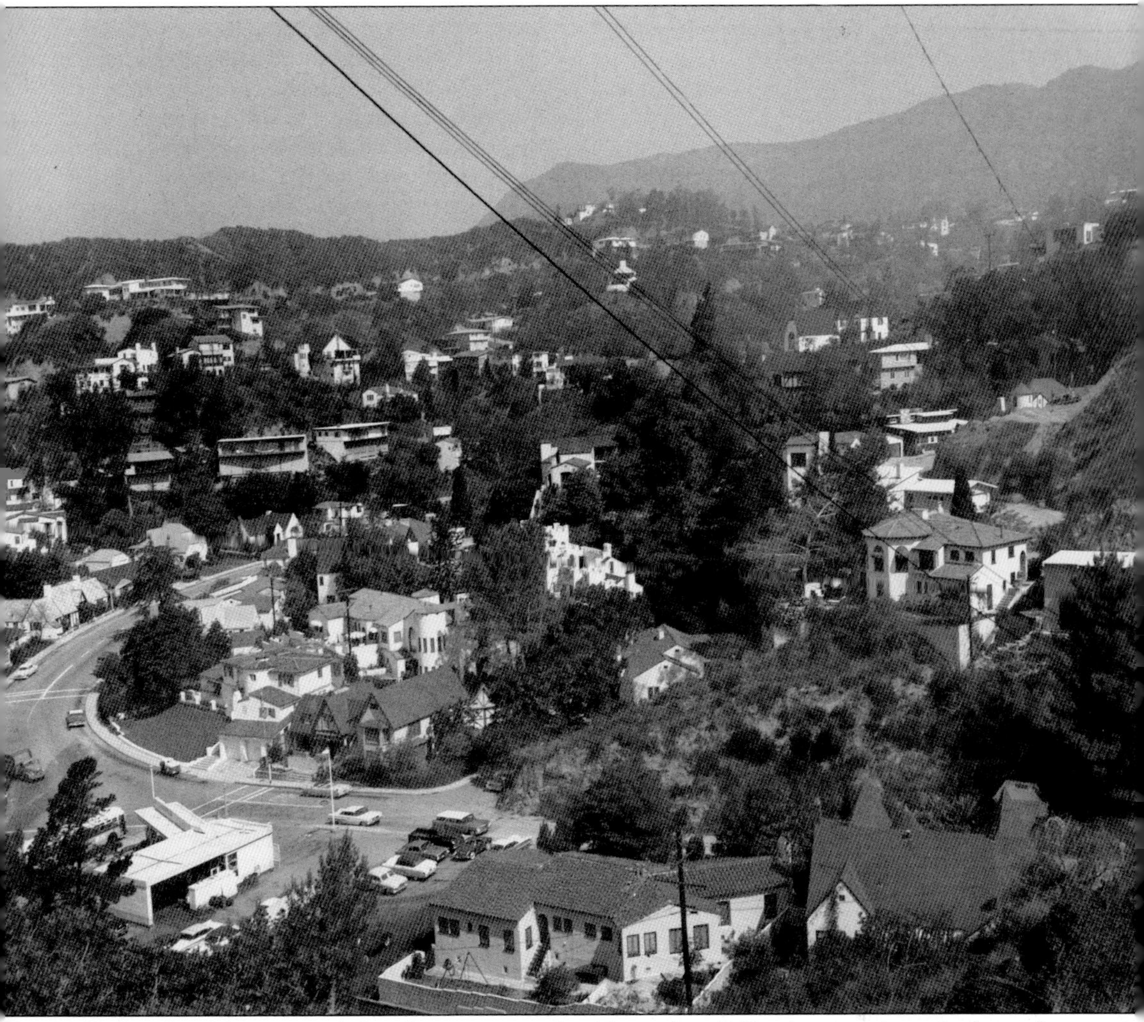

Hollywoodland has expanded and grown considerably in this 1950s photograph, with the real estate office at 2700 North Beachwood Drive and the Einar Petersen house at 2706 North Beachwood Drive visible in lower center. S.H. Woodruff was still promoting Hollywoodland as an excellent place to buy and build as late as 1932. When he and his staff moved on in the mid-1930s, architectural restrictions that permitted only four types of homes ended and several other types could be built. Many more houses dot the landscape in a much denser neighborhood. Later, lot sizes were not as large as the original lots, and homes were more packed together. At this point, not all homes could survey and dominate their domain as they had in the 1920s. By the 1950s, the area was being called Hollywood or Beachwood Canyon rather than Hollywoodland.

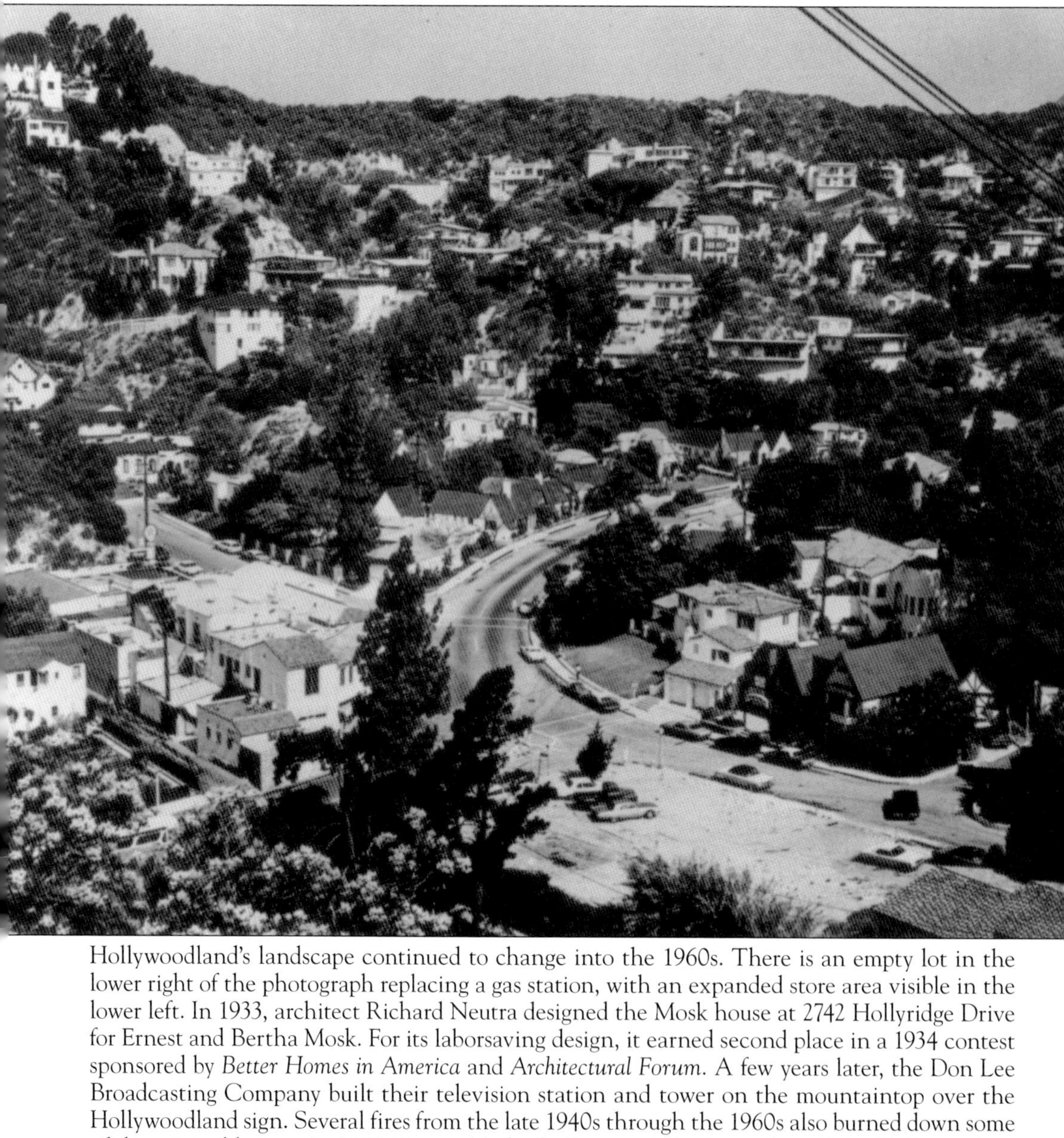

Hollywoodland's landscape continued to change into the 1960s. There is an empty lot in the lower right of the photograph replacing a gas station, with an expanded store area visible in the lower left. In 1933, architect Richard Neutra designed the Mosk house at 2742 Hollyridge Drive for Ernest and Bertha Mosk. For its laborsaving design, it earned second place in a 1934 contest sponsored by *Better Homes in America* and *Architectural Forum*. A few years later, the Don Lee Broadcasting Company built their television station and tower on the mountaintop over the Hollywoodland sign. Several fires from the late 1940s through the 1960s also burned down some of the original homes. In 1962, Bernard Judge built a geodesic dome above Lake Hollywood on Durand Drive. The dome itself was 45 feet in diameter and light enough that six men could carry it. After completion, Julius Shulman photographed it for a July 1, 1962, article in the *Los Angeles Times*.

Three

The Supreme Achievement in Community Building

Tracy E. Shoults, S.H. Woodruff, and their advertising department promoted Hollywoodland as the first hillside development in the United States, one that would "offer more to the seeker of an ideal home environment than any other section of the world." Lot prices ranged from $2,000 to $55,000, with homes costing from $6,000 to over $100,000.

The developers imposed 50-year architectural restrictions on the community and allowed only four types of homes: French Normandy, English Tudor, Mediterranean, and Spanish. The board approved all designs, including interior, exterior, and landscaping. Restrictions gave Hollywoodland a touch more exclusivity and prestige.

In many ways, Hollywoodland resembled Italian towns because of its air of sophistication, intimate feeling, and blending with nature. This more Mediterranean and Spanish architecture appealed to Hollywoodland's architects, who designed both modest bungalows and palatial estates, mostly in the style that hearkened to old California and its missionary days. They took to calling this style California Renaissance, because while it honored the past, layouts and designs were more comfortable and practical for 1920s buyers.

Most of the architects and contractors they hired were either respected in their fields or rising professionals. They appointed John L. (Lucien) DeLario, who had worked with them in Windsor Square, as lead architect.

Many homes sold to successful local residents, but many out-of-town visitors also bought plots to build destination homes, retirement homes, or rental property.

The developers intended to build out Hollywoodland all the way to the eastern shores of Lake Hollywood and the hills overlooking it. These areas they called Lakewood, but financial issues halted the project.

S.H. Woodruff formed a new real estate syndicate to buy, subdivide, and develop Dana Point, a hilly enclave outside of Laguna Beach overlooking the Pacific Ocean. He and most of his top associates shifted their focus there but continued selling in Hollywoodland until at least 1932. Financial problems in the mid-1930s caused him to abandon Dana Point and turn the remaining undeveloped parts of Hollywoodland back over to the M.H. Sherman Company.

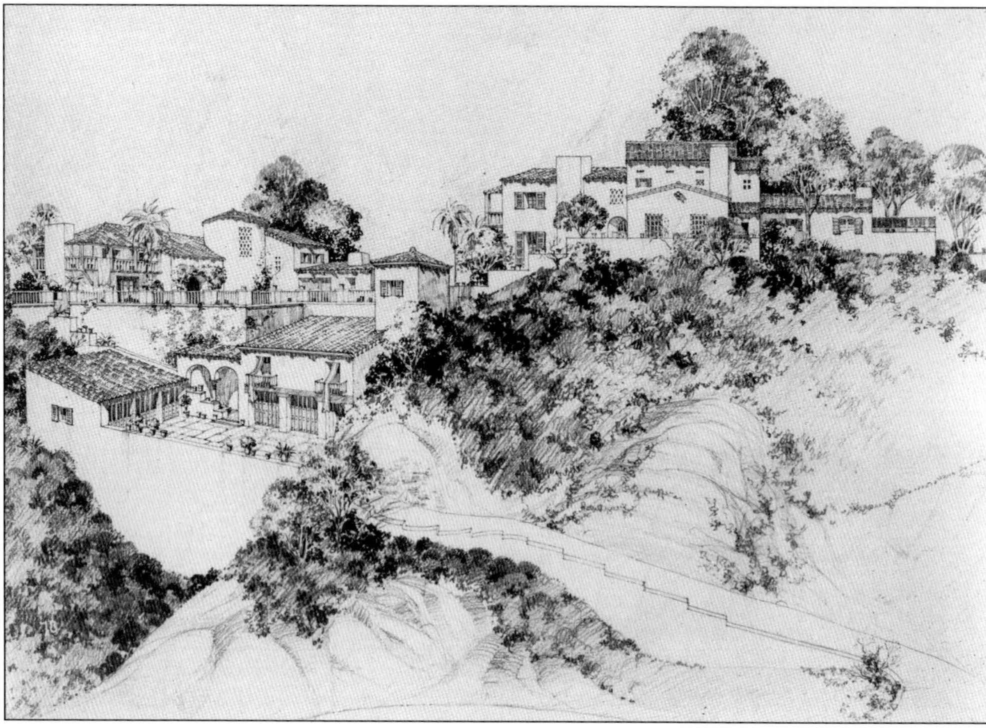

Home construction in Hollywoodland began almost as soon as permits and lots were offered for sale. The developers planned to make the development "into one of the most attractive residential sections of the city," according to an April 1, 1923, *Los Angeles Times* article. They envisioned something similar to European hillside towns, with a concentration of California Spanish-style homes, as evidenced in this drawing.

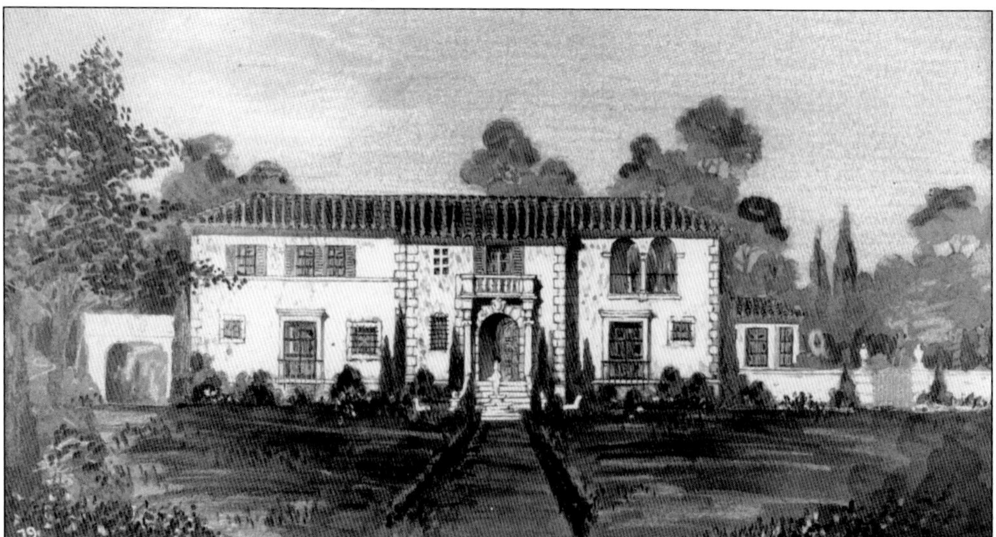

Tracy E. Shoults and S.H. Woodruff advertised for potential clients "to live where California means the most." Adding a touch of elegance and exclusivity to their hillside development, an architectural committee would approve all exterior and landscaping plans. Only four architectural styles were allowed: French Normandy, English Tudor, Mediterranean, and Spanish.

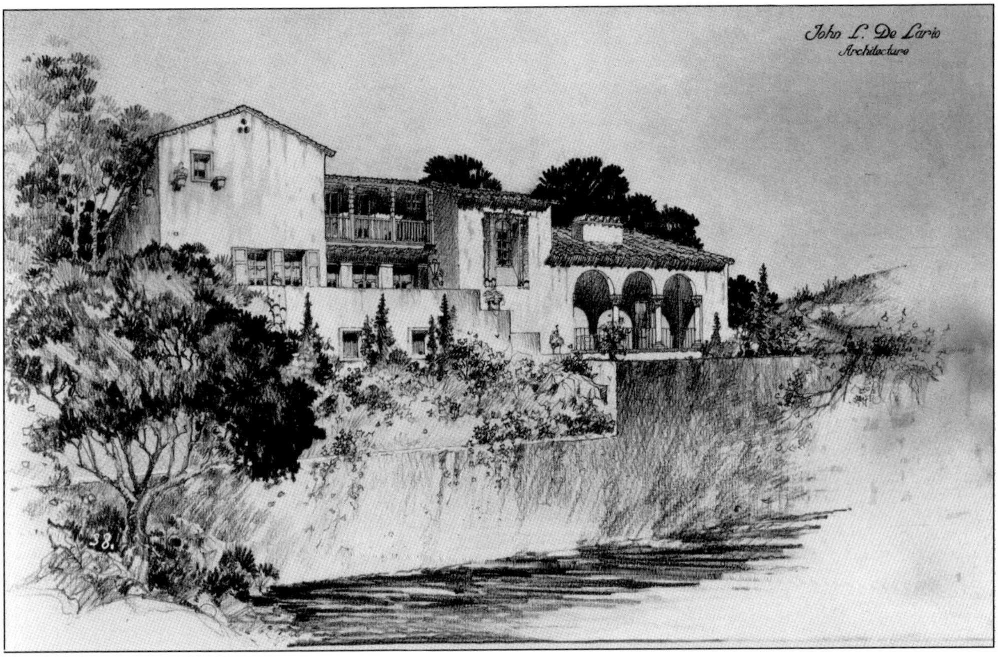

Tracy E. Shoults and S.H. Woodruff hired John L. DeLario as the lead architect for the housing development. DeLario had worked with them in their Windsor Square subdivision, designing English-style and Spanish-style homes. For Hollywood, DeLario preferred Spanish-style homes that hearkened to California's mission past.

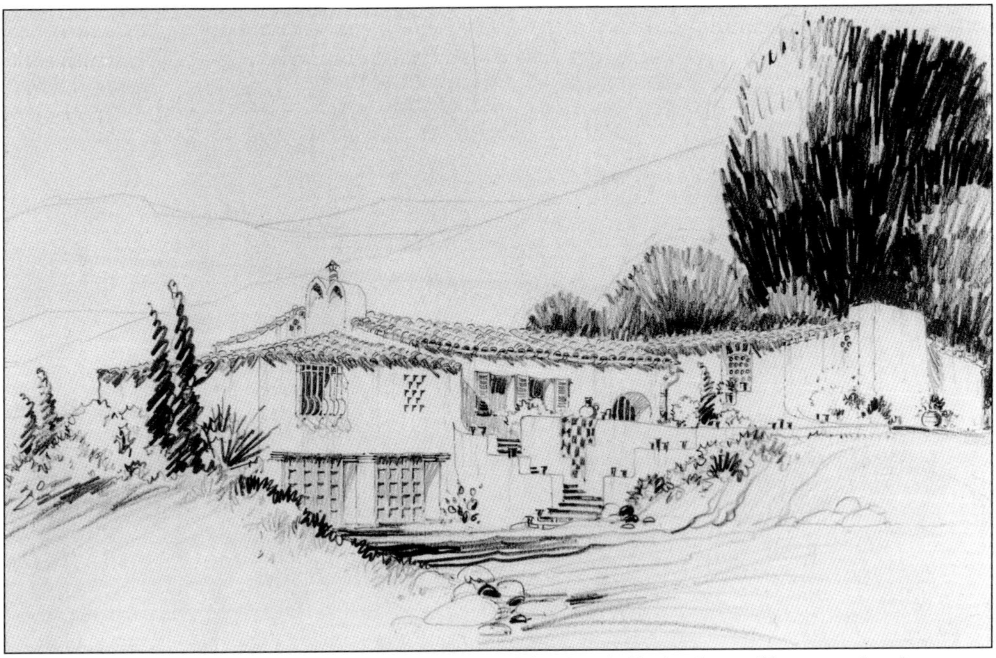

The developers promoted Hollywoodland as one of the first hillside-themed housing developments in the United States, a restricted neighborhood full of attractive homes with an abundance of social and recreational activities. As an architect, S.H. Woodruff favored an organic style of architecture in which the home complements the environment.

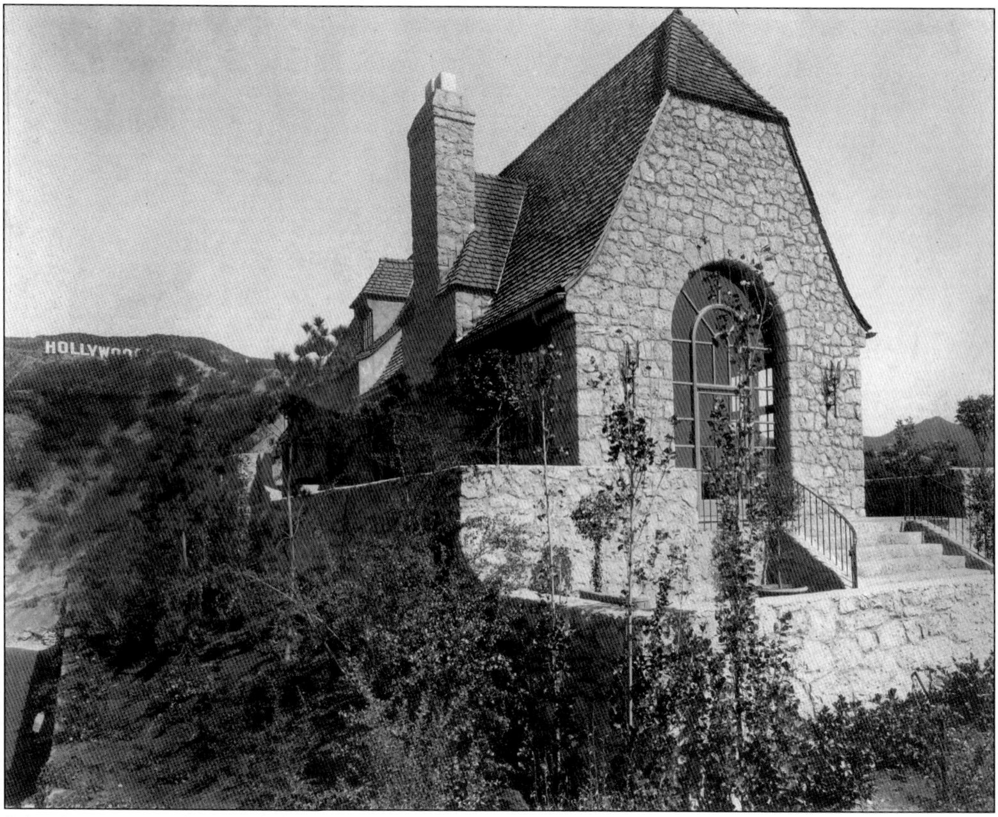

John L. DeLario designed this nine-room demonstration home for the Hollywoodland real estate tract. It was built on one of the most prominent hilltops as a showcase for Hollywoodland's architecture and hillside building. Developers filmed the entire construction process so that the motion picture could display the opportunities of successful foothill home building.

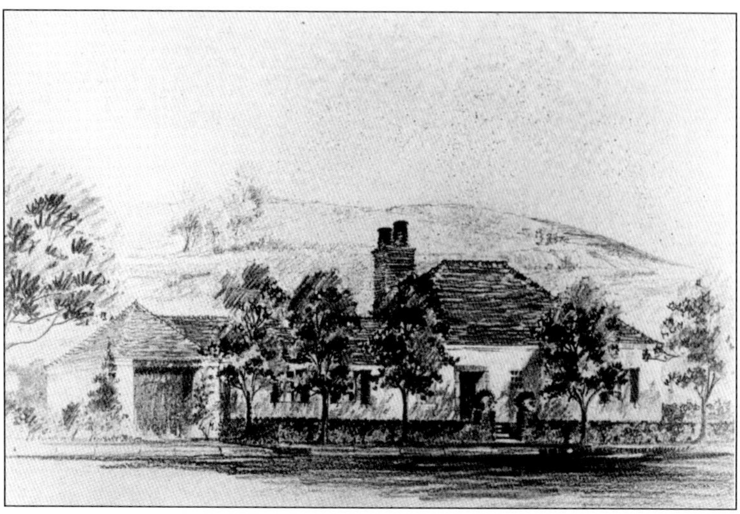

Home sizes and prices were affordable for middle class as well as upper middle class people. Prices ranged from $2,000 to $55,000 for lots, with homes costing $10,000 and up. Deeds cost $6,000, with restrictions lasting 50 years. This modest home was constructed at 2805 Beachwood Drive.

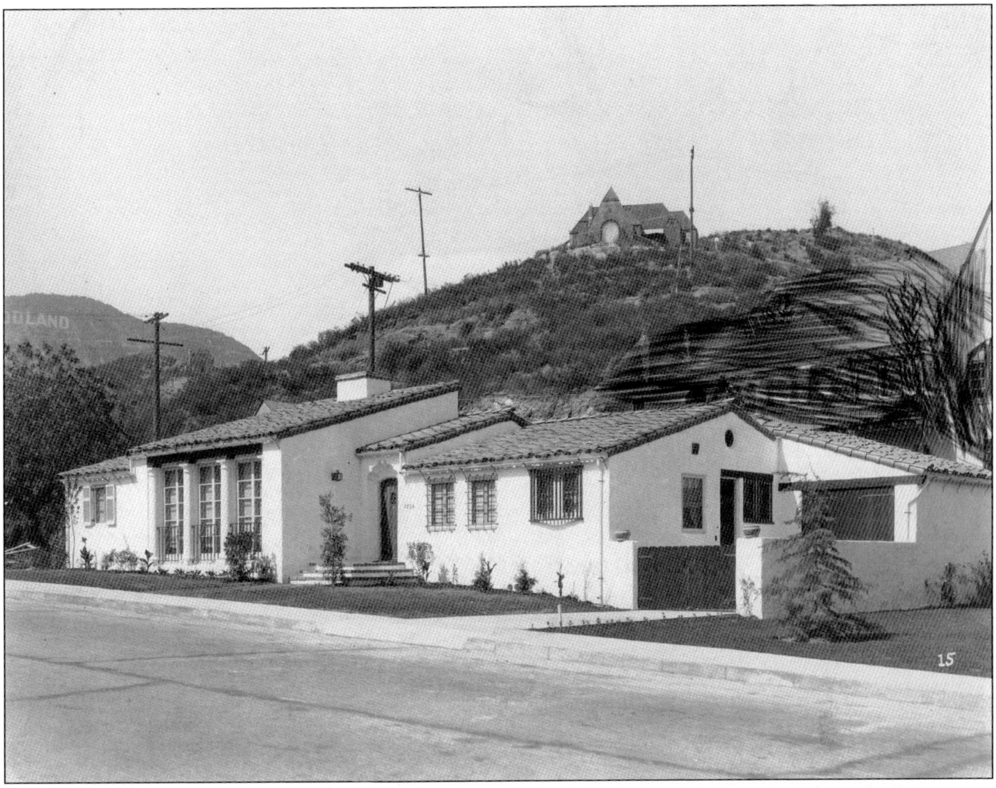

Several salesmen and other employees of the Hollywoodland development bought homes in the subdivision. Salesman Gilbert A. Miller and his wife purchased this home at 2734 North Beachwood Drive designed by architect John L. DeLario. The demonstration house sits on the top of the hill behind the Miller house.

This home at 3185 Durand Drive was planned by architect John L. DeLario to blend into the hillside around it and featured a Spanish architectural style. As DeLario stated to a *Los Angeles Times* columnist, "It is true that a purely California architecture, partly Spanish–partly Italian, really seems to be the best fitted for our needs in the Southland."

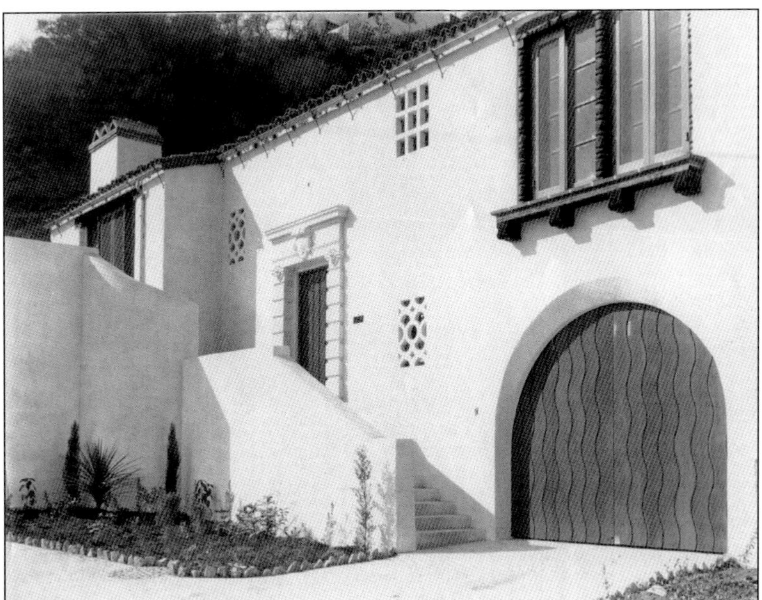

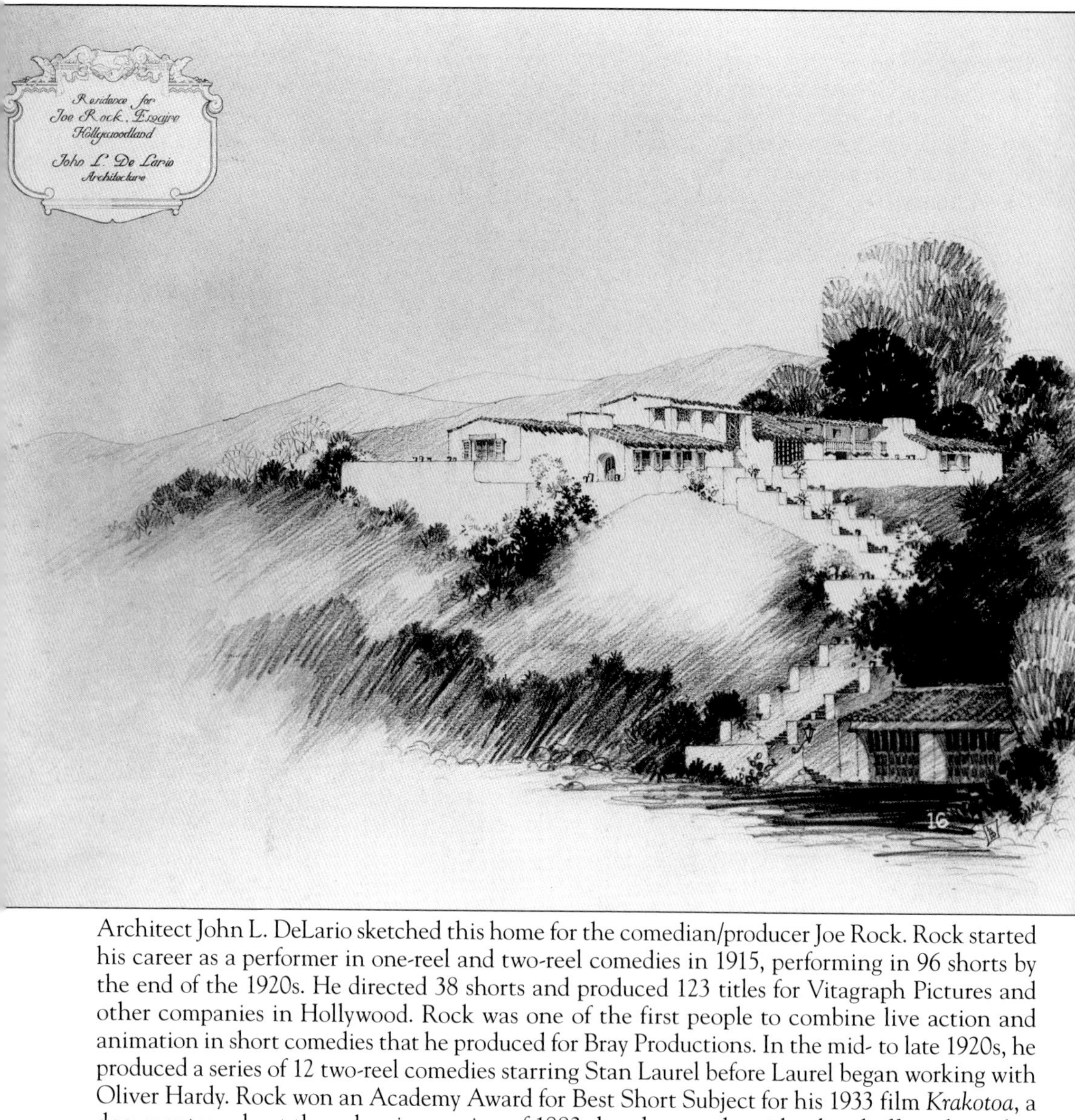

Architect John L. DeLario sketched this home for the comedian/producer Joe Rock. Rock started his career as a performer in one-reel and two-reel comedies in 1915, performing in 96 shorts by the end of the 1920s. He directed 38 shorts and produced 123 titles for Vitagraph Pictures and other companies in Hollywood. Rock was one of the first people to combine live action and animation in short comedies that he produced for Bray Productions. In the mid- to late 1920s, he produced a series of 12 two-reel comedies starring Stan Laurel before Laurel began working with Oliver Hardy. Rock won an Academy Award for Best Short Subject for his 1933 film *Krakotoa*, a documentary about the volcanic eruption of 1883 that destroyed an island and affected weather patterns around the world for several months.

Designed by John L. DeLario, this home for Clara Shatto was located near the top of the Hollywoodland development. Shatto bought the northeast corner of Wilshire Boulevard and Western Avenue in Los Angeles in 1929 and, in 1930, donated land where the First Congregational Church and MacArthur Park are located.

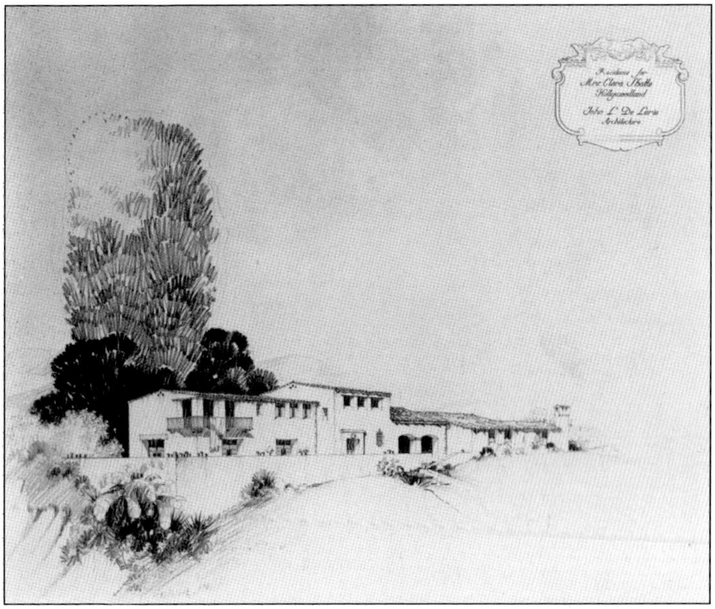

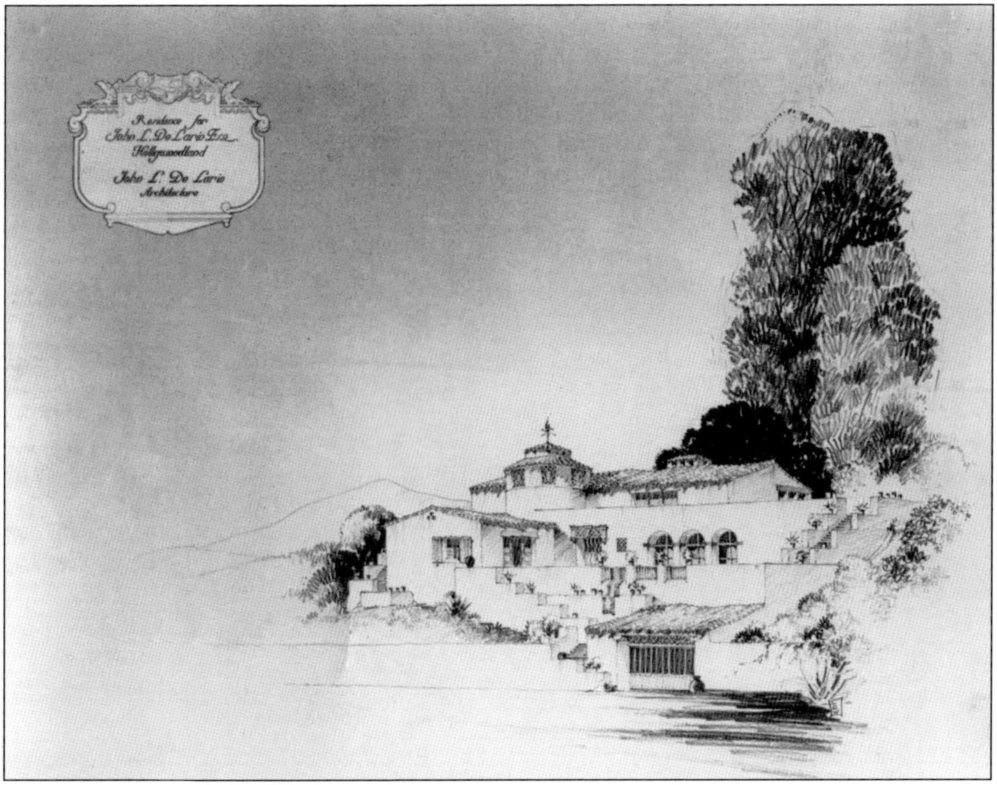

John L. DeLario designed his own California Spanish-style home on Rodgerton Drive in Hollywoodland. He coined the term California Renaissance to describe this style, "which tends to create a home delightful, beautiful, and comfortable, with the combination of modern comforts and conveniences and the early romance and enchantment of history."

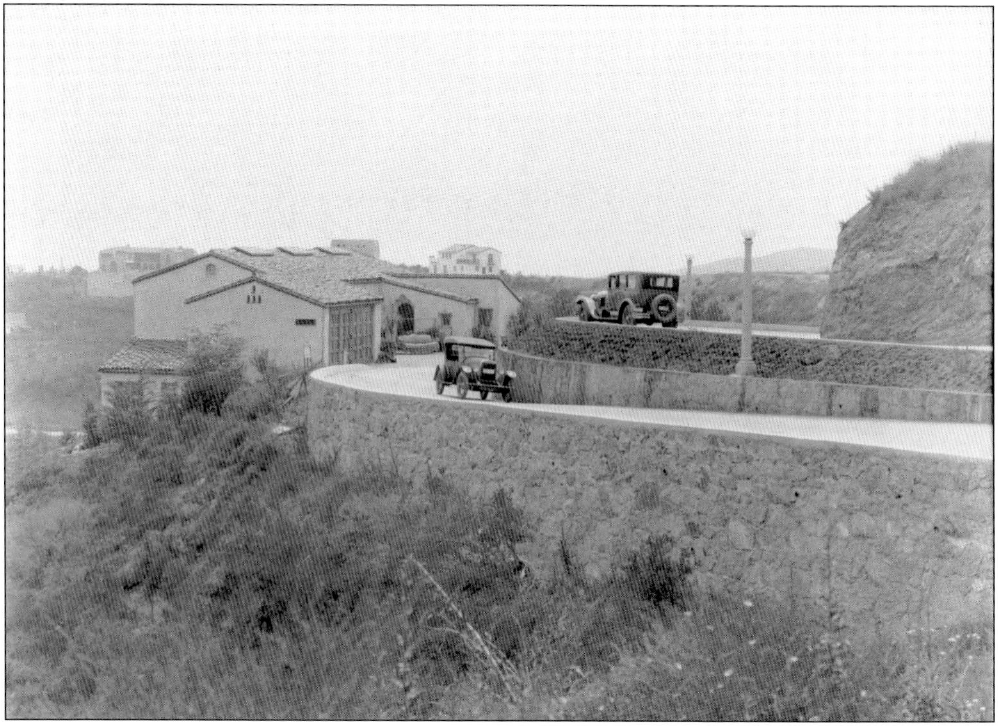

Construction began June 14, 1924, on the Kanst Art Gallery, located at 6182 Mulholland Highway with views in all directions. Granite retaining walls supported the roads while also providing a special artistic touch. Architects John L. DeLario and Harbin F. Hunter designed this home for art gallery owner J.F. Kanst to both work and live in.

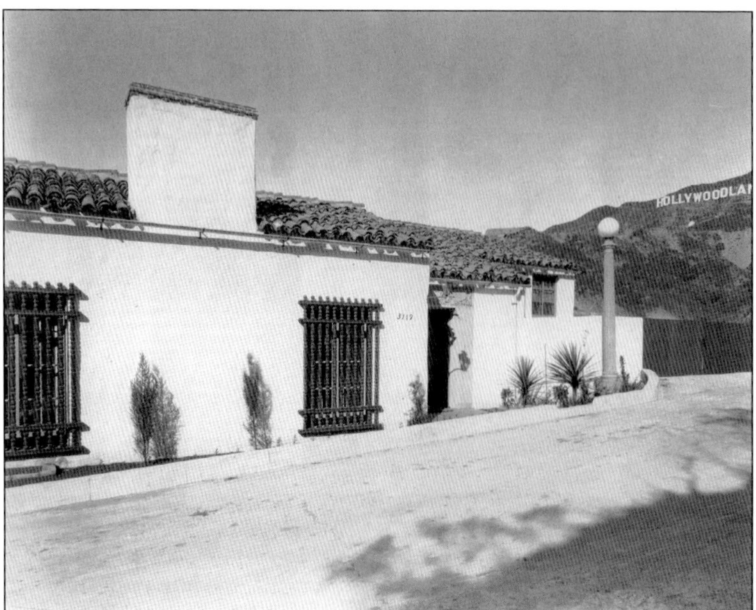

Conceived by John L. DeLario in 1925, the Kathryn and Dr. Edwin R. Kibler home at 3119 Hollyridge Drive looks up at the Hollywoodland sign. The Kiblers bought the property after seeing a *Los Angeles Times* advertisement in March 1925. The home was built by the Atlas Construction Company and cost $21,500.

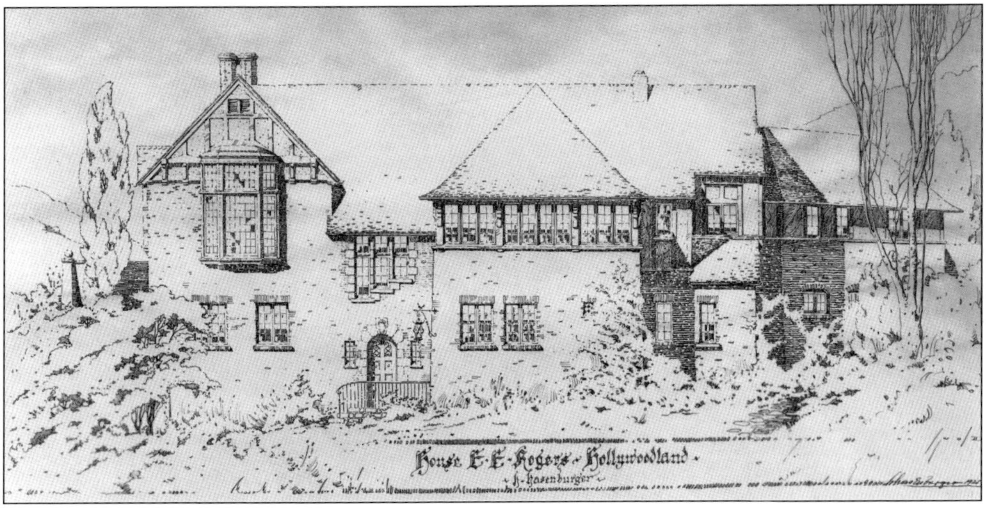

According to Hollywoodland advertising manager L.J. Burrud in the February 14, 1926, issue of the *Los Angeles Times*, architect H. Hasenberger was so precise in designing the English Tudor Ernest E. Rogers home that he built an exact miniature in color and detail so that every vantage point of the site could be studied and utilized.

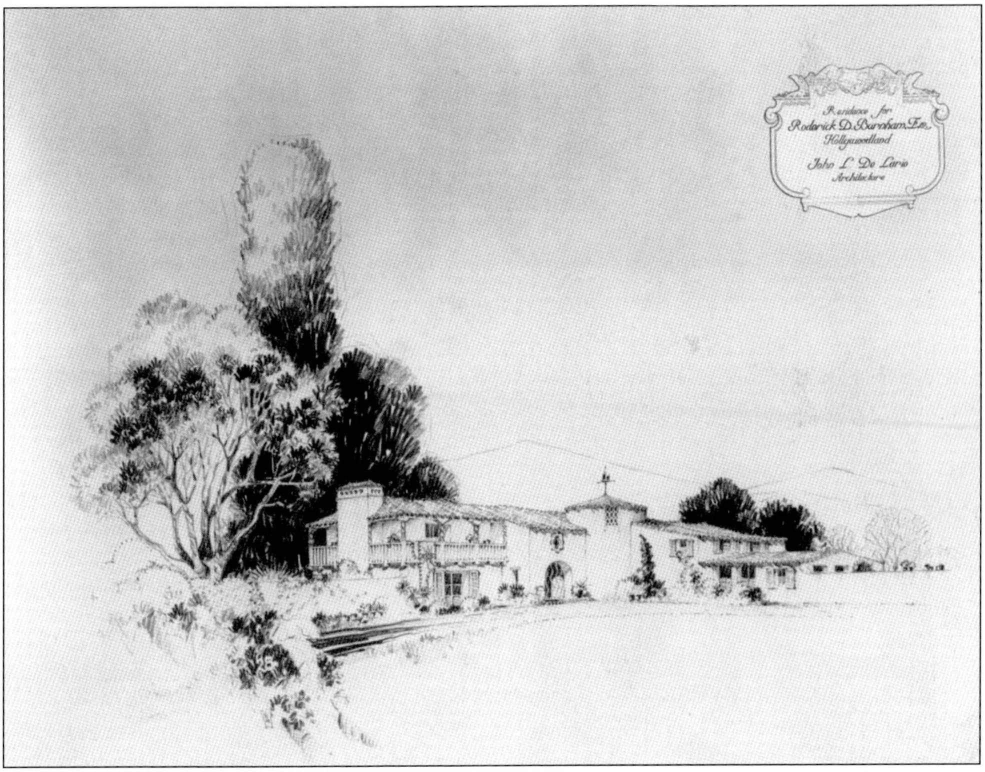

The Roderick D. Burnham home located at 3129 Durand Drive was conceived in 1925 by architect John L. DeLario in 1925 to overlook the San Fernando Valley, Lake Hollywood, and Los Angeles. Burnham was a manager of oil lands in Venezuela for Union Oil and later in California. In 1929, he served as photographer on a tour of British game preserve areas in Africa with his father, Maj. Frederick Burnham.

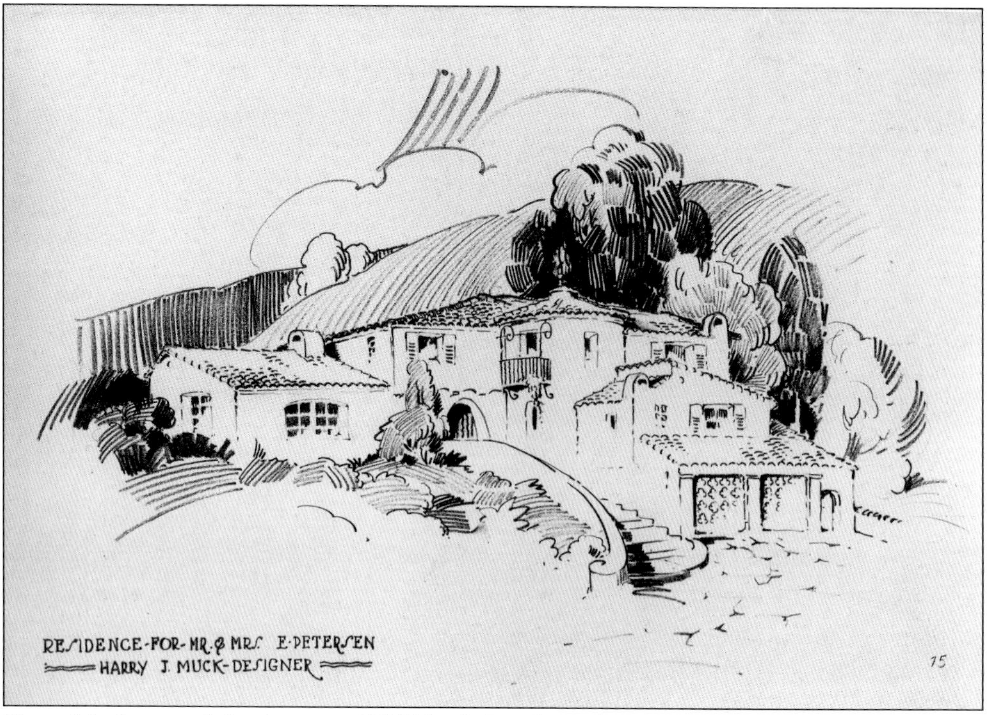

Harry Muck created this home at 2706 North Beachwood Drive in 1927 for Kirstine and Einar C. Petersen. Muck would later design the George R. Kress home in Beverly Hills. Petersen was a well-respected muralist from Denmark who had studied in Europe. He painted murals for the "new" Rosslyn Hotel in 1915, Clifton's "Brookdale" Cafeteria, and the Spring Street Guaranty Building and Loan Association in downtown Los Angeles.

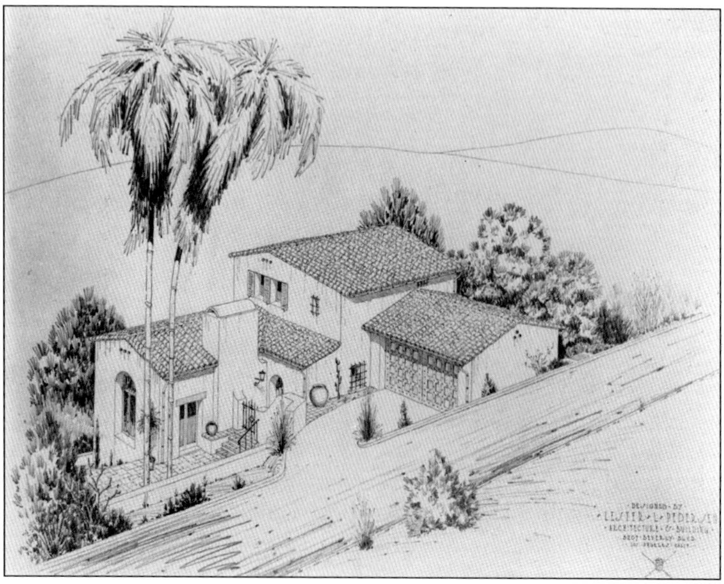

Lester L. Pedersen sketched this California Spanish-style home in the hills of Hollywoodland. Pedersen was a top architect for homes in another exclusive hillside housing development in the western hills of Hollywood, Outpost Estates, on behalf of the C.E. Toberman Company. He was one of several architects recognized in that outfit for their Spanish home designs.

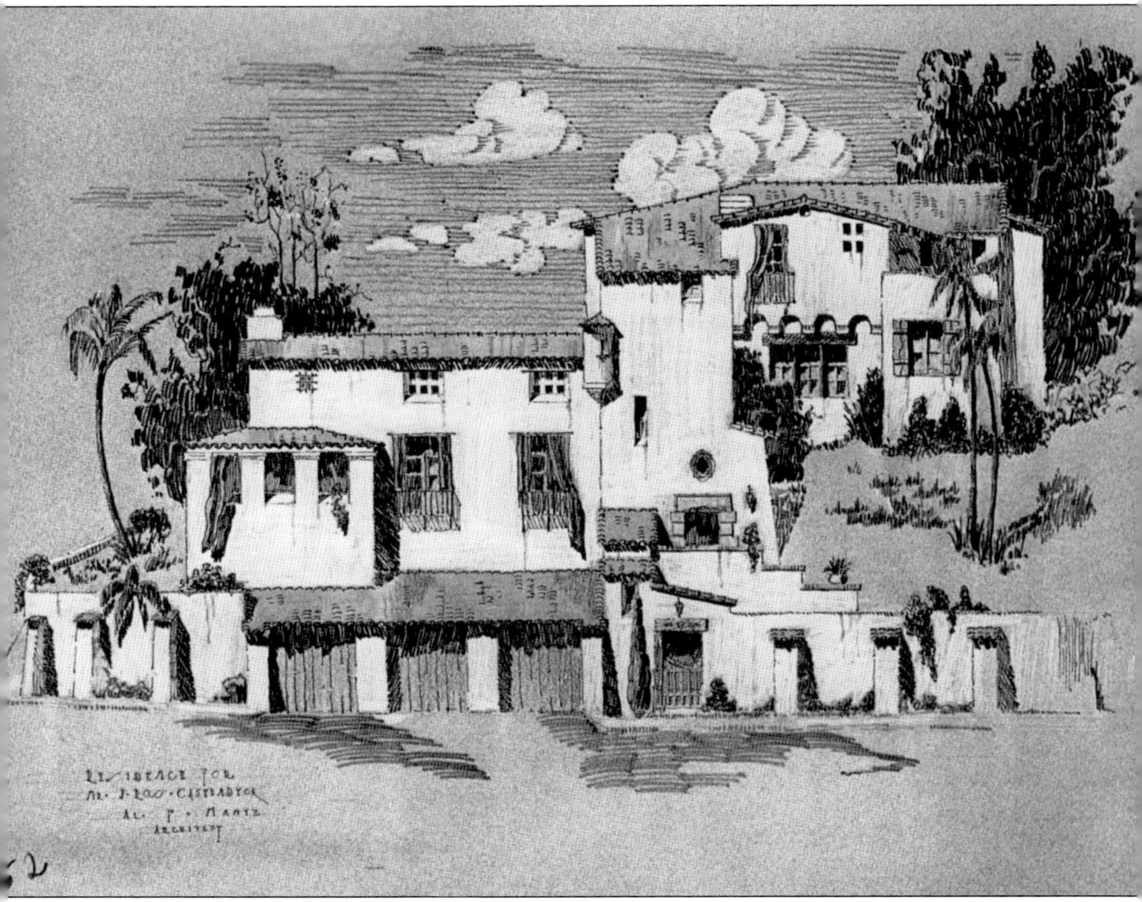

Architect Al F. Mantz drew two elevations for the front and side of a Hollywoodland home for homebuilder J. Ross Castendyck. Mantz, a manager of a Spring Street hotel in 1919, was awarded $2,125 from the owner, Francisca Jesserun, who accused him of allowing gambling and other vices at the hotel. He became an architect in the early 1920s. Mantz remodeled the Berwilla Studios at 5821 Santa Monica Boulevard for Richard Thomas in 1925, adding a second floor to the building and stuccoing the exterior for a cost of $100,000. He was also one of 50 local architects, including fellow Hollywoodland architect Vincent Palmer, who exhibited works in a show sponsored by the Hollywood Chamber of Commerce in 1927. Castendyck constructed upscale homes throughout Los Angeles. He erected a $60,000 home in Hancock Park in 1929 that was designed by Milton J. Black. Castendyck also built homes in C.E. Toberman's Outpost Estates.

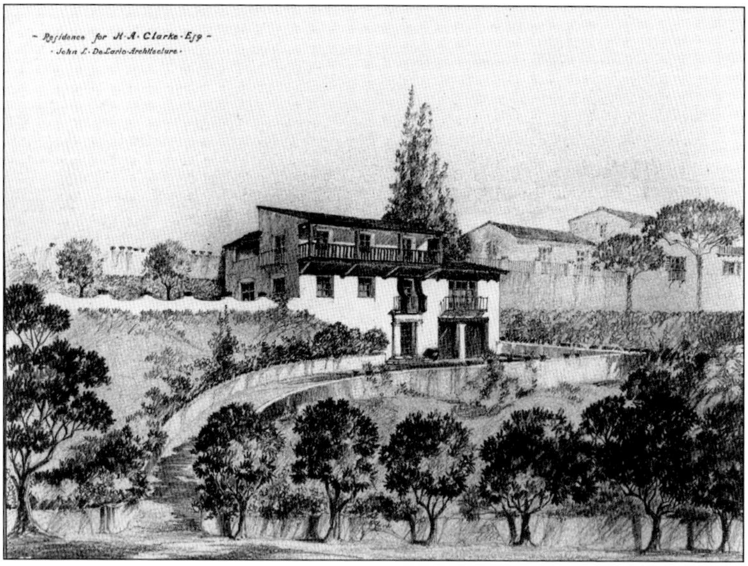

John L. DeLario designed this home in Hollywoodland for fellow architect Harrison Clarke. Clarke was an up and coming young architect in Los Angeles. He was the winner of the Los Angeles Civic Center Plan, as well as a winner in the 1924 Small Houses design building. Clarke placed second in the 1929 National Better Homes Competition.

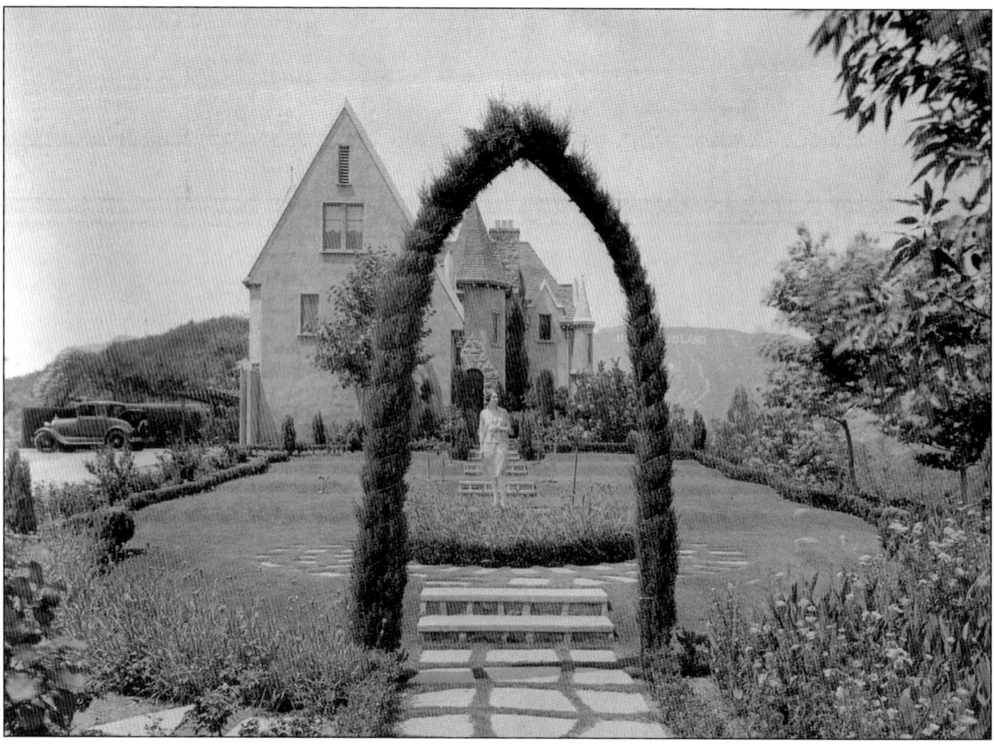

Wolf's Lair, the French Normandy home planned and built for developer Milton Wolf in 1927, resembles a fairy tale castle with the Hollywoodland sign just to the right of it in the background of the photograph. Located at 2869 Durand Drive, the house has been home to several entertainment-related owners over the years.

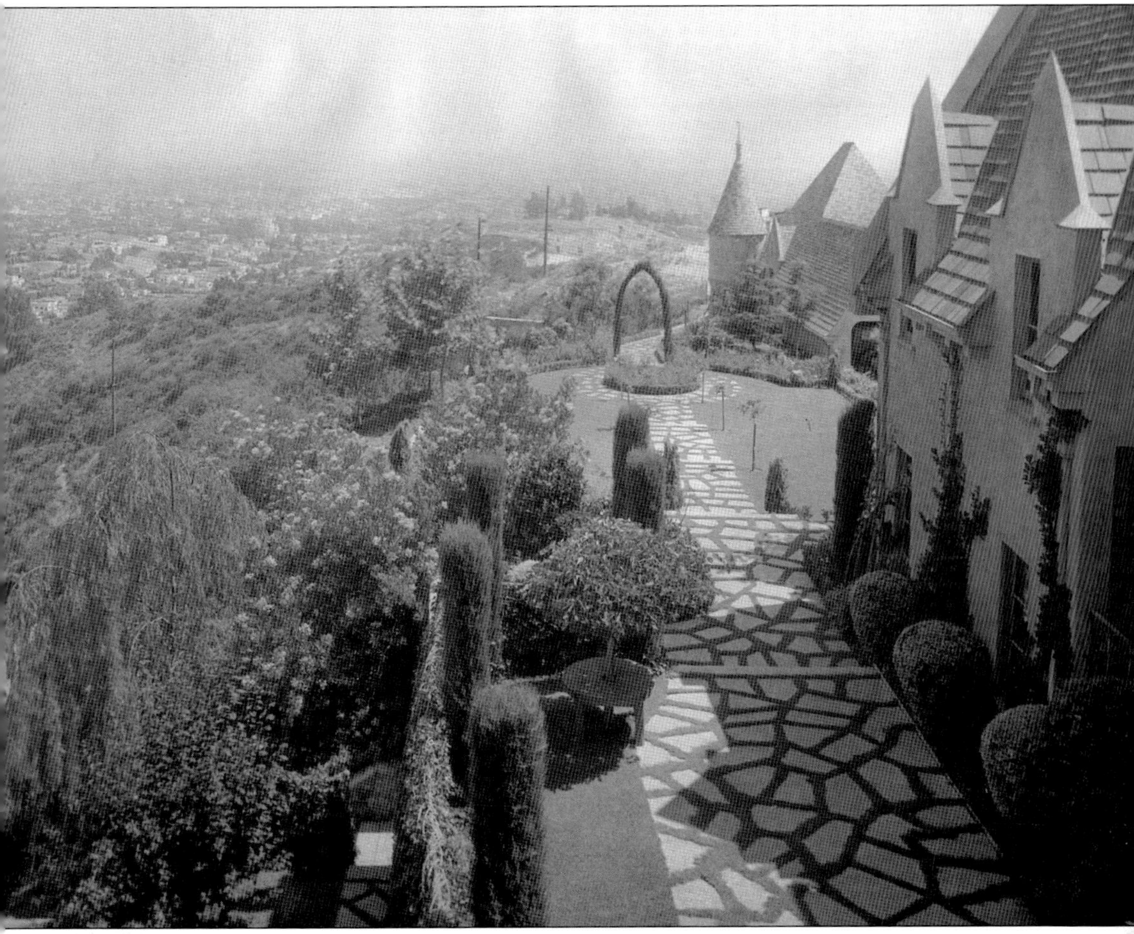

Now owned by the musician Moby, the Norman castle Wolf's Lair, built in 1927, contains extensive grounds to go along with its storybook architecture. The grounds, as well designed as the home, include fountains, fishponds, walking paths, promenades, a nature preserve, and views of both Lake Hollywood and the Hollywood sign. These outside touches help make the large home more intimate and private, adding to its otherworldly quality. Inside the home is just as elegant, containing many interesting little touches. It contains secret stairways and a 1920s-era speakeasy that is a tiki bar, complete with bamboo piano. These additions allowed the owners a chance to enjoy an alcoholic drink in the privacy of their own home during the heyday of Prohibition. During the 1950s, architect John Lautner designed a separate two-bedroom guesthouse in the gardens of the estate. (Bison.)

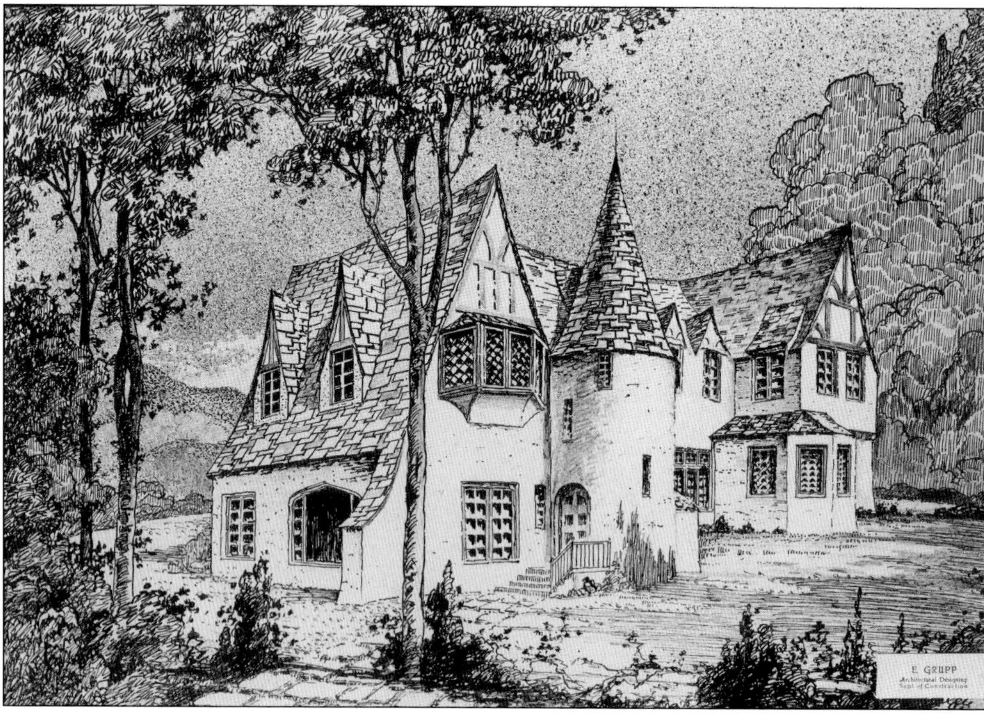

This combination Norman castle and English Tudor home demonstrates the fairy tale atmosphere of Hollywoodland. Elmer Grupp, the architectural designing superintendent of construction, was general manager of the Hollywood Architectural and Engineering Service, which built homes and apartments through Hollywood. Hollywoodland developers promoted the theatricality and beauty of the neighborhood's storybook architecture.

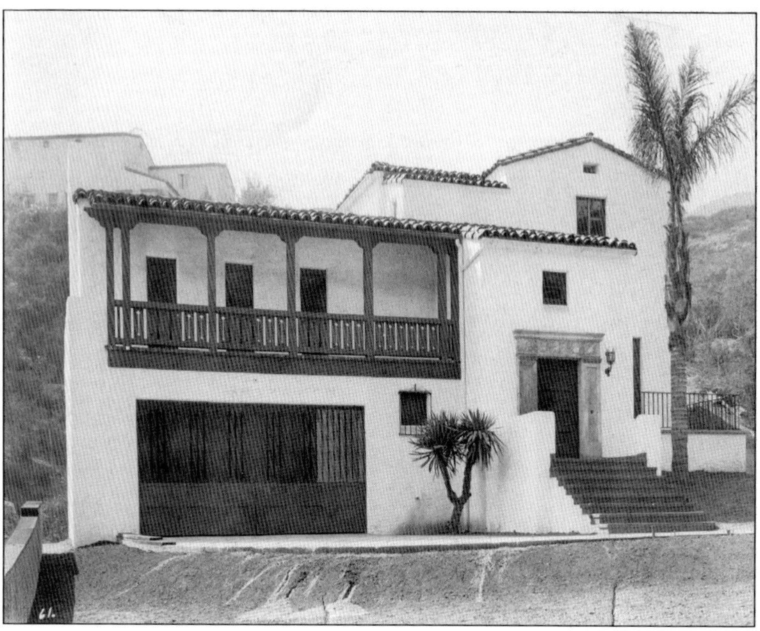

The home at 3323 Ledgewood Drive takes advantage of its views with a porch and a small terrace to the side. The developers employed a photograph of the home in the brochure *Hollywoodland: Five Minutes from Hollywood's Great White Way* to promote how "quaint balconies and interesting entrance ways" reflected the charm of the subdivision.

The home at 6384 Rodgerton Drive exists on three different levels. Architect John L. DeLario wrote in a July 5, 1925, *Los Angeles Times* column that careful planning would allow for constructing a hillside home for the same price as a home on flat land, if the home was designed to fit the site.

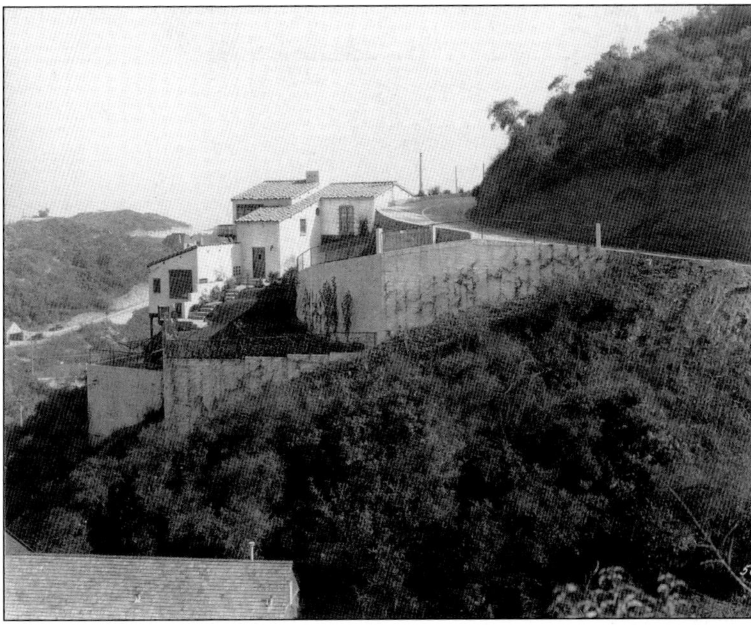

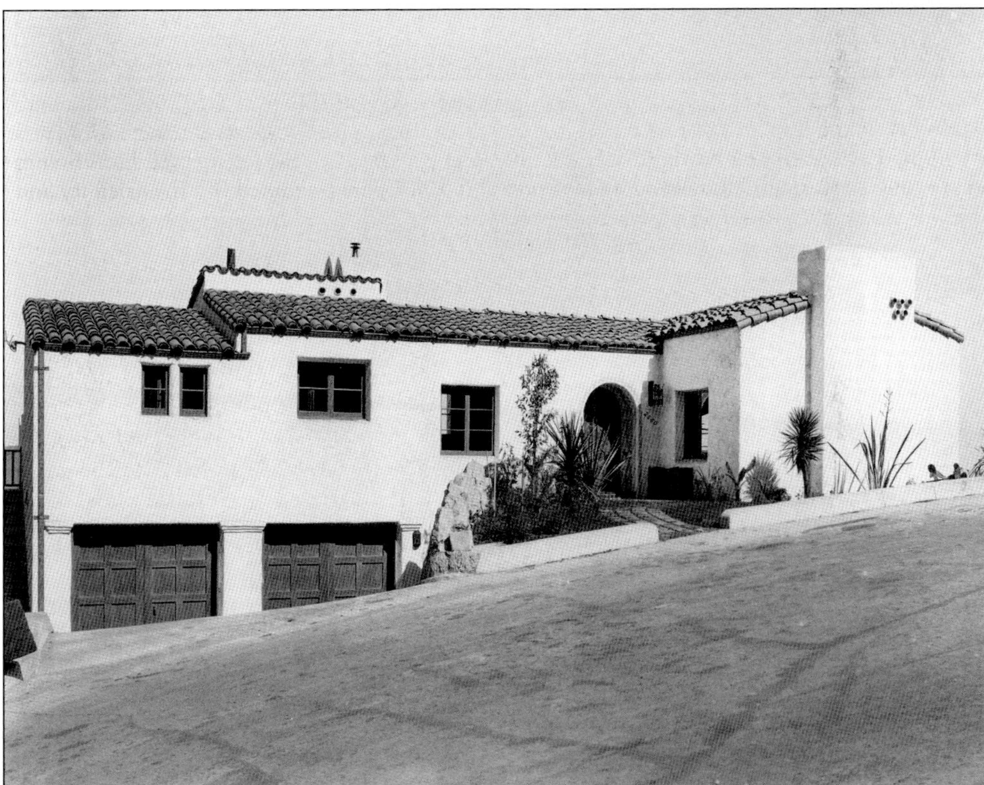

This Hollywoodland home was constructed for George S. Colley, according to a July 11, 1926, article in the *Los Angeles Times*. The home was open for inspection for those interested in Spanish architecture. The article stated that the home "combines architectural and artistic individuality with a very convenient and practical interior arrangement."

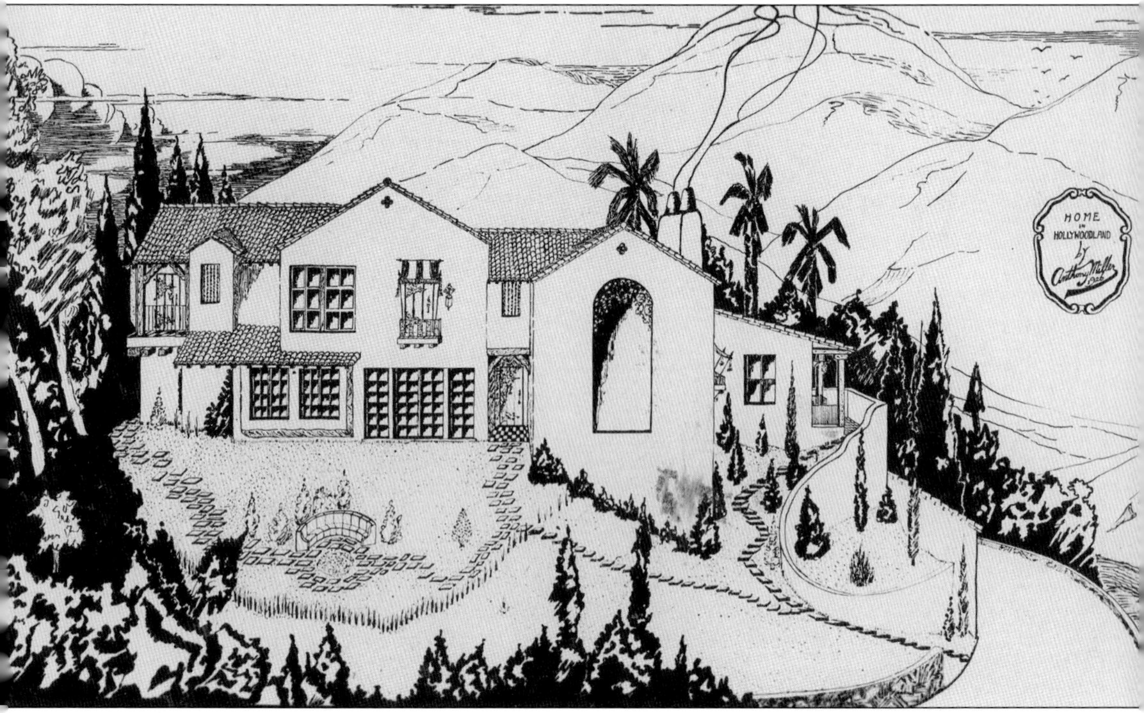

Architect Anthony Miller designed this home at 3267 Ledgewood Drive for actress Fritzi Ridgeway. Ridgeway, wife of musical conductor Constantin Bakaleinikoff, hired Miller in March 1928 to build houses for her. Deputy district attorney J.W. Joos filed a complaint against Miller on Ridgeway's behalf on June 8, 1928, accusing him of taking $734 by padding expense costs. Ridgeway first appeared in western two-reelers in the mid-teens before going on to feature player status for major studios. She and husband Bakaleinikoff lived at 2836 Beachwood Drive. Bakaleinikoff, born in Moscow, served in the Russian Army during World War I. Soon after, he came to the United States and joined the Los Angeles Philharmonic as viola player, leaving in a few years to conduct the orchestra at Sid Grauman's Million Dollar Theatre. Bakaleinikoff conducted Grauman's Egyptian Orchestra in the mid-1920s before acting as musical director for such musicals as *Oh Kay* in 1927. He composed scores and directed orchestras at several film studios for over 30 years, earning four Oscar nominations for his work.

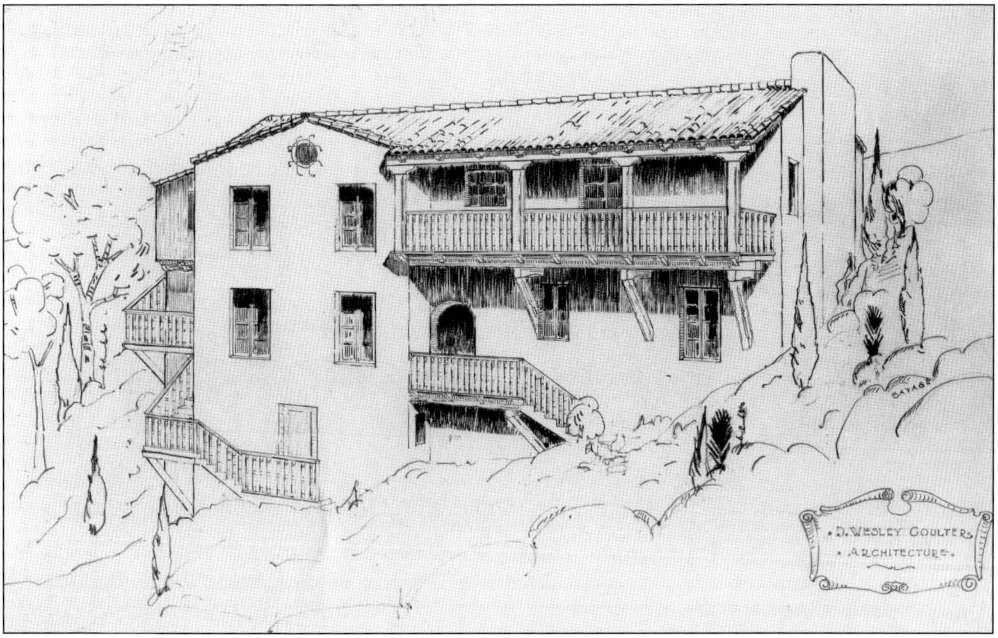

Architect D. Wesley Coulter planned this home to be built for himself in Hollywoodland. The elevation ran in the January 3, 1926, edition of the *Los Angeles Times* and demonstrated how the home followed the contours of the hills around it. The *Times* also ran a second story that day promoting Coulter as an outstanding builder in Southern California.

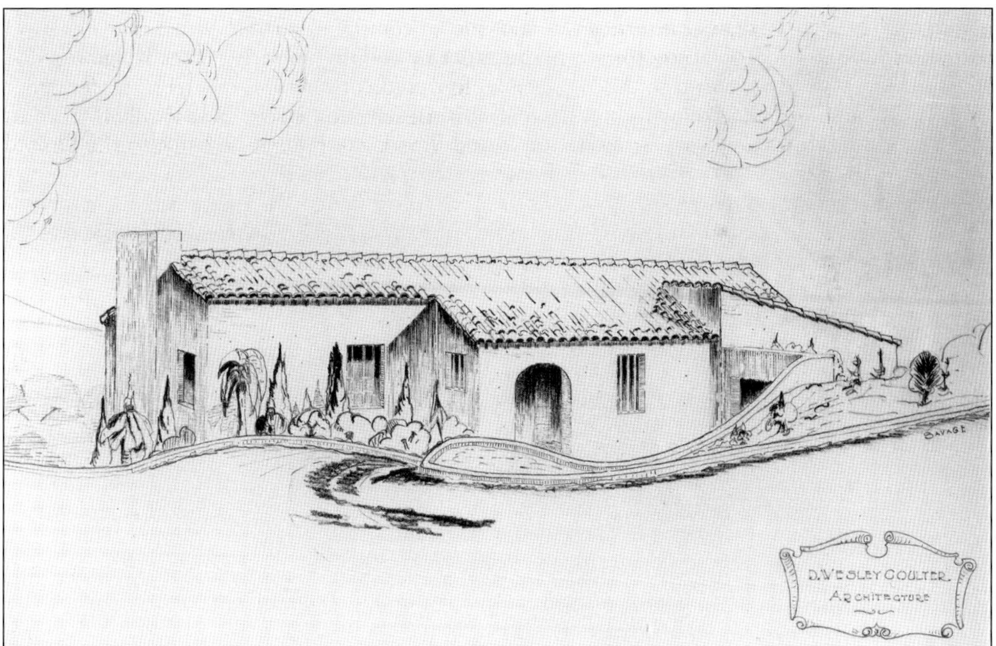

The *Los Angeles Times* printed a letter from architect/builder D. Wesley Coulter on January 3, 1926, in which he stated he planned to build several Spanish-style homes in Hollywoodland. He described the vista from Hollywoodland as "a magnificent, never-to-be-forgotten view that would thrill the most inert to the joys of living."

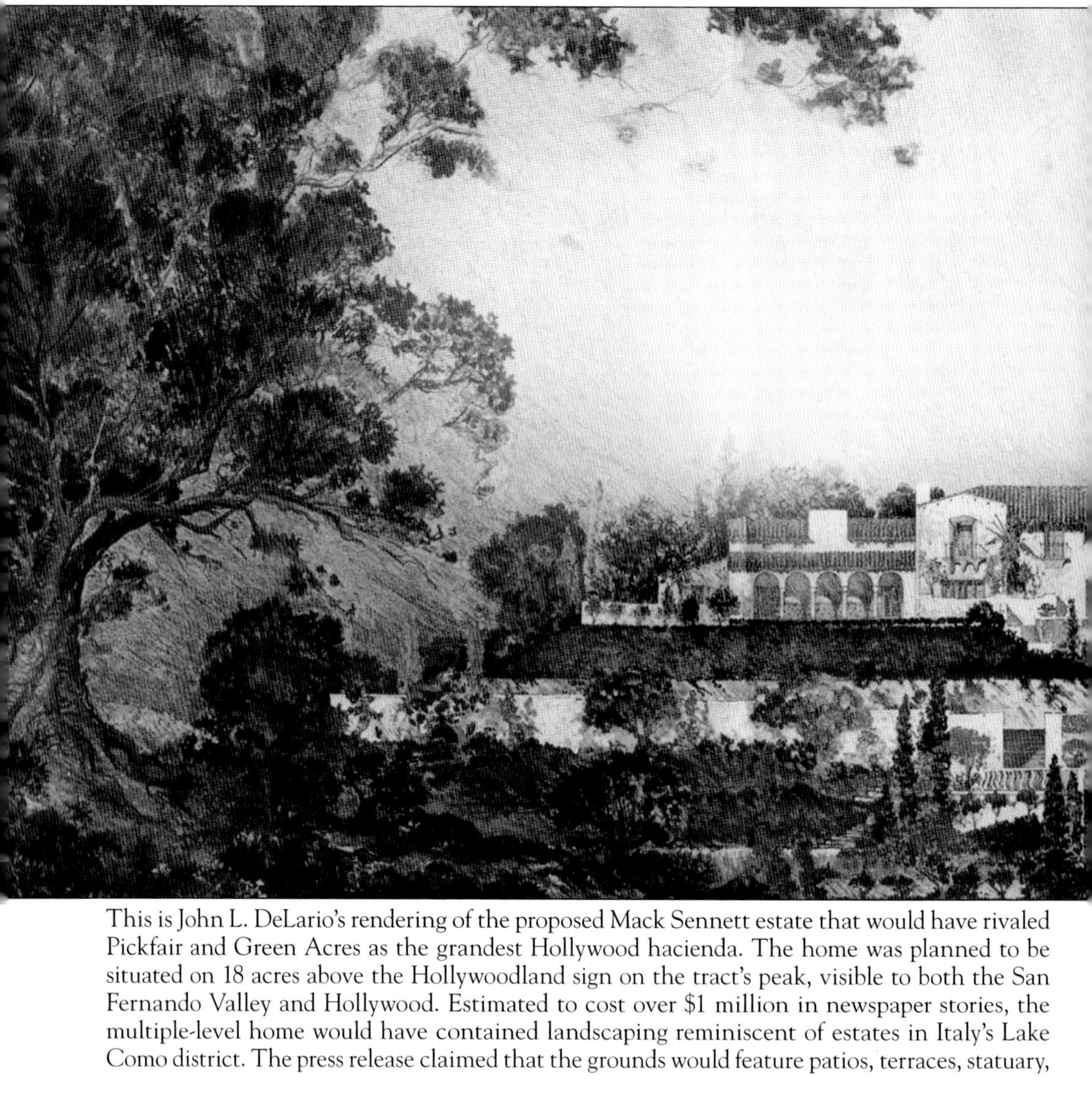

This is John L. DeLario's rendering of the proposed Mack Sennett estate that would have rivaled Pickfair and Green Acres as the grandest Hollywood hacienda. The home was planned to be situated on 18 acres above the Hollywoodland sign on the tract's peak, visible to both the San Fernando Valley and Hollywood. Estimated to cost over $1 million in newspaper stories, the multiple-level home would have contained landscaping reminiscent of estates in Italy's Lake Como district. The press release claimed that the grounds would feature patios, terraces, statuary,

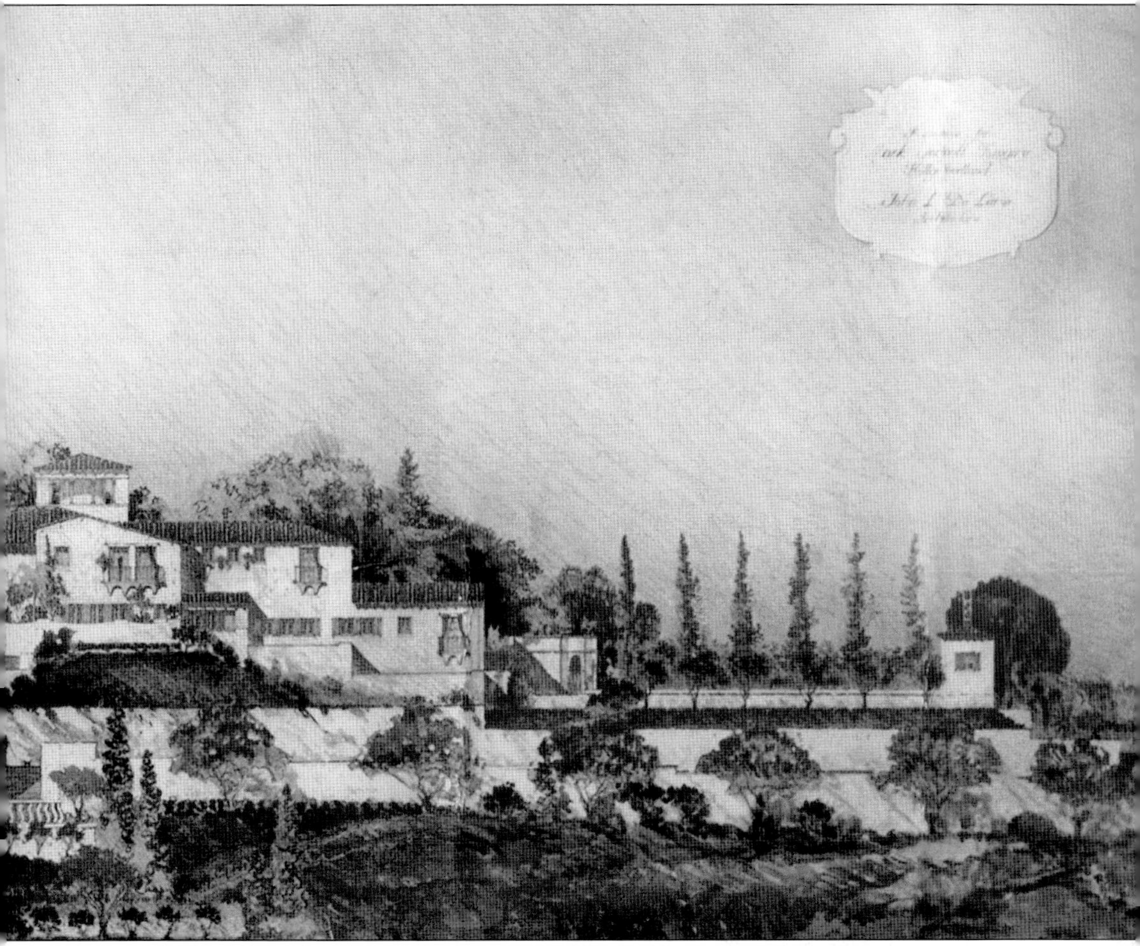

cloistered loggia, fountain, 40-by-75-foot swimming pool with sand beach, tennis courts, open-air theater, and miniature golf course. The interior would include patios, cloister, living room, dining room, conservatory, library, drawing room, kitchen, guest suites, a suite for his mother, and a master suite to include steam room, dressing room, and loggia. No motion picture theater was mentioned. (AMPAS.)

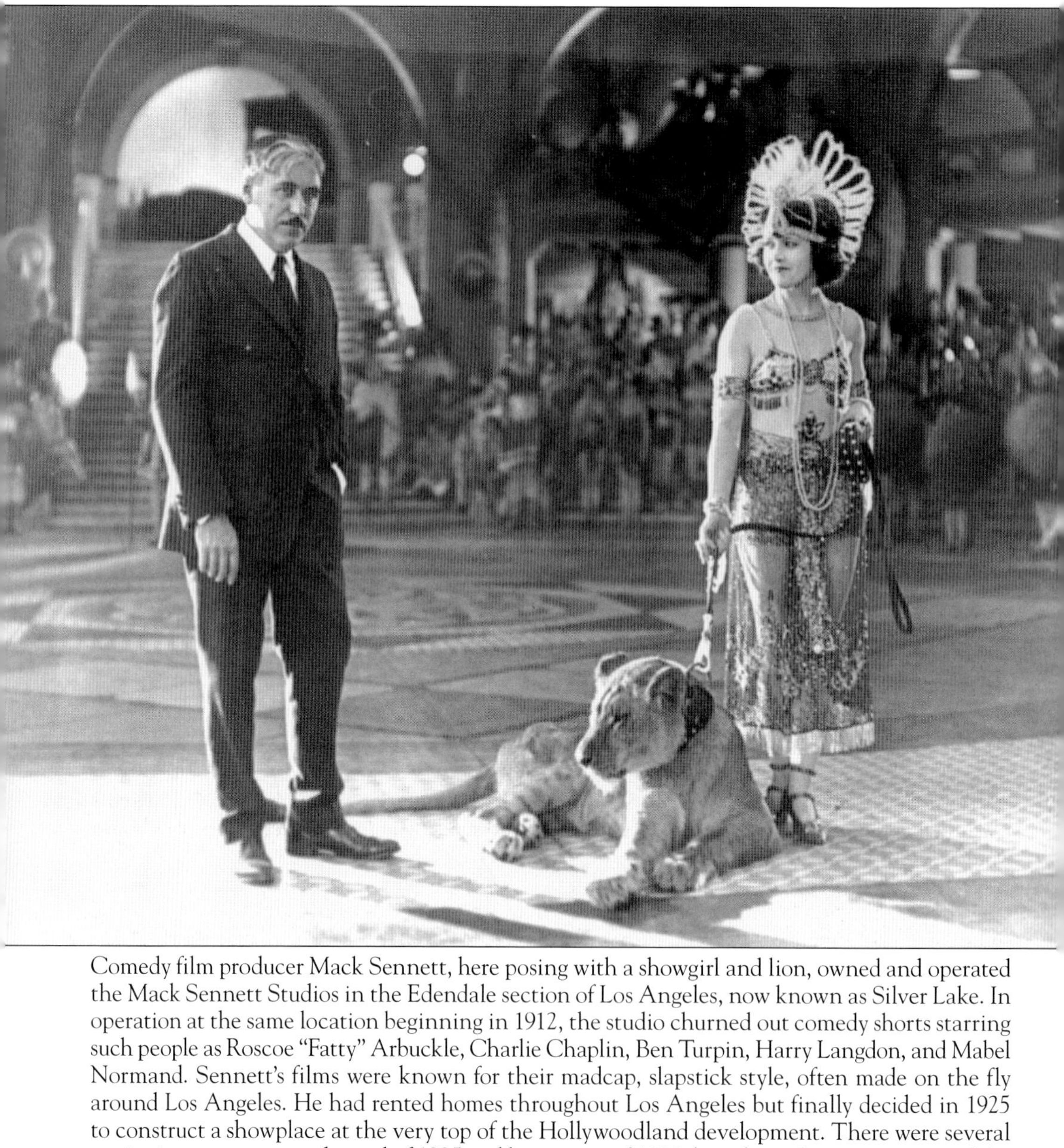

Comedy film producer Mack Sennett, here posing with a showgirl and lion, owned and operated the Mack Sennett Studios in the Edendale section of Los Angeles, now known as Silver Lake. In operation at the same location beginning in 1912, the studio churned out comedy shorts starring such people as Roscoe "Fatty" Arbuckle, Charlie Chaplin, Ben Turpin, Harry Langdon, and Mabel Normand. Sennett's films were known for their madcap, slapstick style, often made on the fly around Los Angeles. He had rented homes throughout Los Angeles but finally decided in 1925 to construct a showplace at the very top of the Hollywoodland development. There were several stories in newspapers at the end of 1925 and beginning of 1926 describing the construction of the road to the future home as well as the proposed home plan. Sennett suffered financial problems, and the home was never built. (MM.)

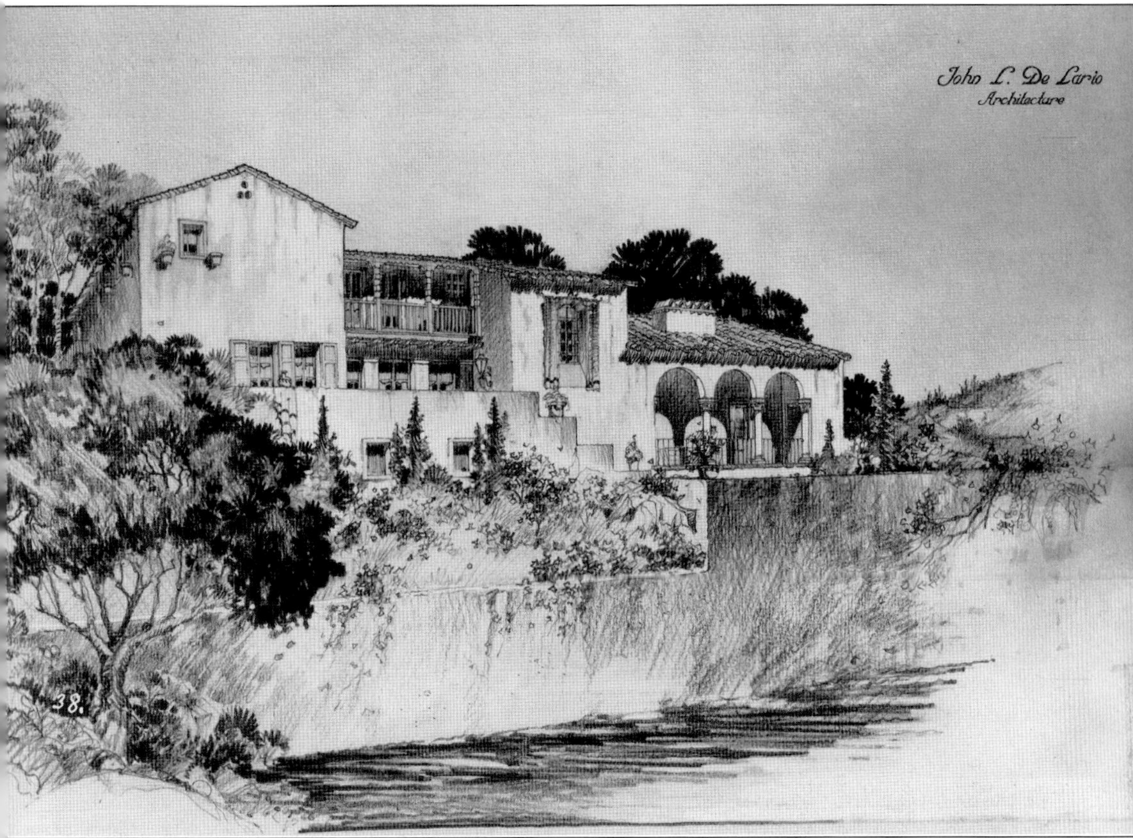

Carrie and Clyde R. Franklin built this $25,000 John L. DeLario–designed home at 6171 Rockcliff Place in 1926. According to a December 27, 1925, article in the *Los Angeles Times*, the house would be steeped in Spanish atmosphere, finished in white and employing tile, ornamental ironwork and stairway, wood-truss ceiling, terraces, patios, balconies, and old padre handmade red tile roof. The first floor would include large living room with fireplace and open wood-truss ceiling, loggia, terrace, entrance hall, breakfast room, kitchen, pass pantry, service porch, and maid's room, with a separate room below for games or billiards. The second floor would include master suite with bedroom, tile bath, separate shower, dressing room, closets, guest rooms, and bath. A two-car garage and landscaping were included in the cost. Tile and iron work would be employed throughout to add to the "charming effect."

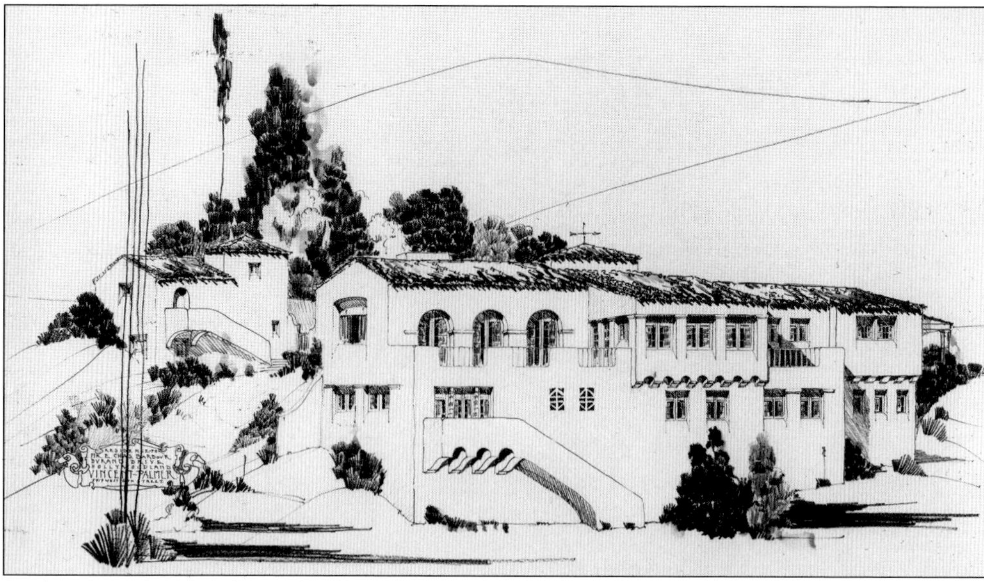

Architect Vincent Palmer planned this residence for E. Charles Barbour on Durand Drive in 1926, but it was not completed until 1927. The elevation ran in a November 14, 1926, story about Hollywoodland in the *Los Angeles Times*. It typified the style of California Renaissance architecture that was popular in Hollywoodland.

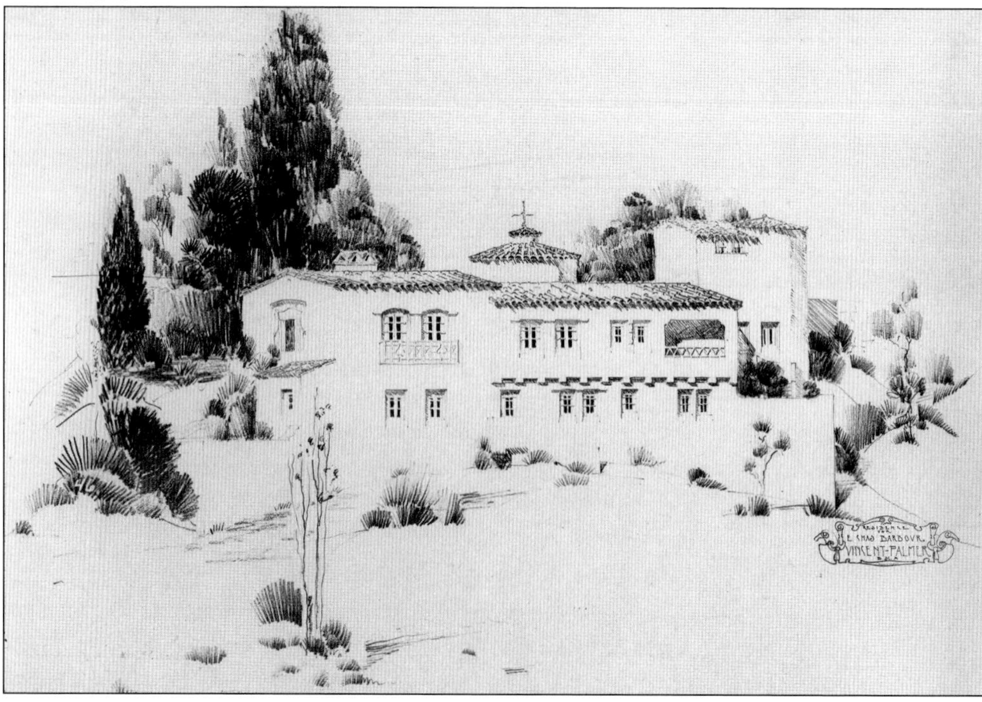

Vincent Palmer designed this elevation of the back of the E. Charles Barbour home. Such architecture, or "frozen music" as the developers of Hollywoodland called it, drew fame to the real estate tract. This Spanish-style architecture was considered the "most adaptable to the hillside property, principally because of the simplicity which is the keynote of its rich elegance," they told the *Los Angeles Times* on January 23, 1927.

Architect Vincent Palmer sketched this residence for builder H.S. Beiland. In 1924, Beiland constructed a two-story building at Rodeo Drive and Burton Way in Beverly Hills. He planned to build 10 houses in Hollywoodland, most designed by Palmer. This home was located at 3206 Deronda Drive and cost $40,000 when built in 1926.

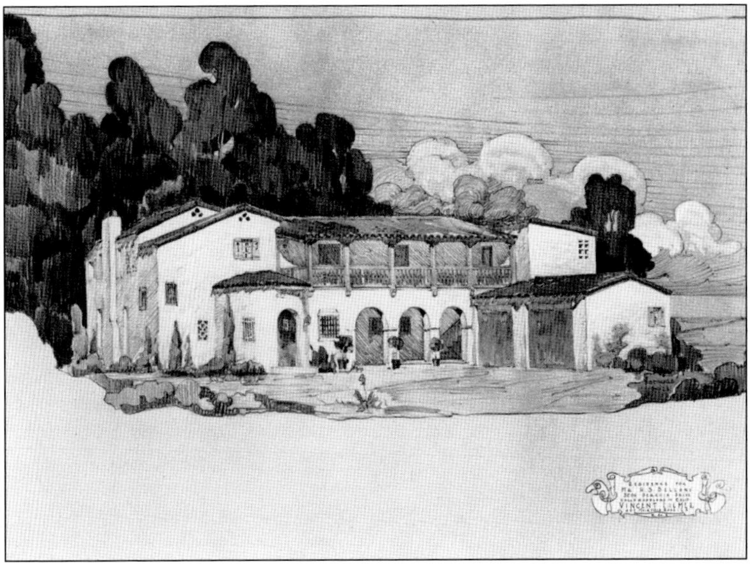

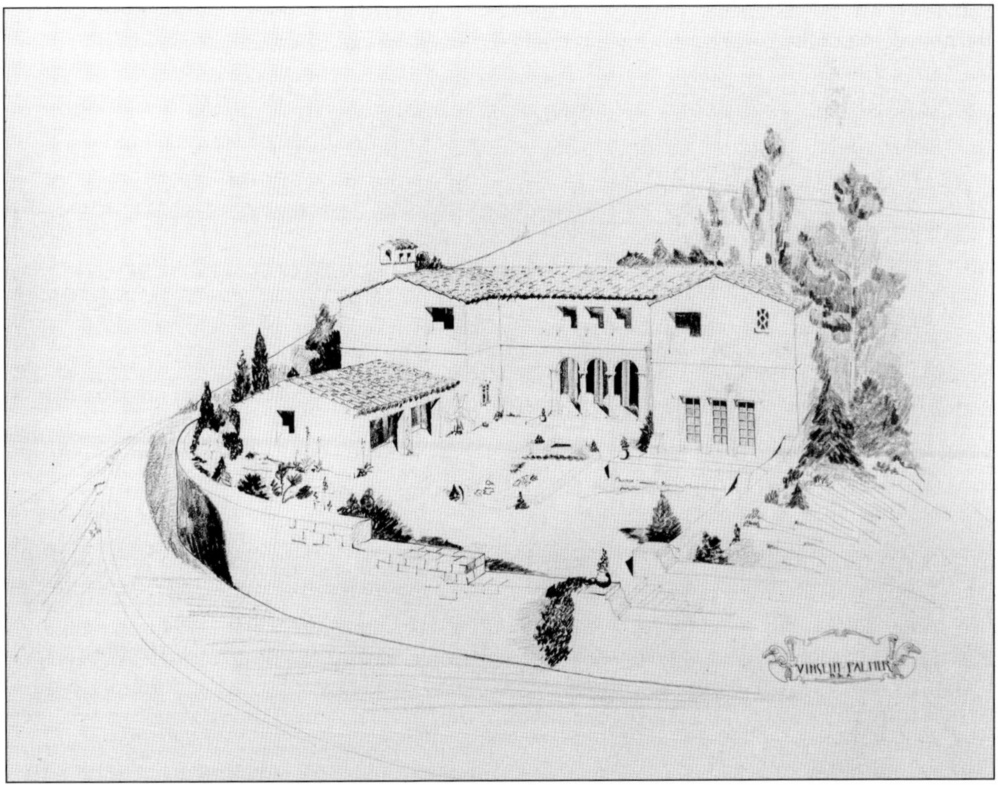

The homes Vincent Palmer designed for H.S. Beiland took advantage of the hillsides by featuring terraces, patios, balconies, and outdoor sleeping areas. Beiland enhanced the exterior as well, by incorporating landscaping, rare flowers, and shrubbery into the designs. He described selecting Hollywoodland as a building site because "it offered me most in beauty, location, convenience, improvements, and value."

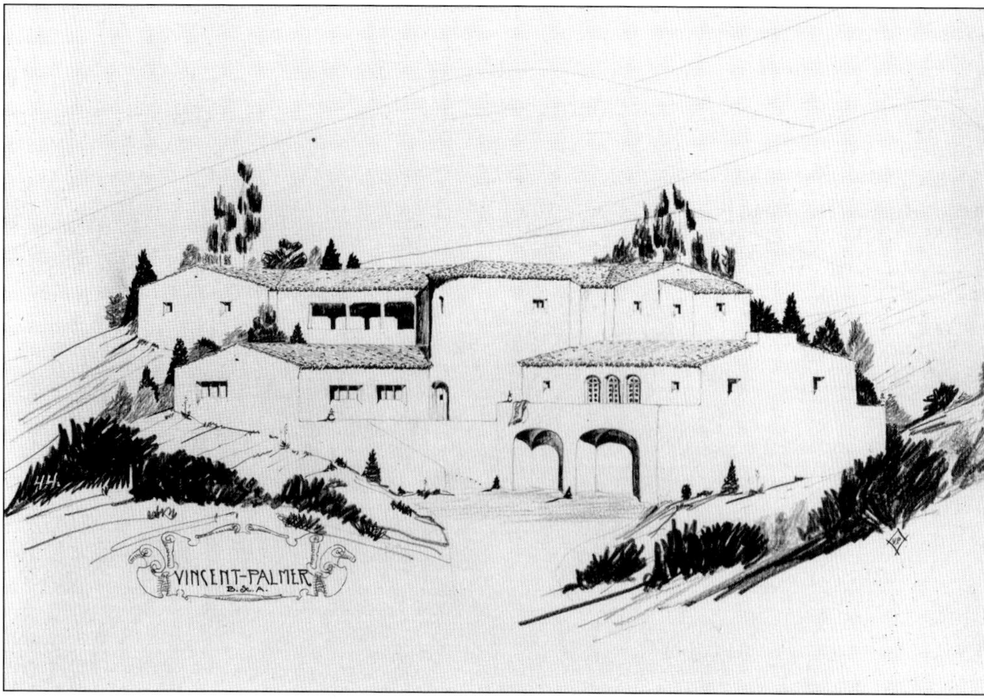

Vincent Palmer drew homes in the California Spanish style in the late 1920s. He followed more classical styles of architecture and belonged to the Hollywood Architects' League. On February 18, 1929, he and Vernon McClurg represented classical architecture and Richard Neutra and R.M. Schindler represented modern architecture in a debate sponsored by the California Art Club at Barnsdall Park.

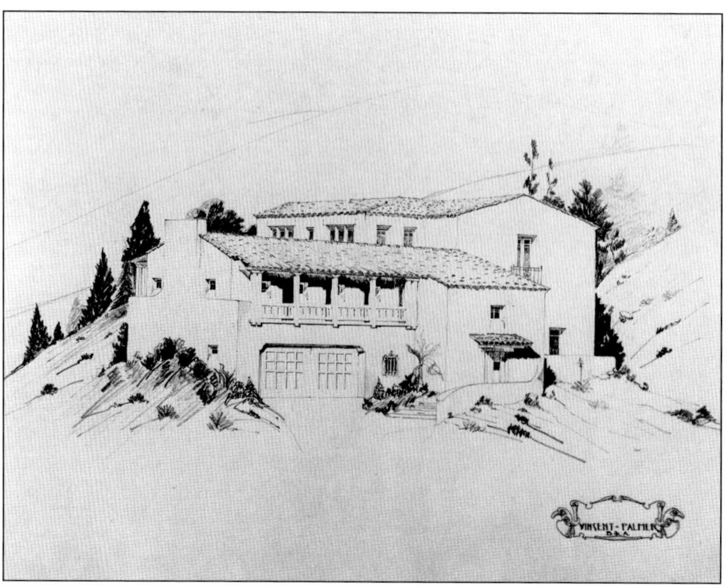

Architect Vincent Palmer's work was included in the Hollywood Architects' League exhibit in 1927. His work was also exhibited in the Architects' Building Material exhibit in 1930 that included Roland Coate, Myron Hunt, Gordon B. Kaufmann, and Wallace Neff. He designed an office tower for California Estates, Inc. that year that was supposed to be built on Wilshire Boulevard.

By 1934, Vincent Palmer established Palmer Steel Buildngs, Inc. to build steel homes. His company opened a demonstration home at Wilshire and Windsor Boulevards that year. He would later design a YWCA building at the University of Southern California as well as lead the Los Angeles branch of the American Institute of Architects.

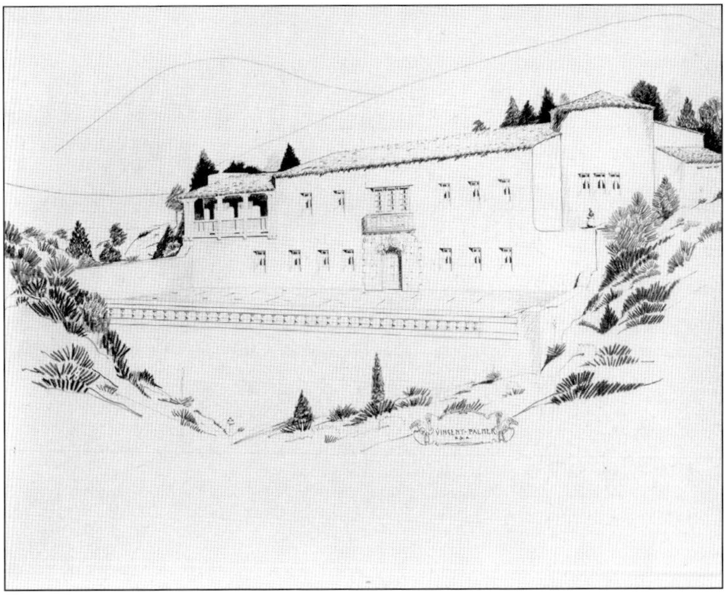

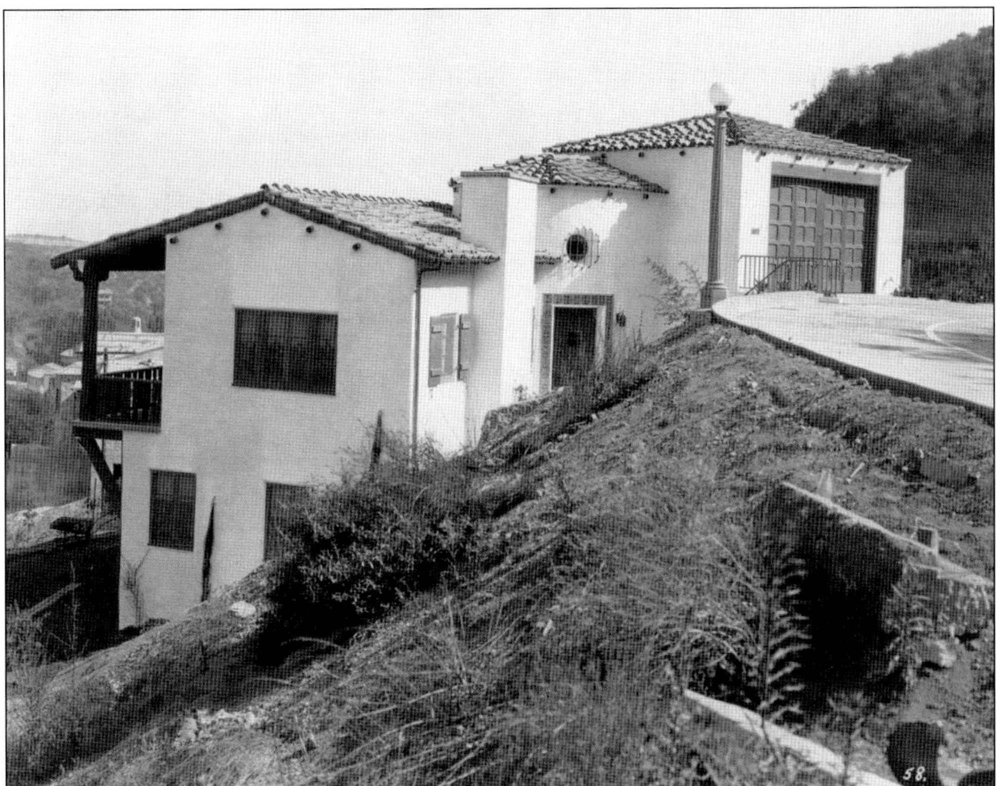

This Spanish-style home is located at 2910 Belden Drive in Hollywoodland. The developers explained in the *Los Angeles Times* that "the Spanish architecture which has become the vogue is not Spanish architecture at all; but is purely a rebirth of the early Spanish haciendas crystallized into a strictly Californian architecture which preserves all the color and romance of the early California homes."

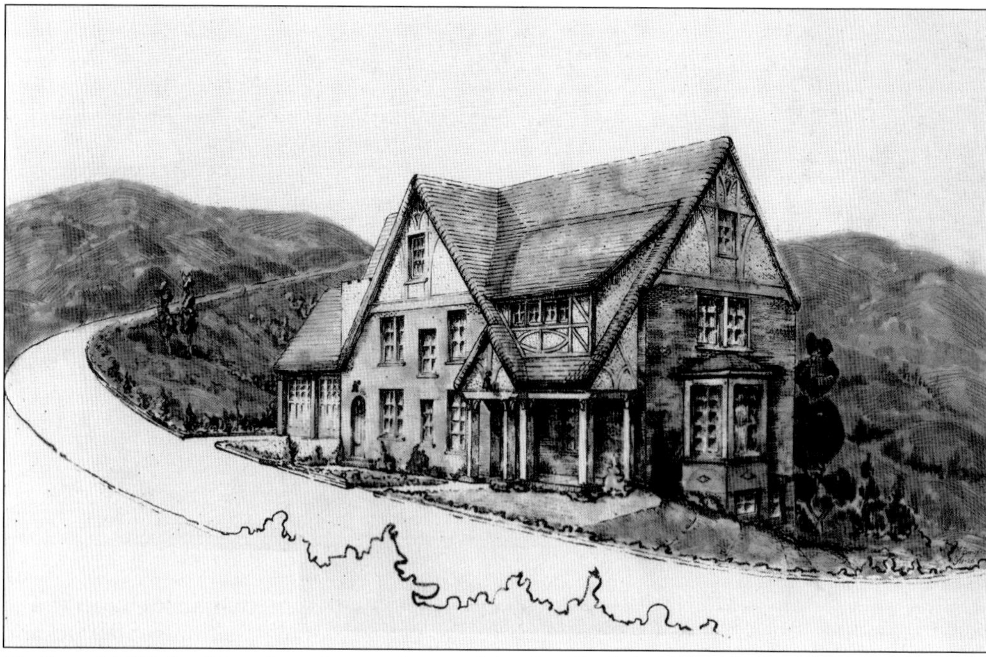

J.J. (Joseph) Blick of Pasadena designed one of the few English Tudor homes in Hollywoodland, which is located at 6010 Lechner Place. Blick drew homes in the West Adams and Wilshire-Westlake districts around 1910 and in Westwood and Los Feliz in the 1930s. He designed Pasadena's police and jail facilities in 1930.

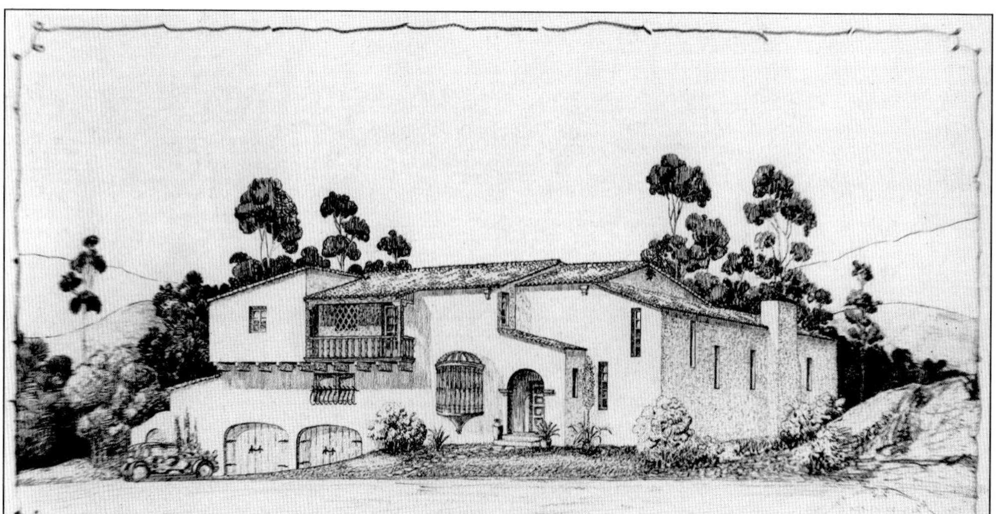

This elevation ran with a story about Hollywoodland in the May 16, 1926, edition of the *Los Angeles Times*. The article promoted hillside development. Developer S.H. Woodruff explained, "The charm and distinctive beauty that attend the Hollywoodland tract is largely the result of its distinctive setting in the hills of Hollywood."

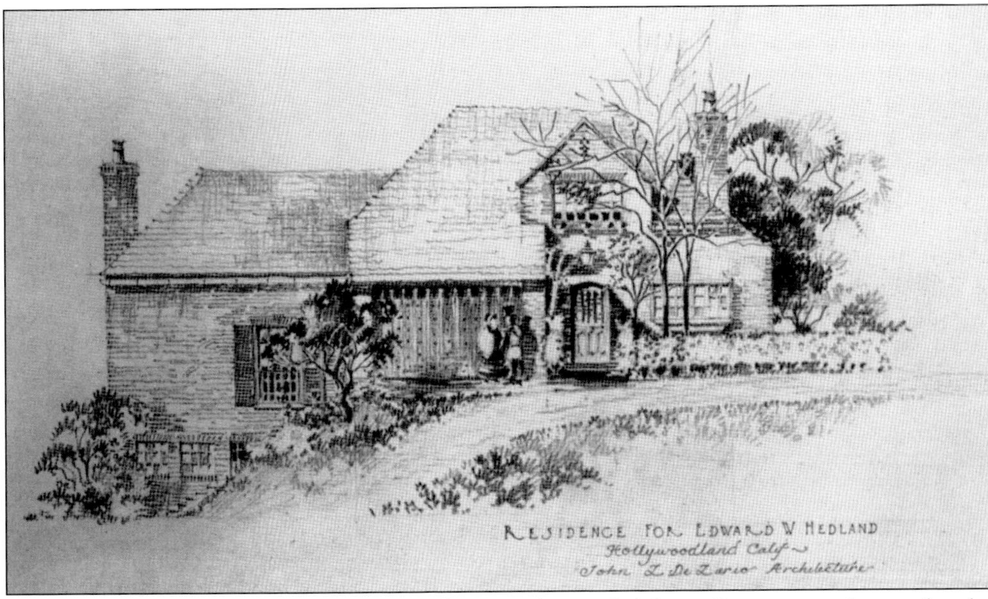

Architect John L. DeLario could do more than just design California Renaissance homes; he also drew this English Tudor home for Edward Hedland. Instead of using retaining walls, DeLario designed it to fit into the hillside terrain and become a part of the landscaping. The house contained stone fireplaces, nooks, and window openings.

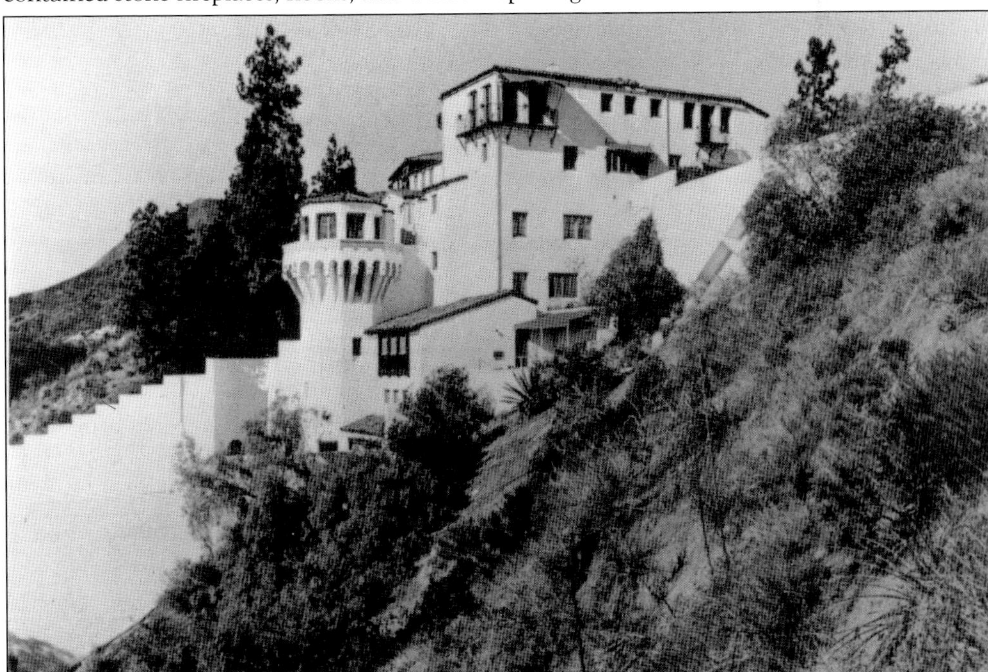

This photograph reveals the massive Castillo del Lago still under construction. Located at 6342 Mulholland Highway, the home was designed by John L. DeLario and constructed by Western Construction Company between 1925 and 1926 for oilman Patrick M. Longan. The house cost over $250,000, containing 20 rooms on nine different levels and standing 106 feet tall at its highest point. (Bison.)

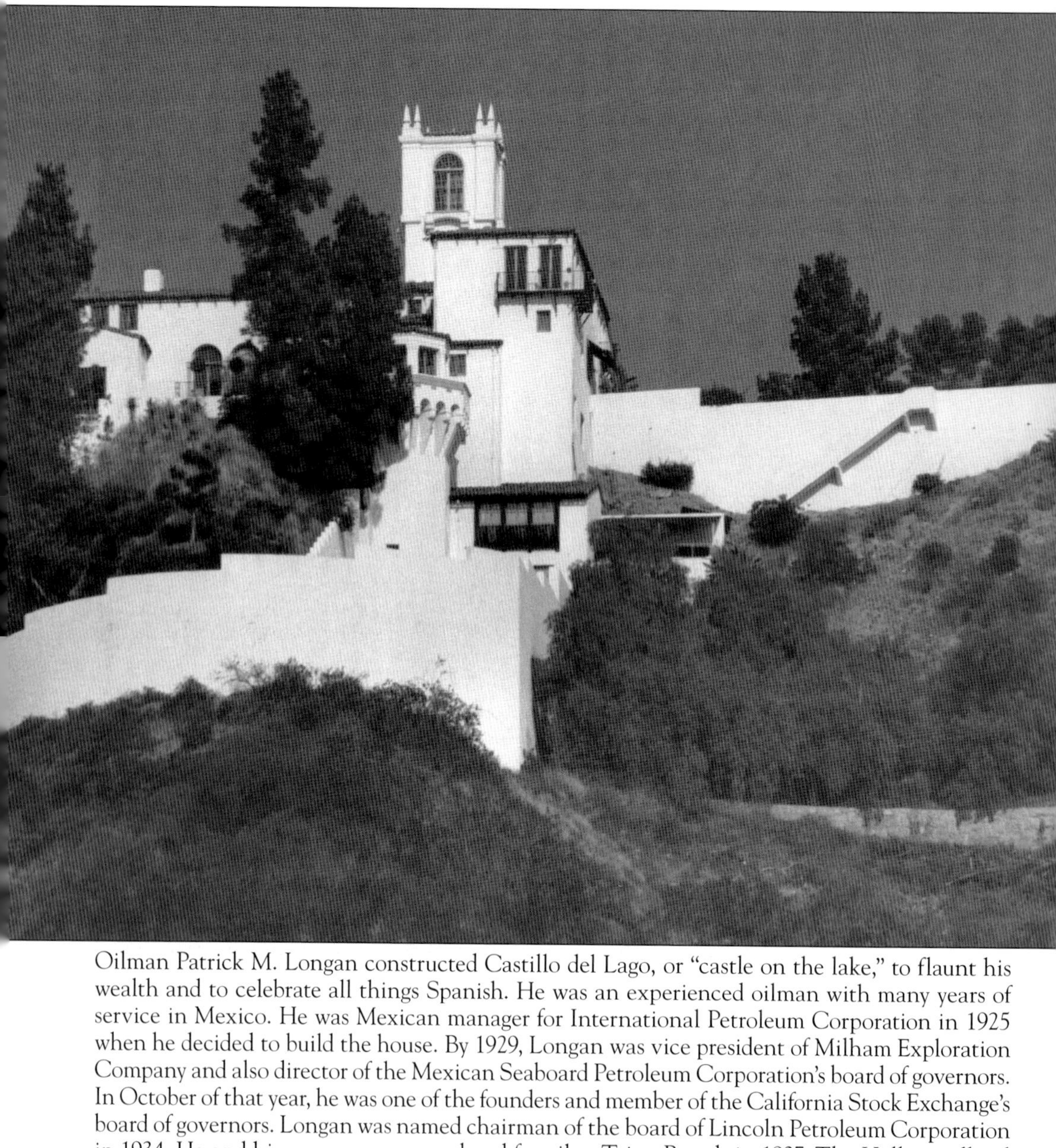

Oilman Patrick M. Longan constructed Castillo del Lago, or "castle on the lake," to flaunt his wealth and to celebrate all things Spanish. He was an experienced oilman with many years of service in Mexico. He was Mexican manager for International Petroleum Corporation in 1925 when he decided to build the house. By 1929, Longan was vice president of Milham Exploration Company and also director of the Mexican Seaboard Petroleum Corporation's board of governors. In October of that year, he was one of the founders and member of the California Stock Exchange's board of governors. Longan was named chairman of the board of Lincoln Petroleum Corporation in 1934. He and his new company explored for oil at Tejon Ranch in 1937. The Hollywoodland sales staff claimed in newspaper stories that the home commanded views of the Pacific Ocean, Sierra Madre Mountains, and Los Angeles. Bugsy Siegel supposedly operated a gambling joint here in the 1930s. (Bison.)

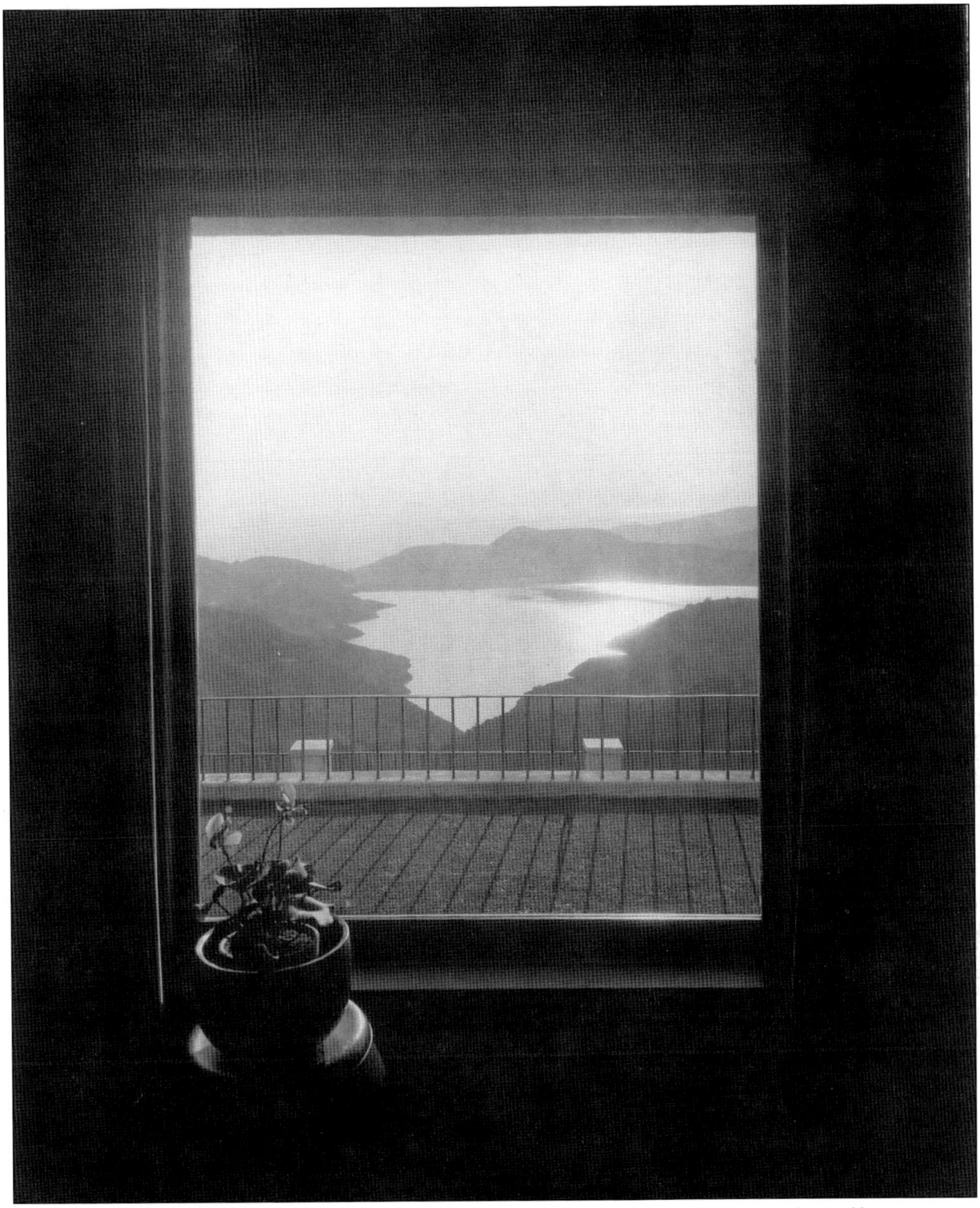

A Neuschwanstein-inspired castle, Castillo del Lago contained 20,000 square feet of living space with over 7,700 square feet in its outdoor grounds. The residence contained an elevator rising two stories from the garage to the living quarters, two-story living room, library, dining room, guest apartments, sewing room, nursery, master suites with private baths, dressing rooms, sleeping porches, and servants' quarters. The Longans traveled to the East Coast to purchase furniture, tapestries, and art objects. The home combined Spanish and Mediterranean architecture and was designed to take advantage of the outdoors; it blended gardens, patios, and 32 terraces to bring areas of privacy and serenity while also providing views in every direction. The grounds included pool, aviary, and an open air grill in Andalusian gardens, for which shrubs, flowers, and rare plants had been imported. Giorgianna Longan died in 1931, not long after the couple moved in. A view of Lake Hollywood can be glimpsed out of a window. (Bison.)

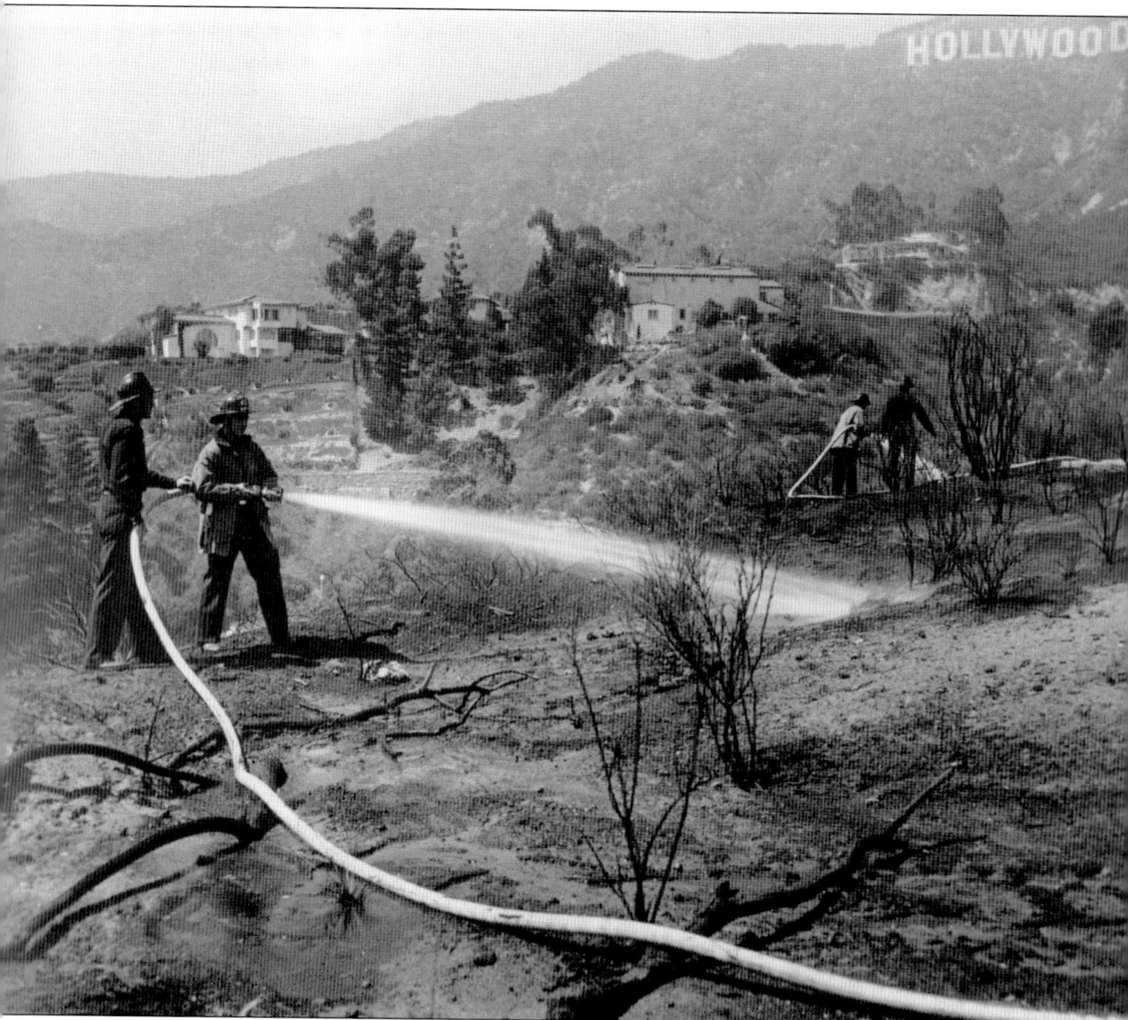

This photograph displays the downside of living in a hillside home: the threat of fire. The *Los Angeles Times* reported on July 15, 1941, that a brush fire originating in an abandoned shed on Canyon Drive spread rapidly to surrounding property before racing up a 400-foot hillside to Hollyridge Drive. No homes were damaged. In 1947, over 25 acres on the north end of Beachwood Drive burned and two homes were slightly damaged, including painter Edward Biberman's. Firefighters doused the flames just below the Hollywoodland sign and Don Lee television station. A 1956 fire caused by a carelessly flipped cigarette severely damaged a home at 2760 Westshire Drive, but two other homes were prevented from catching fire. On May 12, 1961, a fire damaged 30 homes and destroyed 24 others, including that of writer Aldous Huxley, who lost nearly all his manuscripts. A horse also died in the fire. Massive mudslides deluged the neighborhood in February 1962 as a result of this fire. (Bison.)

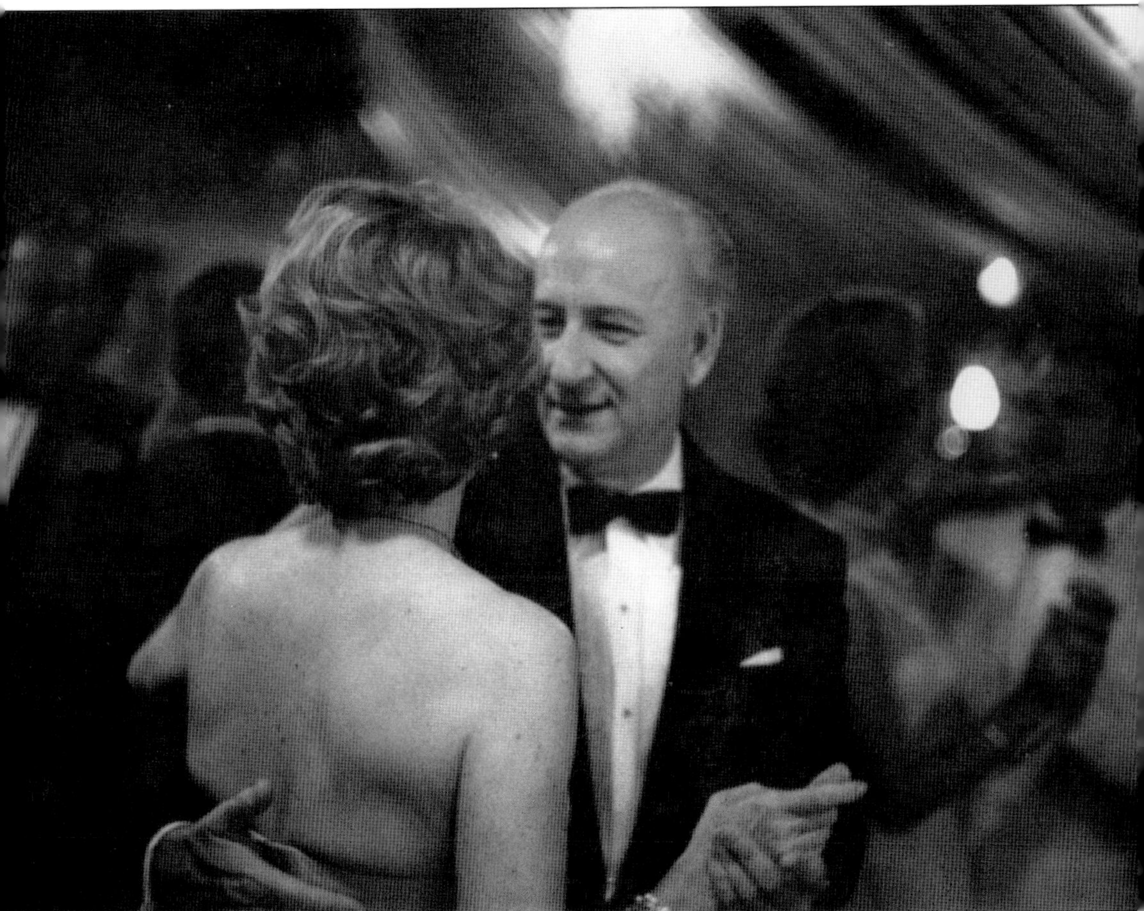

S.H. Woodruff enjoys an elegant evening out in this undated photograph. Woodruff and his staff effectively employed all types of media to help promote the Hollywoodland development, including press releases and planted stories in newspapers. He advocated the use of new media in attracting potential customers for the real estate tract. Newsreel cameramen captured demolition of hillsides as well as the construction of the Hollywoodland sign. Advertising manager L.J. Burrud arranged the filming of the entire construction process of the demonstration house. The developer launched the Hollywoodland Community Orchestra in 1924 that played on KHJ radio under the leadership of Al Wesson, bringing in over 20,000 letters from around the country. In 1929, Woodruff established the Hollywoodland–Dana Point Marimba Symphony Orchestra that played pioneer songs on radio station KMTR for a short time. These shows gained the development free advertising due to the use of Hollywoodland in the music groups' names.

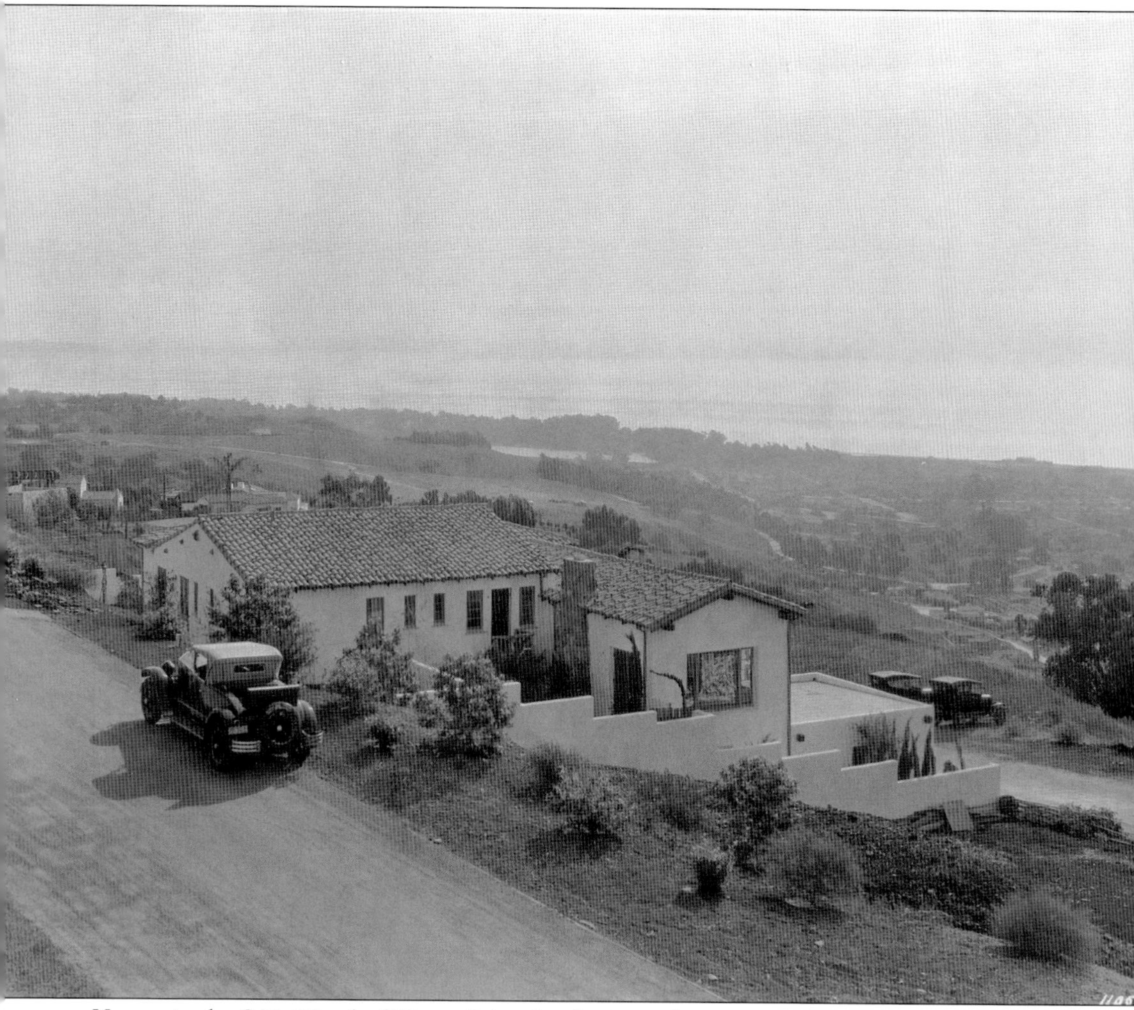

Homes in the S.H. Woodruff Dana Point development face toward the Pacific Ocean. In 1926, Woodruff formed a new real estate syndicate to buy, subdivide, and develop land at Dana Point, California, just south of Laguna Beach on the Pacific Ocean. Most of the homes featured California Spanish architecture that nestled into the foothills just like Hollywoodland. Woodruff envisioned Dana Point as a smaller version of resort towns located along the French and Italian Rivieras. The stock market crash dashed Woodruff's hopes, and in the mid-1930s, he returned undeveloped Hollywoodland property to the M.H. Sherman Company. The new company did away with architectural restrictions, allowing for more modern designs. Architect Richard Neutra designed the Ernest Mosk house in 1934. Bernard Parker built a geodesic dome at the top of Durand Drive in 1962 that was destroyed several years later.

Four

Skyline of the Hills

Originally intended as a temporary billboard, the Hollywoodland sign has taken on many meanings over the years: location setting, city landmark, and fame magnet. It has evolved from advertising symbol to worldwide icon.

Influenced by two large real estate signs promoting developments, the *Los Angeles Times* publisher and Hollywoodland investor Harry Chandler hired advertising man John Roche to create a giant billboard visible from Wilshire Boulevard. He designed one composed of letters 50 feet high and 30 feet wide, and a potent promotional tool debuted in late November 1923.

The sign gained notoriety on September 16, 1932, when actress Lillian Millicent "Peg" Entwistle leaped to her death from the "H" of the sign.

The sign first appeared in film during construction in 1923 and inadvertently appeared onscreen in the background of the 1939 Three Stooges short *A-Ducking They Did Go*. The gritty 1954 film noir *Down Three Dark Streets* contains the first lengthy feature film appearance of the Hollywood sign.

Owners and caretakers never properly maintained the sign for over 50 years, and it required numerous touchups. The M.H. Sherman Company donated the Hollywoodland sign in 1945 to the City of Los Angeles, and in 1949, the Hollywood Chamber of Commerce removed the word "land" to create today's treasured icon. In 1978, the old wooden letters, telephone poles, and wire were replaced with sheet metal letters and steel framework.

In the 1970s, the sign inspired artists such as Edward Ruscha to use its image in prints and Dory Previn to compose a musical about it. Novelists such as Clive Barker, Michael Connelly, and Robert Crais continue to highlight it in their works. Mischief-makers were also inspired to cloak letters of the Hollywood sign to create tongue-in-cheek messages.

After its 1978 face-lift, the Hollywood sign became an integral part of films shot in and about Los Angeles. To the world, the Hollywood sign operates as a symbol just as powerful as Big Ben, the Eiffel Tower, and the Statue of Liberty. It signifies a land of dreams, success, and potential happiness.

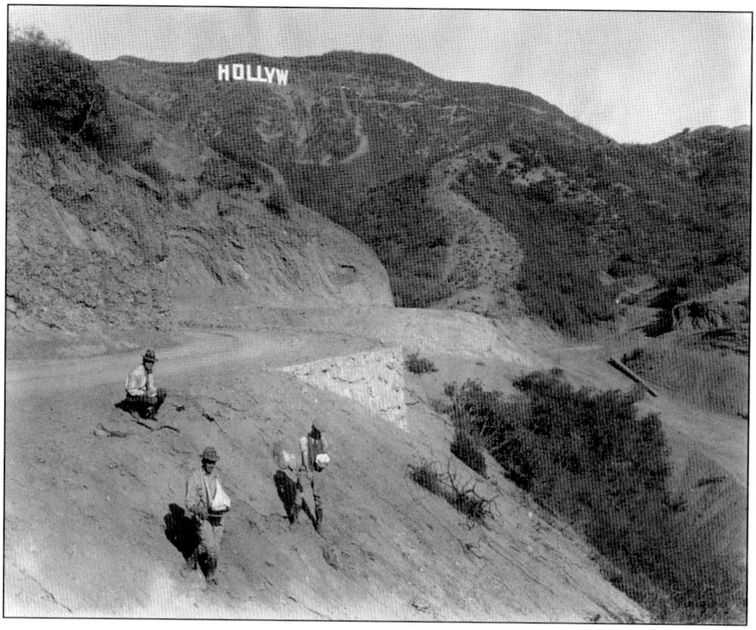

Three unidentified construction workers walk down the hill with the unfinished Hollywoodland sign behind them at the top of the photograph. Because of the steep grade of the hillside, men on foot and on Caterpillar tractors carefully carried telephone poles, sheet metal, wire, and pipes up to the construction site. (Bison.)

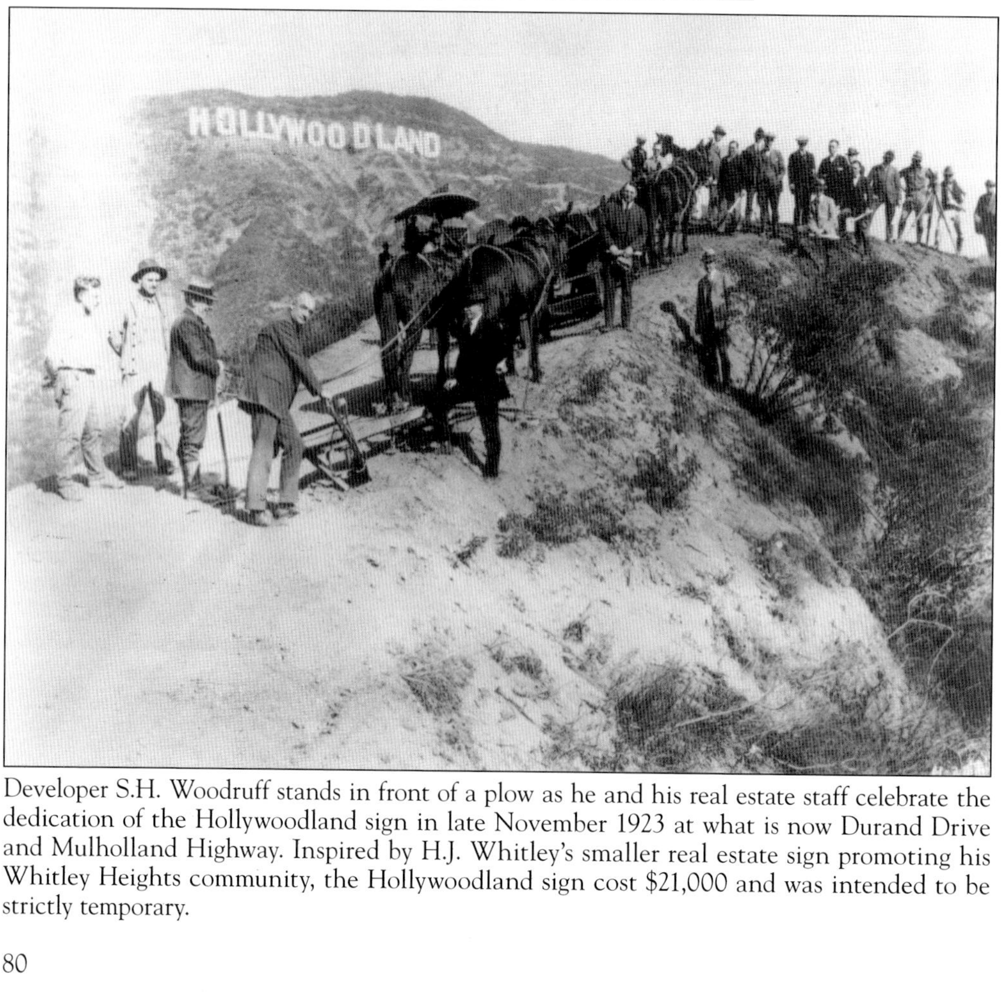

Developer S.H. Woodruff stands in front of a plow as he and his real estate staff celebrate the dedication of the Hollywoodland sign in late November 1923 at what is now Durand Drive and Mulholland Highway. Inspired by H.J. Whitley's smaller real estate sign promoting his Whitley Heights community, the Hollywoodland sign cost $21,000 and was intended to be strictly temporary.

Surveyors standing east of the sign on top of Bronson Canyon measure the Hollywoodland sign with Mulholland Highway visible beneath it. The developers added the eye-catcher later not far below it, a circular 35-foot-diameter piece of sheet metal painted white and circled by 20-watt bulbs that lit up. (Bison.)

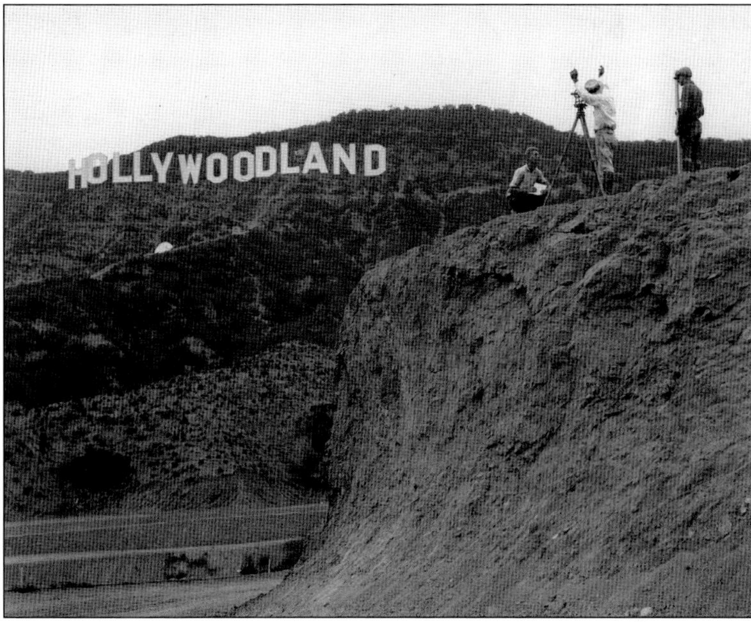

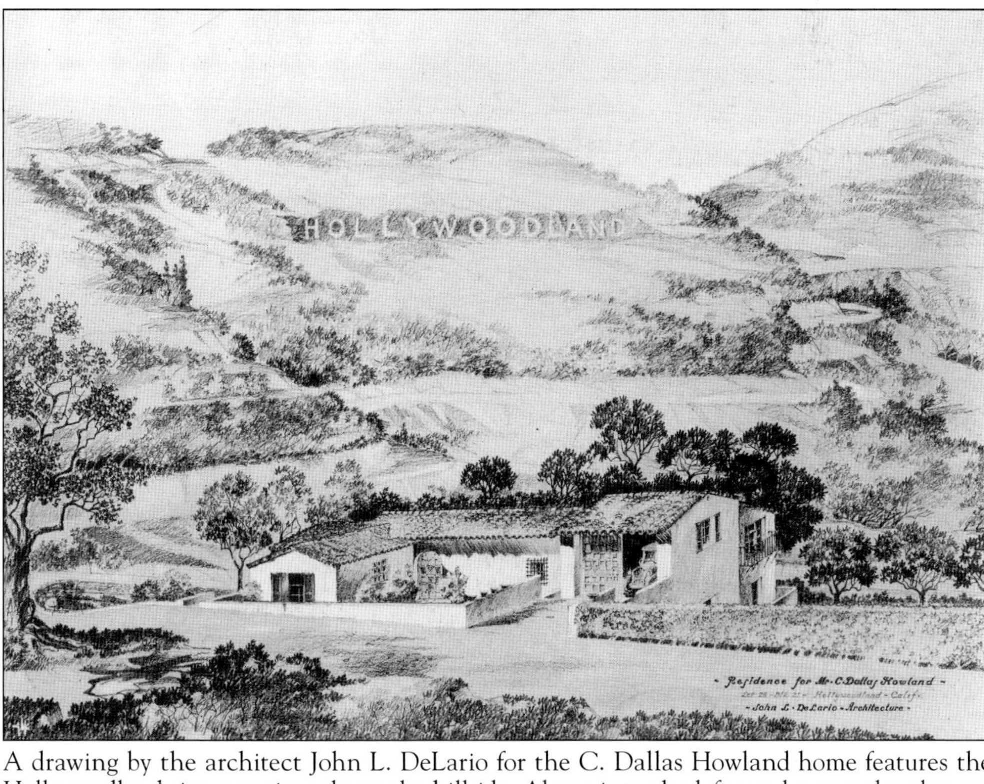

A drawing by the architect John L. DeLario for the C. Dallas Howland home features the Hollywoodland sign prominently on the hillside. Above it to the left can be seen the planned road to the proposed Mack Sennett house. At the right of the picture, Mulholland Highway can be seen connecting with Griffith Park, a part never completed.

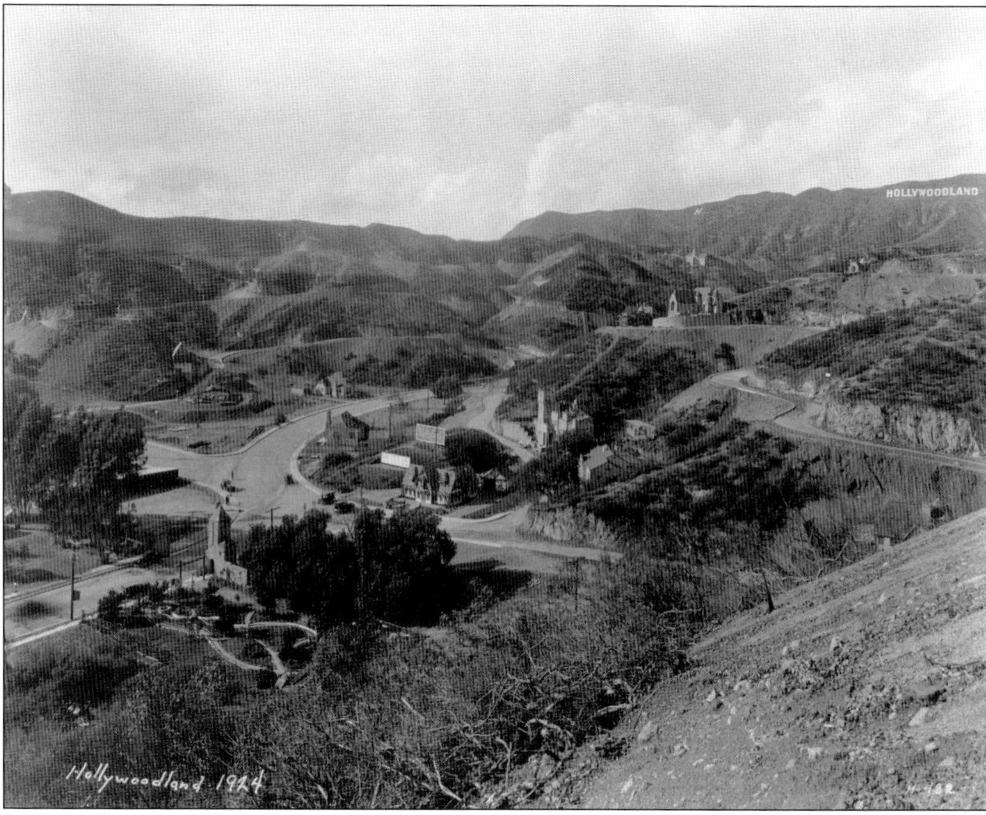

The Hollywoodland sign rises high over Hollywoodland in 1924 in this photograph taken from Pelham Place. The real estate office at 2700 North Beachwood Drive is visible in the center of the photograph, along with the entrance gates, billboard, demonstration house, and many other homes. The sign was intended as a temporary billboard to last approximately 18 months.

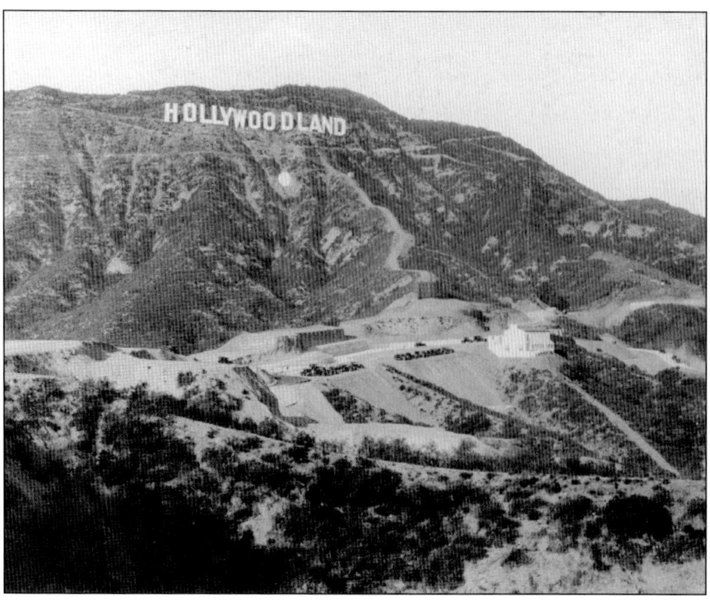

The Hollywoodland sign dominates the hillside. Harry Chandler, publisher of the *Los Angeles Times*, paid publicity man John Roche to create a sign trumpeting the real estate development that was visible from Wilshire Boulevard. Roche took Chandler literally and figuratively, designing a sign composed of individual letters 50 feet high and 30 feet long that spelled out the word Hollywoodland. (Bison.)

The Hollywoodland sign rises over Mulholland Highway. Employing telephone poles, pipes, 3-by-9-foot sheet metal squares, scaffolding, and wire as the sign's chief components, construction workers and tractors carried the material up the steeply angled hillside where each letter was constructed, drilled, and then risen into place as a temporary real estate beacon. (Bison)

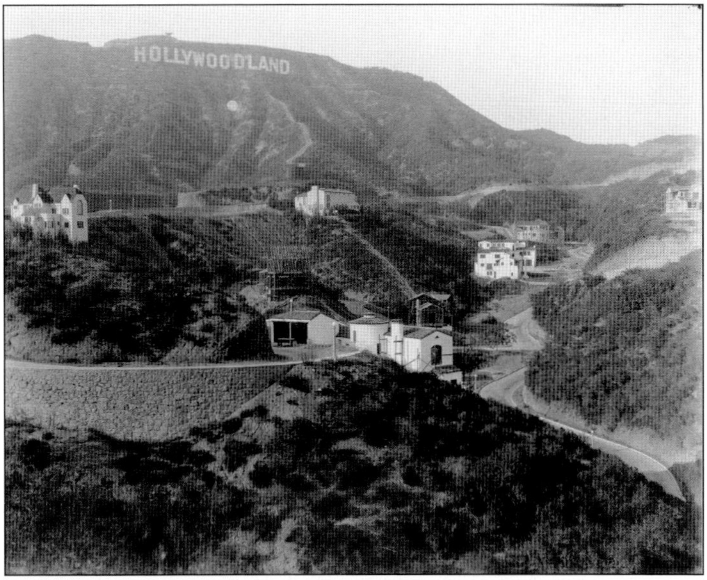

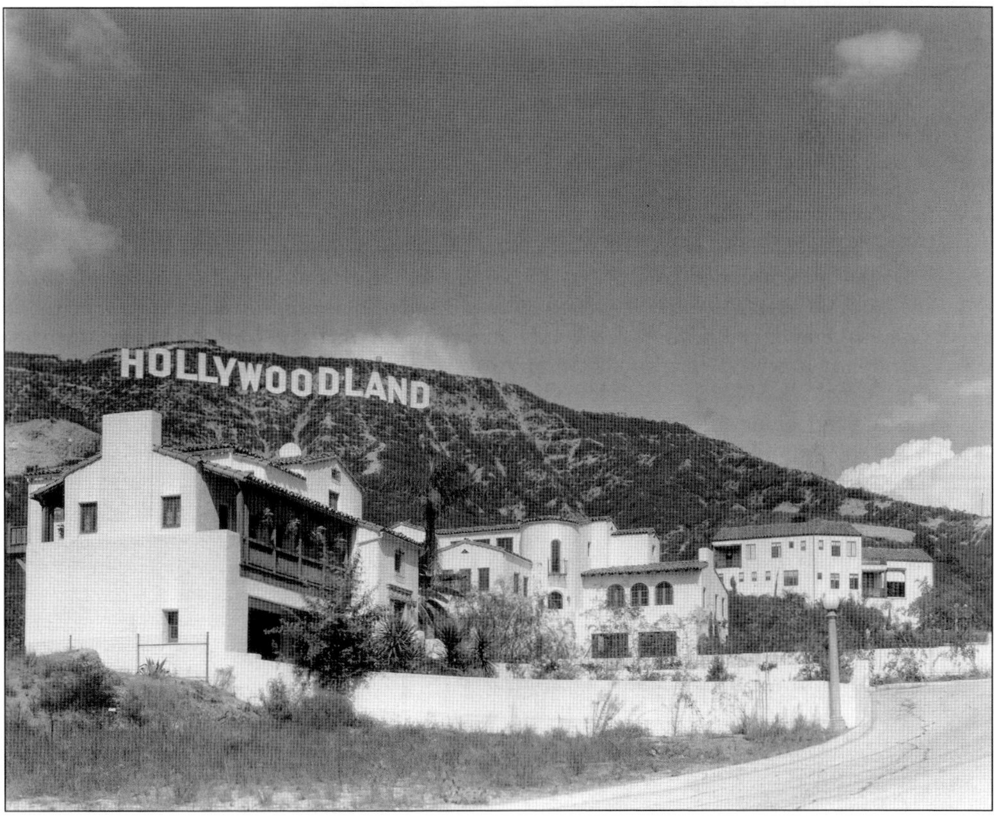

The Hollywoodland sign towers over homes below. Developers hired Albert Kothe, a recent immigrant from Germany, as the caretaker and maintenance man for the sign. He was charged with patrolling the area, repairing vandalism, replacing light bulbs, painting, and patching. Kothe lived in a small shack directly behind one of the letter "L"s in the 1930s, before moving to a home off Beachwood Drive in the 1950s. (Bison.)

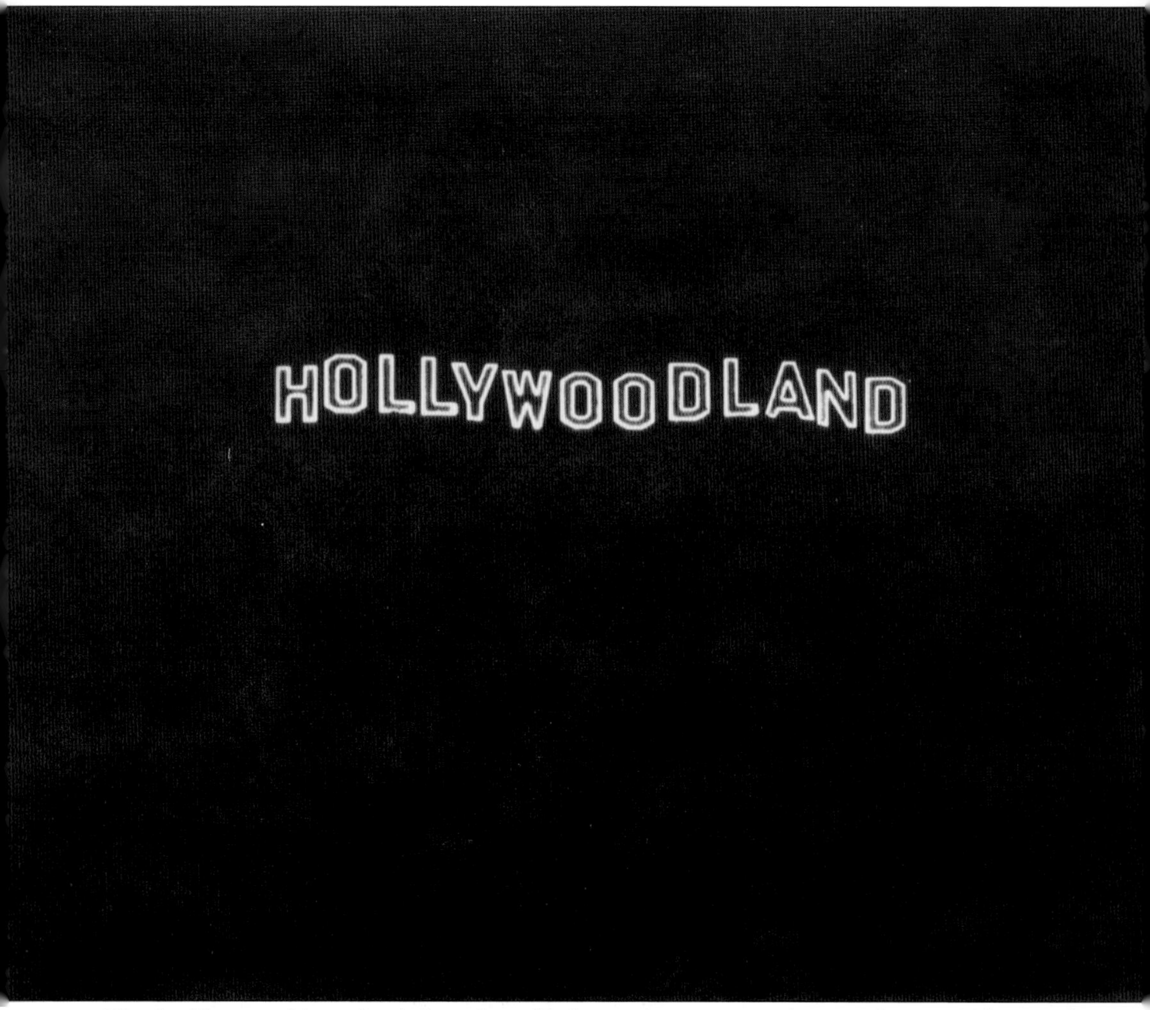

The builders quickly realized the value of lighting the sign at night to make it a 24-hour-a-day beacon promoting the Hollywoodland development. In effect, it was one of the world's largest electric billboards, larger than the lit-up marquees of New York's Times Square or London's Piccadilly Circus. Employing 4,000 twenty-watt light bulbs at eight-inch intervals to completely encircle each letter, the lights spelled out the words "Holly," "wood," and "land" in sequence before forming the single word "Hollywoodland." The eye-catcher below the sign, composed of a circular 35-foot-diameter piece of sheet metal painted white and also encircled by 20-watt bulbs, blinked after the word "Hollywoodland," acting as both a piece of punctuation and attention grabber. On clear nights, the blazing sign was supposedly visible all the way to Catalina Island, over 42 miles away. (AMPAS.)

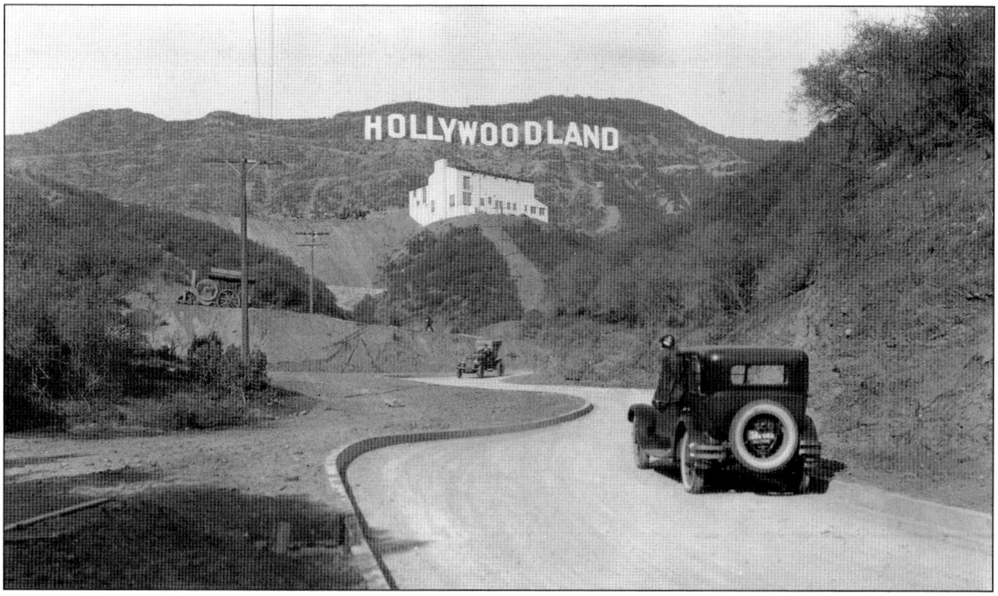

A dramatic, larger-than-life landmark, the Hollywoodland sign towers over Ledgewood Drive and the real estate development in the top photograph as cars drive up and down the winding roads. Touting the community as a tourist attraction in newspaper stories and advertisements brought gawkers up Beachwood Canyon to inspect and hopefully buy property. People from as far away as the East Coast came to admire and inspect the tract, often buying property. The bottom photograph shows an overhead shot of Hollywood with the Hollywoodland sign visible on the hillside at right in a November 8, 1935, photograph from the *Detroit Press*. This image reveals the dramatic impact of the sign on the Hollywood landscape since there are no office towers to compete with it. (Above, Bison; below, MM.)

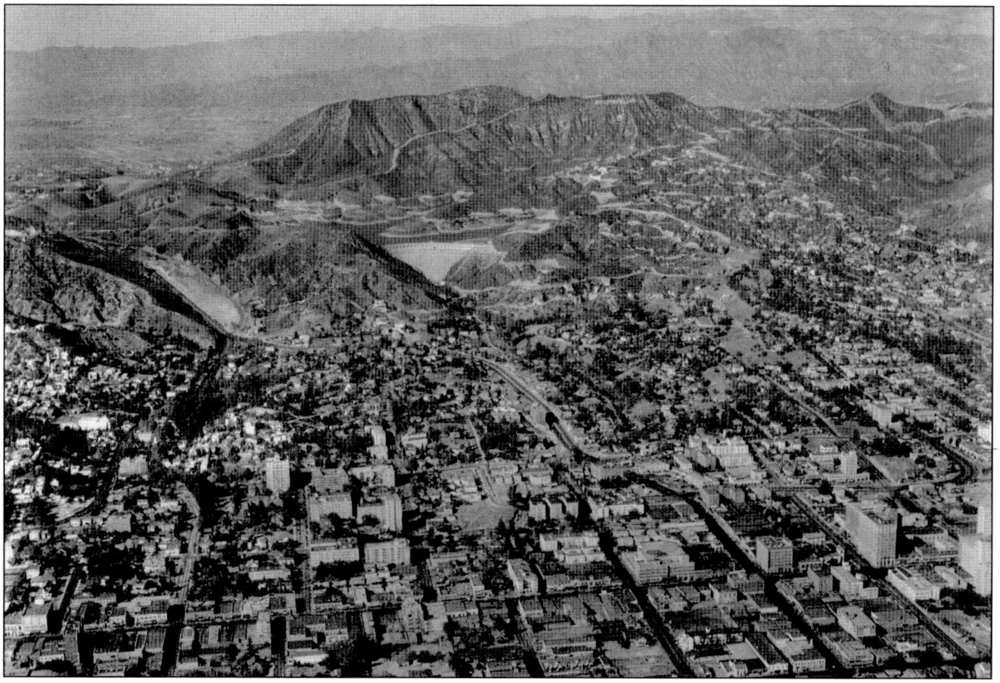

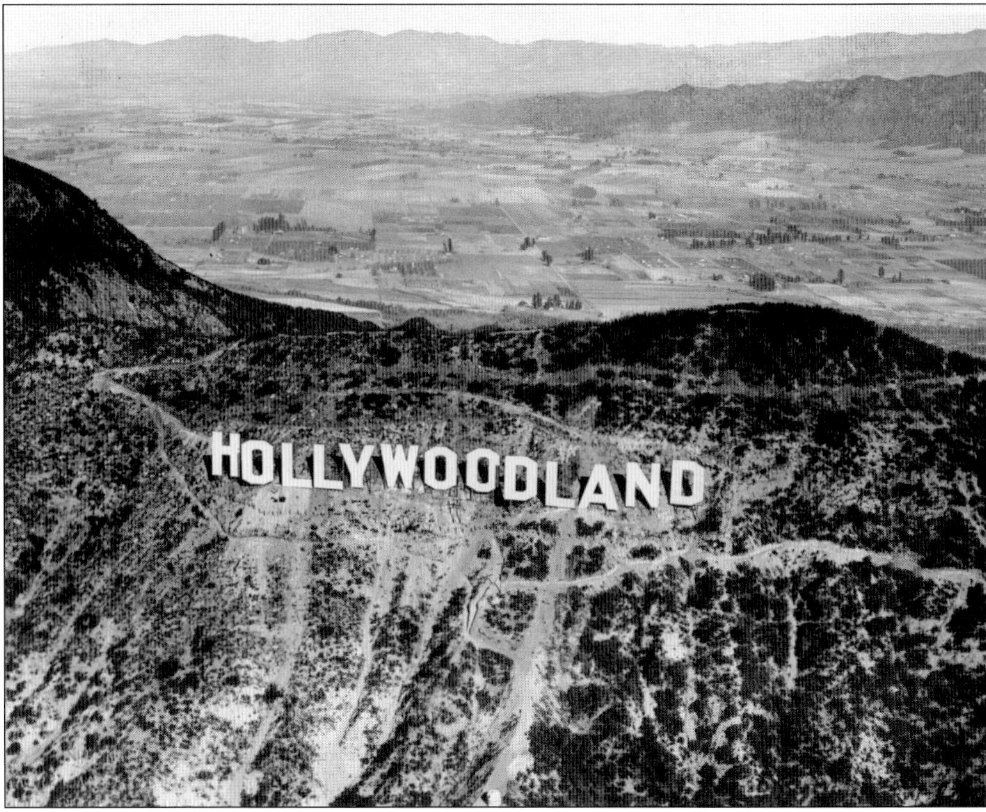

An overhead shot frames the Hollywoodland sign on the hills of Hollywood looking over into the San Fernando Valley. This image was very likely taken by Western Photo Company, a Los Angeles–based photograph studio that traveled the city taking both street and aerial views of local neighborhoods to sell to residents, businesses, and newspapers. (Bison.)

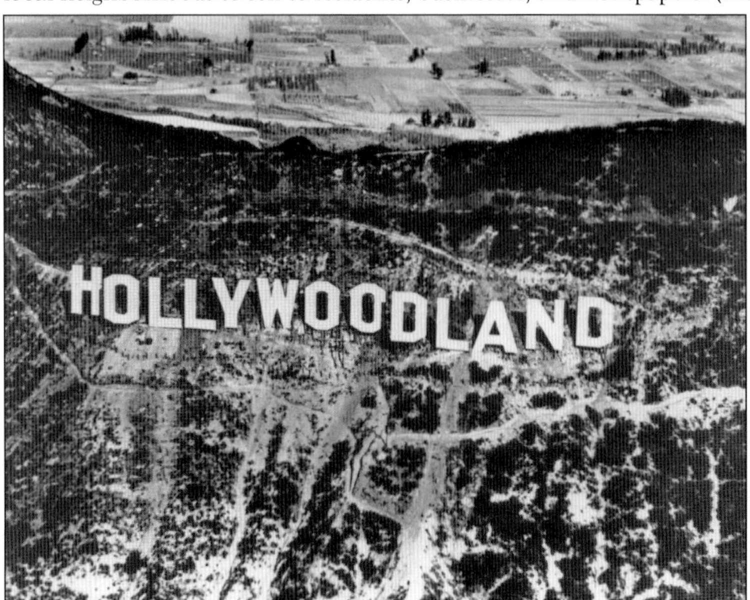

The Hollywoodland sign seems to float on the Hollywood hills while San Fernando Valley can just be glimpsed behind it. Film producer Mack Sennett intended to build a home at the very top of the peak behind it, which would have been visible from the valley side as well as Hollywood and Los Angeles.

A view of the Hollywoodland sign above the real estate tract can be seen in this photograph taken above Pelham Place around 1928. In the lower left of the photograph, the shops in Beachwood Village, the Einar Petersen house, and the real estate office can be glimpsed, along with the neighborhood gates.

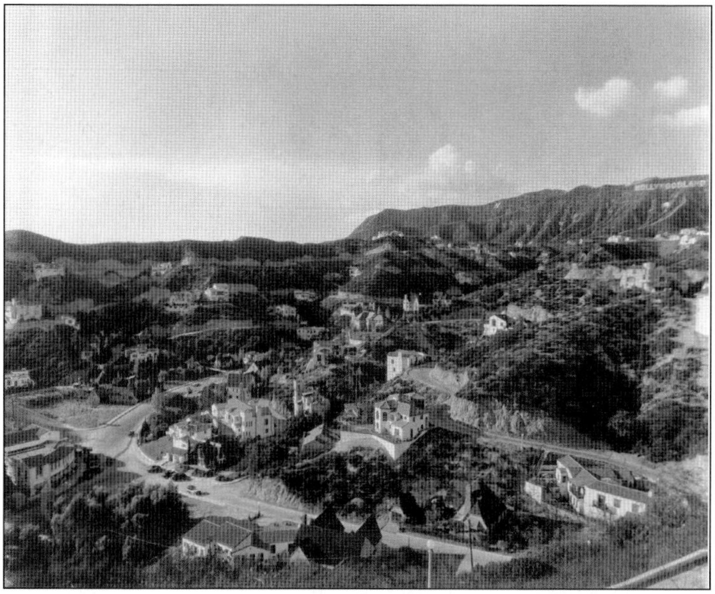

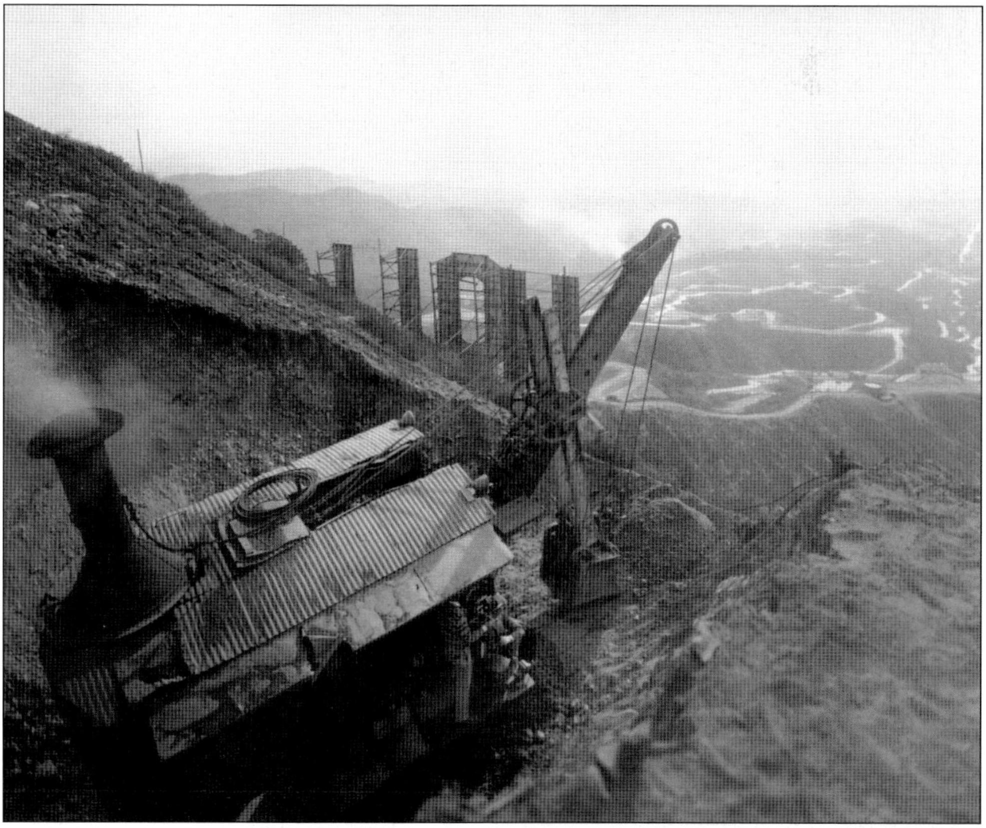

Investor and comedy filmmaker Mack Sennett employed his vast studio publicity machine to help promote the Hollywoodland development in 1925. Here is the giant crane clearing out land behind the Hollywoodland sign, on the road being constructed to the proposed location of the Sennett mansion at the top of the summit. (AMPAS.)

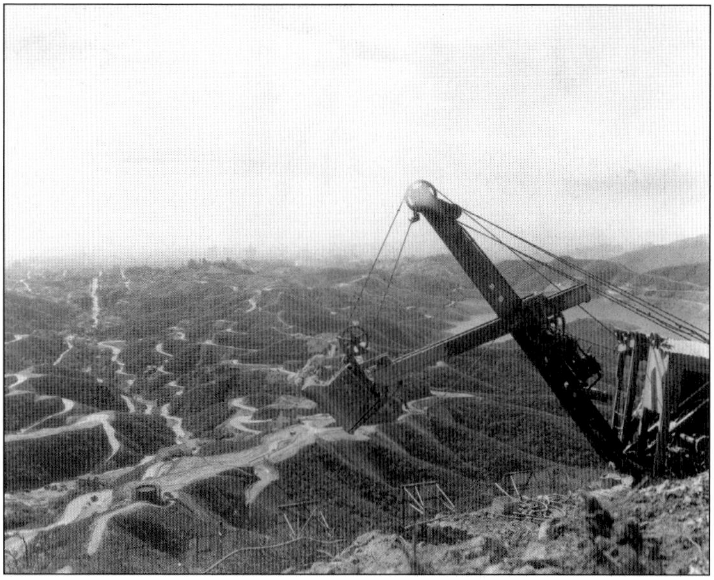

This is a shot taken by the Sennett cameraman from behind the wood and sheet metal Hollywoodland sign down on Hollywood itself. The patchwork of curvy, winding roads constructed up the steep hillsides throughout the development is clearly visible in the photograph, as well as the Beachwood Village area at the bottom of the photograph. (AMPAS.)

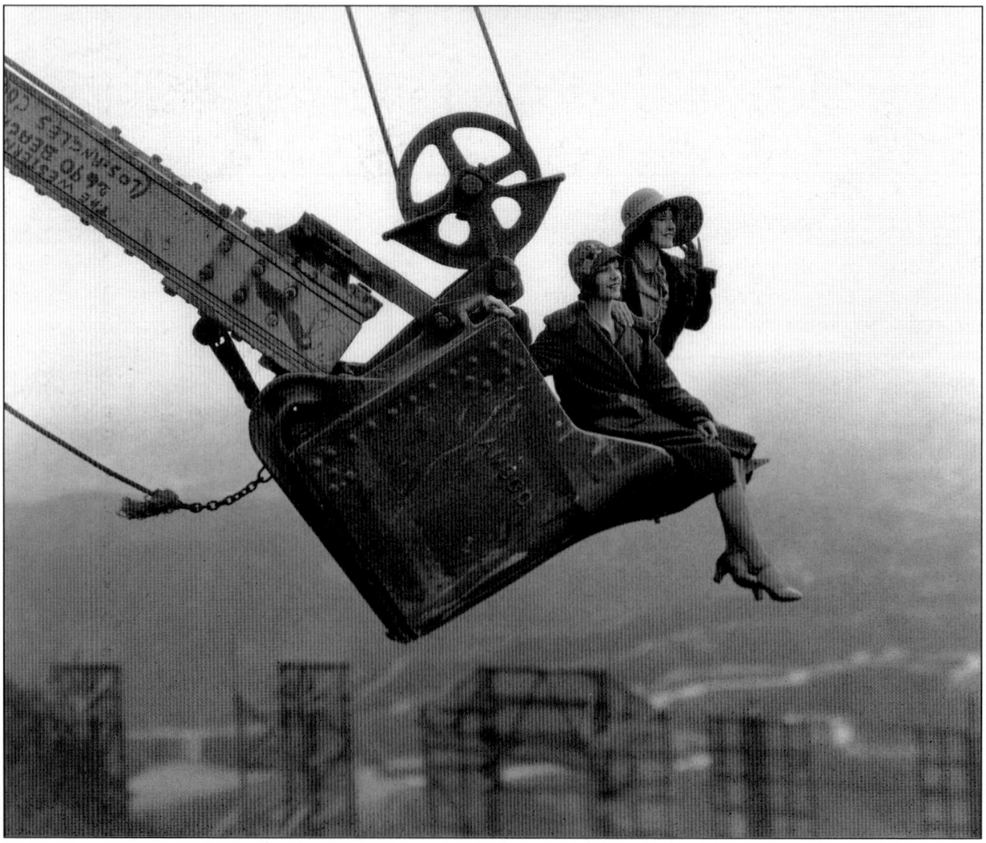

Two unidentified young studio starlets take part in the photo shoot on the road being constructed to the very summit of the real estate development. Posing in the cab of the crane, they tower over the back of the sign, looking down on the development's roads in Beachwood Canyon and beyond. (AMPAS.)

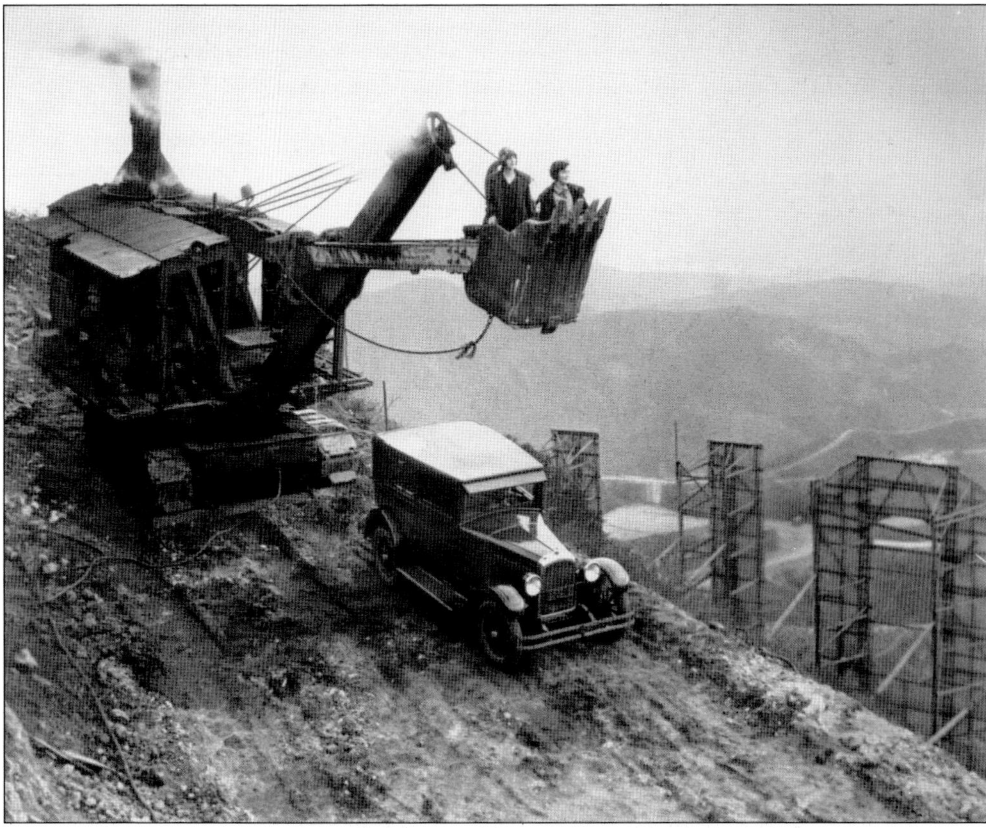

The same two unidentified starlets bravely pose in a giant crane, high above the sign, on the road being cut to the proposed Mack Sennett residence. The view looks down on the lake, which was created when William Mulholland constructed the nearby dam in 1923. Developers intended to build homes to the edge of the lake, but finances later prevented it. (AMPAS.)

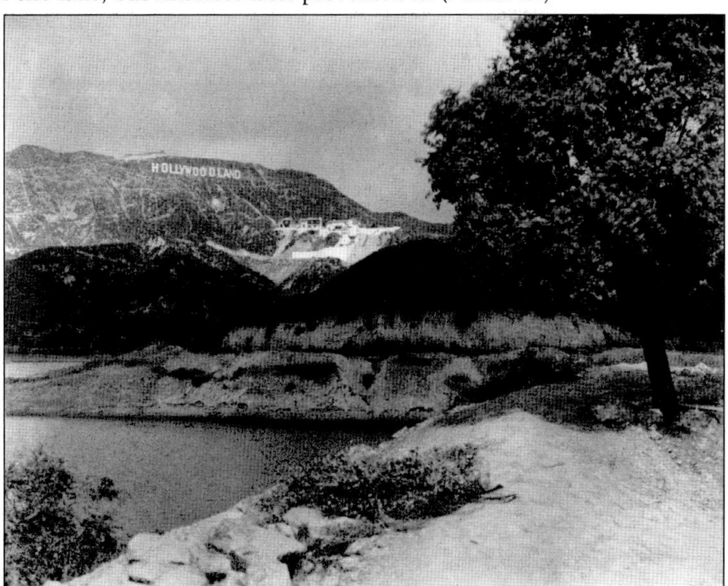

A beautifully framed shot of the Hollywoodland sign is shown here looking up from the shore of Lake Hollywood just east of the development. Developer and builder S.H. Woodruff smartly recognized the value of photographs capturing beautiful views throughout the real estate tract that could be employed as publicity in the development's glossy brochures.

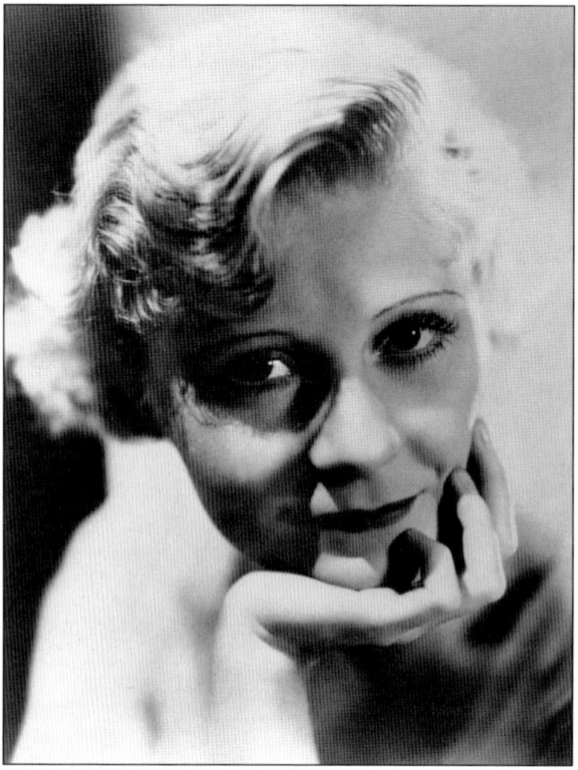

As 24-year-old actress Lillian "Peg" Entwistle left her uncle's bungalow at 2428 North Beachwood Drive on the evening of September 16, 1932, she told him she was meeting a friend at the Hollywoodland Drugstore up the hill. He never saw her alive again. That night was supposed to have been the premiere of RKO Pictures' *Thirteen Women*, a melodrama in which she had her first featured role. Unfortunately, when the film did not test well in previews, RKO had trimmed 15 minutes, including much of Peg's performance. By the time *Thirteen Women* opened belatedly in mid-October, she had written her own indelible part in Tinseltown history by walking up to the top of Beachwood Canyon, climbing the 50-foot-high "H" of the Hollywoodland sign, and leaping into the warm night toward the distant lights of the city that had disappointed her. (Left, Jim Dawson; below, James Zeruk Jr.)

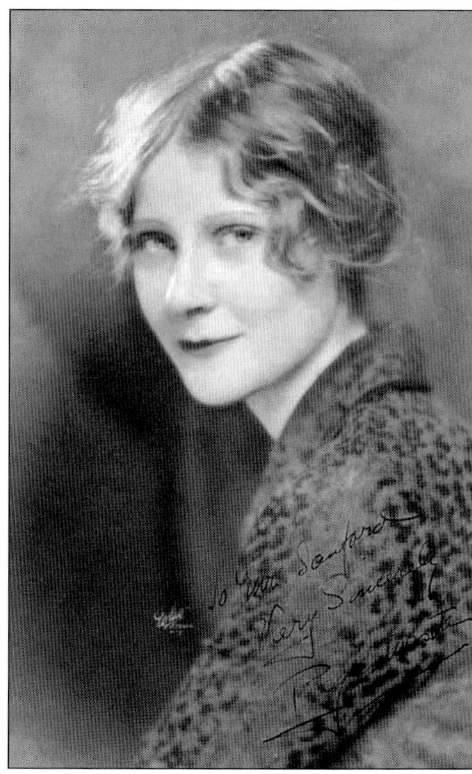

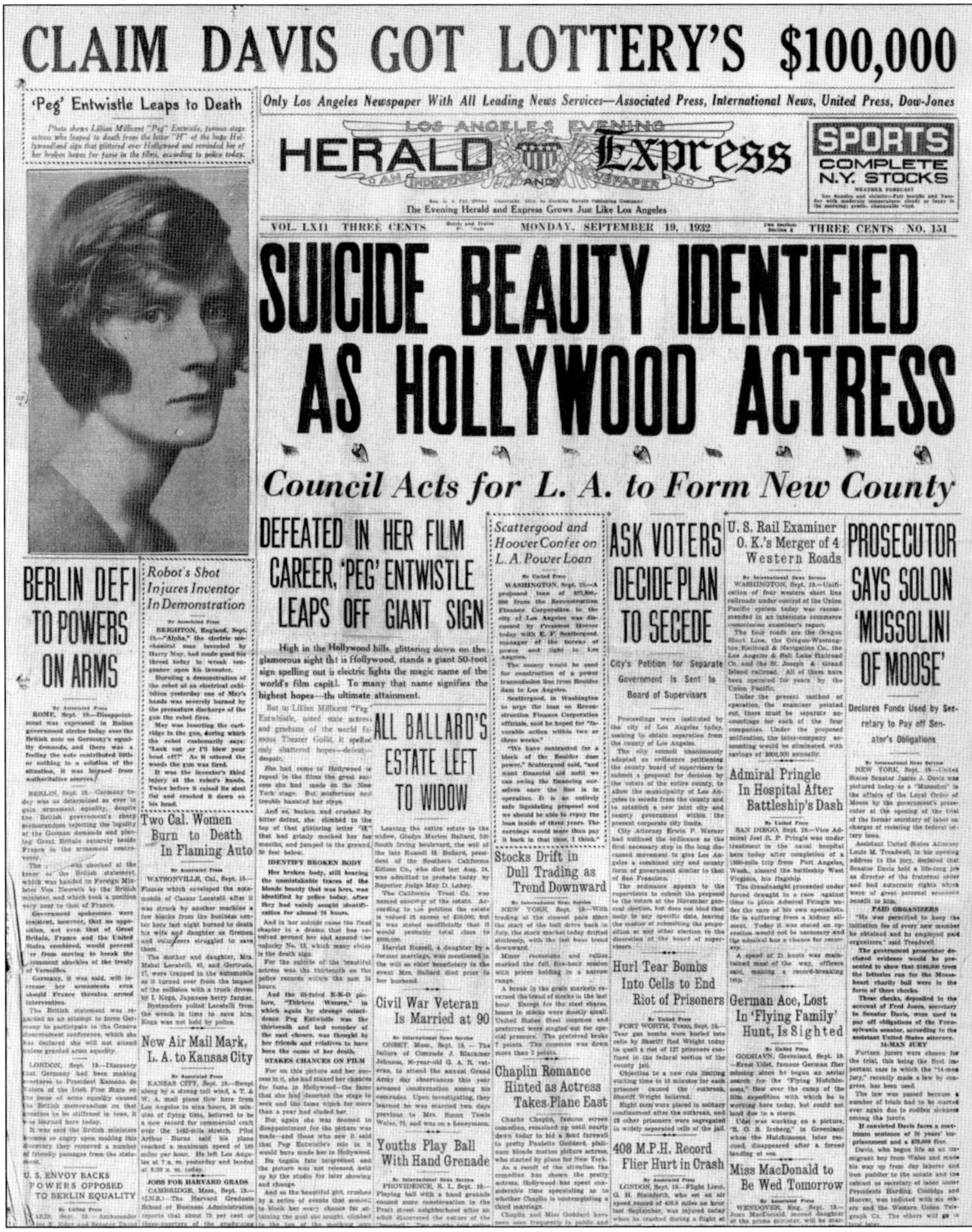

CLAIM DAVIS GOT LOTTERY'S $100,000

'Peg' Entwistle Leaps to Death

Only Los Angeles Newspaper With All Leading News Services—Associated Press, International News, United Press, Dow-Jones

LOS ANGELES EVENING HERALD AND Express

SPORTS COMPLETE N.Y. STOCKS

The Evening Herald and Express Grows Just Like Los Angeles

VOL. LXII THREE CENTS MONDAY, SEPTEMBER 19, 1932 THREE CENTS NO. 151

SUICIDE BEAUTY IDENTIFIED AS HOLLYWOOD ACTRESS

Council Acts for L. A. to Form New County

DEFEATED IN HER FILM CAREER, 'PEG' ENTWISTLE LEAPS OFF GIANT SIGN

High in the Hollywood hills, glittering down on the glamorous sight that is Hollywood, stands a giant 50-foot sign spelling out in electric lights the magic name of the world's film capitl. To many that name signifies the highest hopes—the ultimate attainment.

Scattergood and Hoover Confer on L. A. Power Loan

ASK VOTERS DECIDE PLAN TO SECEDE

City's Petition for Separate Government Is Sent to Board of Supervisors

U. S. Rail Examiner O. K.'s Merger of 4 Western Roads

PROSECUTOR SAYS SOLON 'MUSSOLINI OF MOOSE'

Declares Funds Used by Secretary to Pay off Senator's Obligations

BERLIN DEFI TO POWERS ON ARMS

Robot's Shot Injures Inventor In Demonstration

ALL BALLARD'S ESTATE LEFT TO WIDOW

Two Cal. Women Burn to Death In Flaming Auto

IDENTIFY BROKEN BODY

STAKES CHANCES ON FILM

Stocks Drift in Dull Trading as Trend Downward

Admiral Pringle In Hospital After Battleship's Dash

Hurl Tear Bombs Into Cells to End Riot of Prisoners

Civil War Veteran Is Married at 90

New Air Mail Mark, L. A. to Kansas City

Chaplin Romance Hinted as Actress Takes Plane East

German Ace, Lost In 'Flying Family' Hunt, Is Sighted

Youths Play Ball With Hand Grenade

408 M.P.H. Record Flier Hurt in Crash

Miss MacDonald to Be Wed Tomorrow

U. S. ENVOY BACKS POWERS OPPOSED TO BERLIN EQUALITY

JOBS FOR HARVARD GRADS

PAID ORGANIZERS

14-MAN JURY

Peg Entwistle's tragic suicide was front-page news in all the Los Angeles newspapers on September 18, 1932, two days after her death. According to the papers, she lay in the brush for several hours before being found by a hiker, and then it took the police almost 24 hours to identify her. The *Herald Express* connected the unlucky number 13 to her death, stating that she was the 13th person cast in the film *Thirteen Women*, as well as the 13th person in Los Angeles County to commit suicide in a 24-hour period. The paper also described the Hollywoodland sign as an emblem of success but also death. "High in the Hollywood Hills, glittering down on the glamorous site that is Hollywood, stands a giant 50 foot sign spelling out in electric lights the magic name of the world's film capital. To many that name signifies the highest hopes—the ultimate attainment. But to Lillian Millicent "Peg" Entwistle . . . it spelled only shattered hopes—defeat—despair." (MM.)

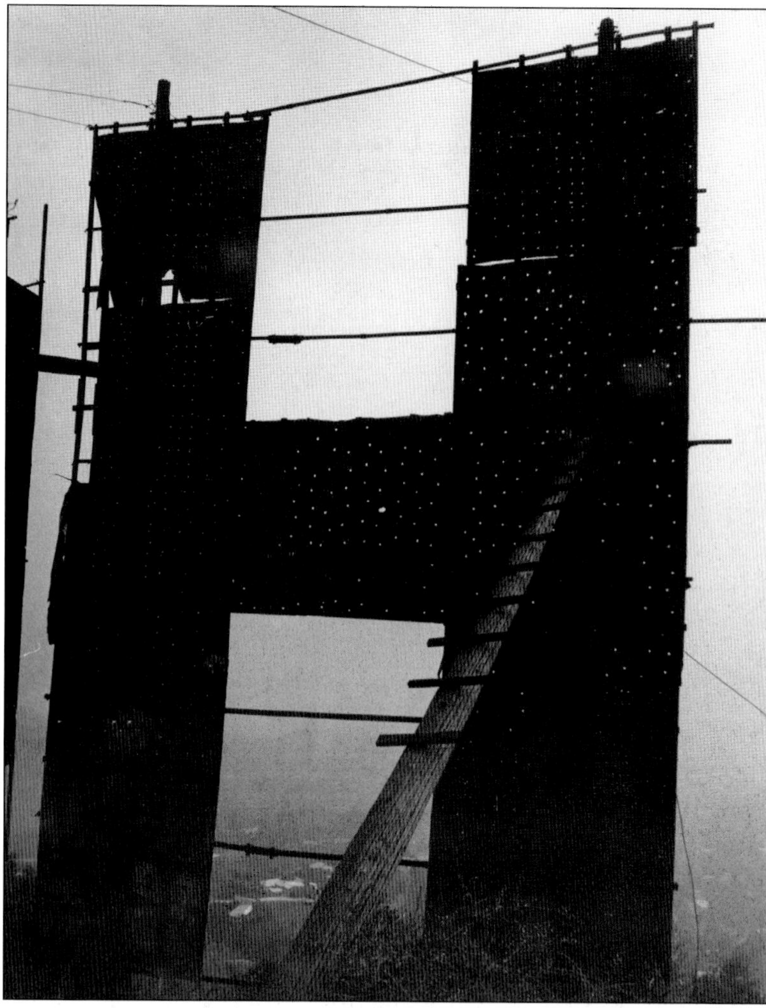

The letter "H" of the Hollywoodland sign shows disrepair in this photograph from the 1940s. Caretaker Albert Kothe climbed a steep ladder once a week with lightbulbs tucked in his shirt to replace the burned-out ones. People stole the light bulbs and vandalized the sign after maintenance ended in 1939. Holes appeared where the sheet metal blew or fell off. (Bison.)

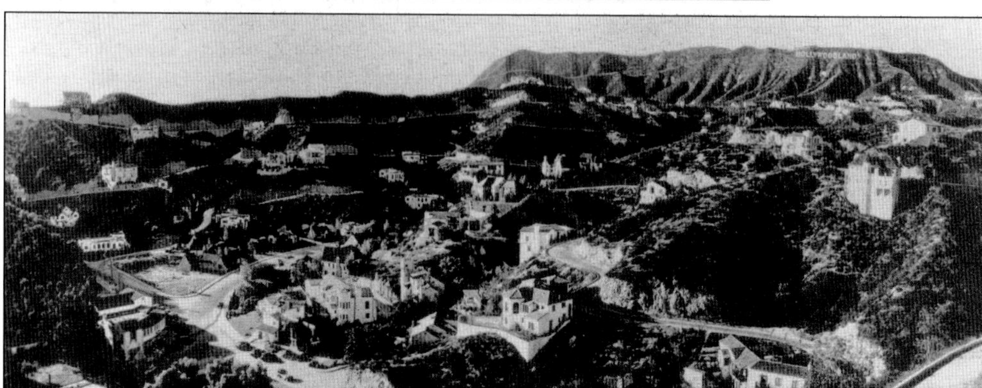

A panoramic shot of Hollywoodland shows the Hollywoodland sign dominating the landscape as it rises high on the hill. The entrance of Hollywoodland at 2690 North Beachwood Drive can be glimpsed as well as the entrance gates in the lower center of the photograph. Homes and apartment buildings dot lower Beachwood Drive.

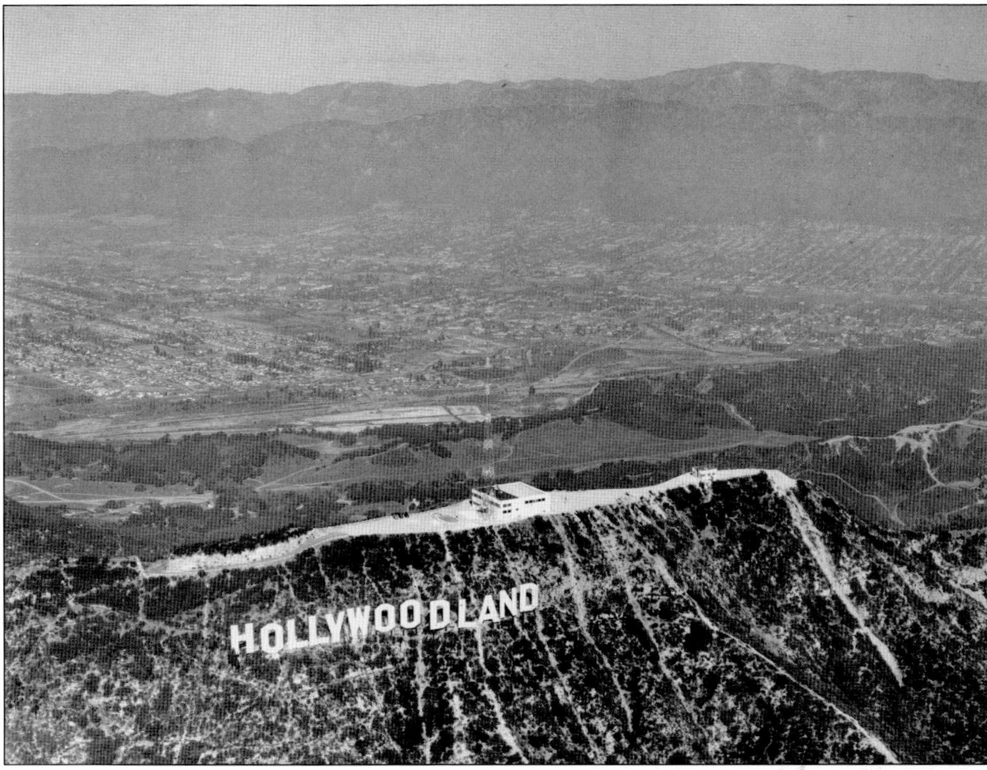

An aerial shot of the Hollywoodland sign taken around 1945 shows the broadcast tower of the Don Lee Mutual Radio Broadcast Company visible on the hill behind it. The M.H. Sherman Company sold the land above Mulholland Highway to Don Lee in 1935, with the mountain being renamed Mount Lee in his honor. The city approved construction of the radio station in 1945. (Bison.)

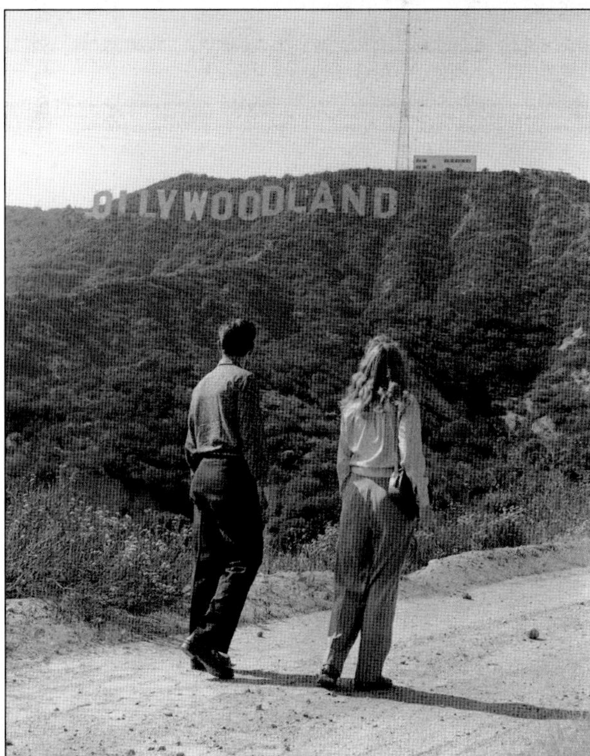

A 1949 photograph of the Hollywoodland sign reveals that the "H" has fallen down and that the rest seems in a state of disrepair. A high wind blew down the "H" and damaged other letters. Ten years of neglect had also caused the white paint to peel off. The sign was beginning to disappear into the hillside.

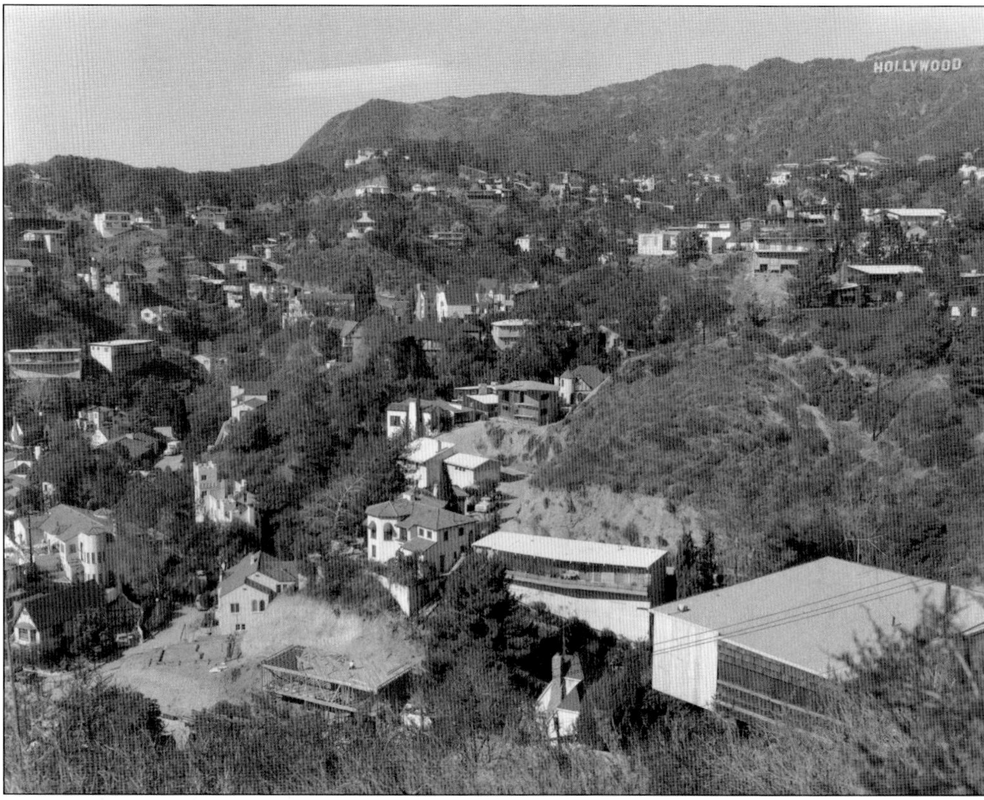

In 1945, the M.H. Sherman Company donated the sign to the City of Los Angeles and the land around it to the city's Recreation and Parks Commission. After the letter "H" blew off the hill in a major storm, the Hollywood Chamber of Commerce paid to renovate the sign in 1949. At that time, the word "land" was removed, and this 1950s photograph reveals the new name. (Bison.)

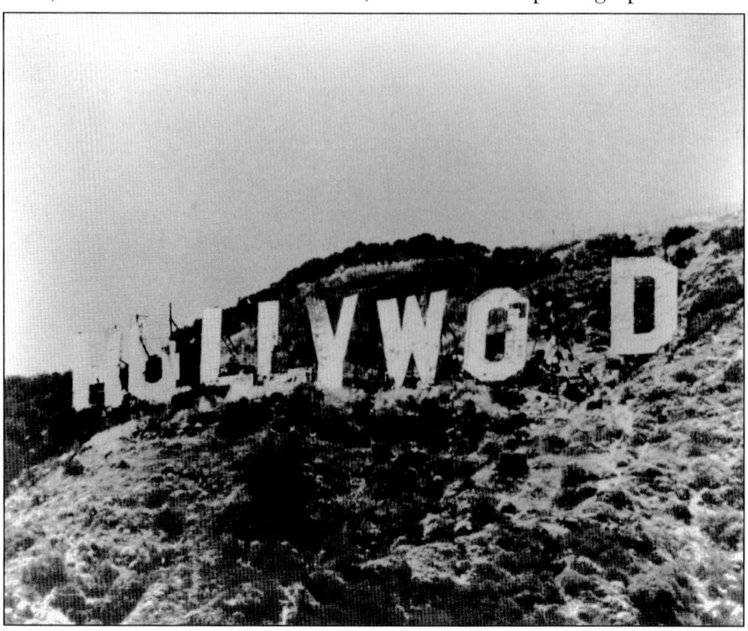

While the Hollywood sign's paint job had been touched up in 1973, major repair work had not occurred in almost 50 years. Heavy rains and terrible storms caused further damage. Letters washed down the hillside, fell off, or contained large holes. The sign deteriorated to such a state that it could no longer be refurbished. (Bison.)

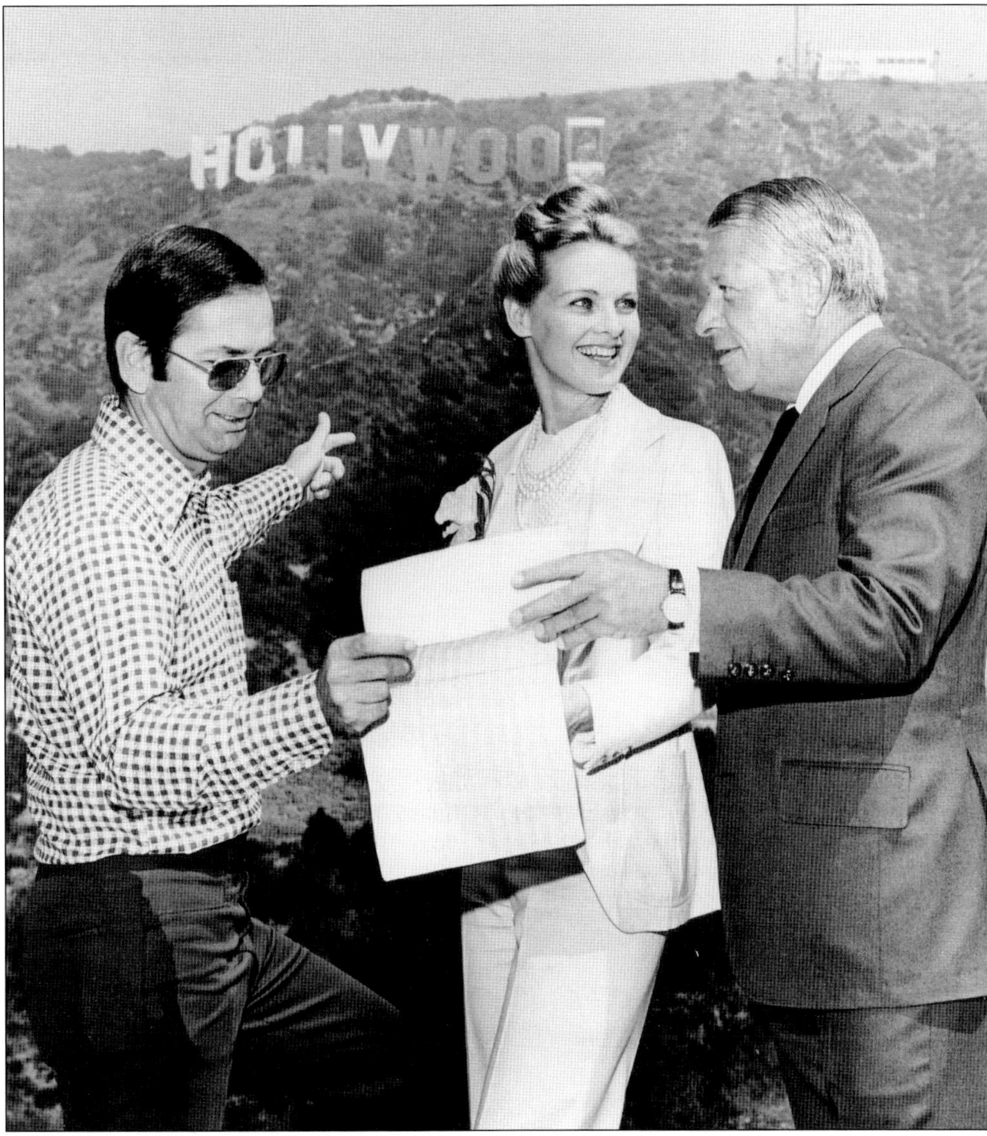

For 50 years, no serious maintenance occurred on the iconic Hollywood sign. Paint touchups were few and far between. In 1973, the sign required a minor patch up and paint job that cost $15,000. R. Lesley Kelley, one of the investors and publishers of the Kelley Blue Book, pledged $1,000 each year for 10 years as an endowment for a sign maintenance fund. The Association of Motion Picture and Television Producers donated $1,500, and the rest of the funds came from small donations by the public. It was somehow fitting that an industry that had become synonymous with the Hollywood sign should help ensure that it look beautiful. Bill Zima (left) of Neon Products Signs; actress Angel Tompkins; and Billy H. Hunt, chief executive officer of the AMPTP, examine the repair work. Neon Products Signs patched, primed, and painted the sign. (Bison.)

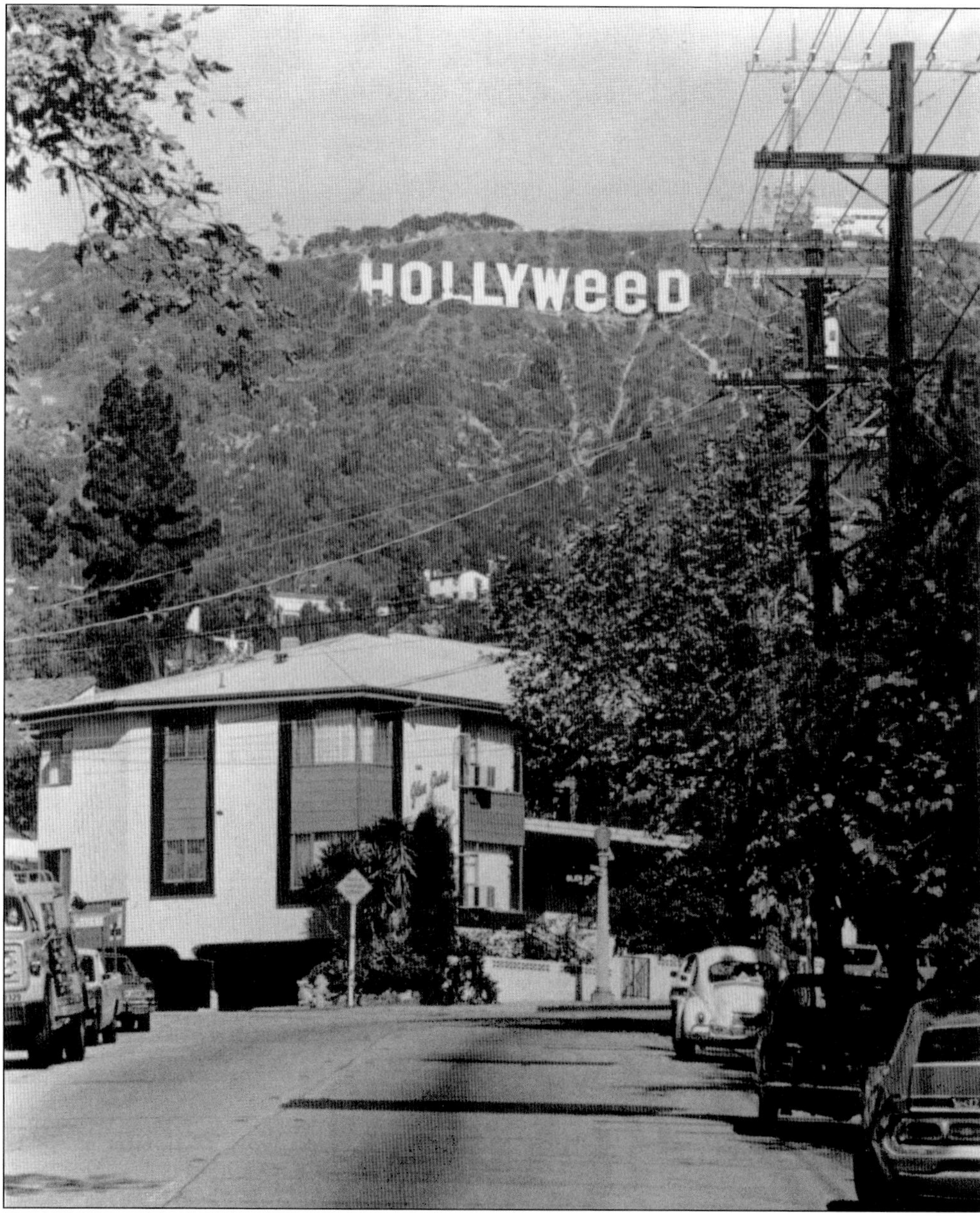

Over the years, several acts of vandalism altered the look and wording of the Hollywood sign. On the morning of January 1, 1976, Hollywood residents awoke and discovered that pranksters had cloaked and modified the "O"s in the Hollywood sign to spell the name "Hollyweed," which celebrated the deregulation of marijuana in California. The authorities quickly responded, removing the sheets and returning the sign to its original appearance. On Easter that year, vandals cloaked the first "L", which changed the wording to "Holywood." When Pope John II visited in 1987, pranksters altered it to say "Holy wood." In December 1983, Navy midshipmen altered it to say "Go Navy" for the only West Coast appearance of the Army-Navy game. The Hollywood Sign Trust allowed it to be altered to "Fox" in April 1987 for a television promotion. Other altered spellings include "Ollywood," "Oil War," "Go UCLA," "Caltech," and "Save the Peak." (Tommy Lamey.)

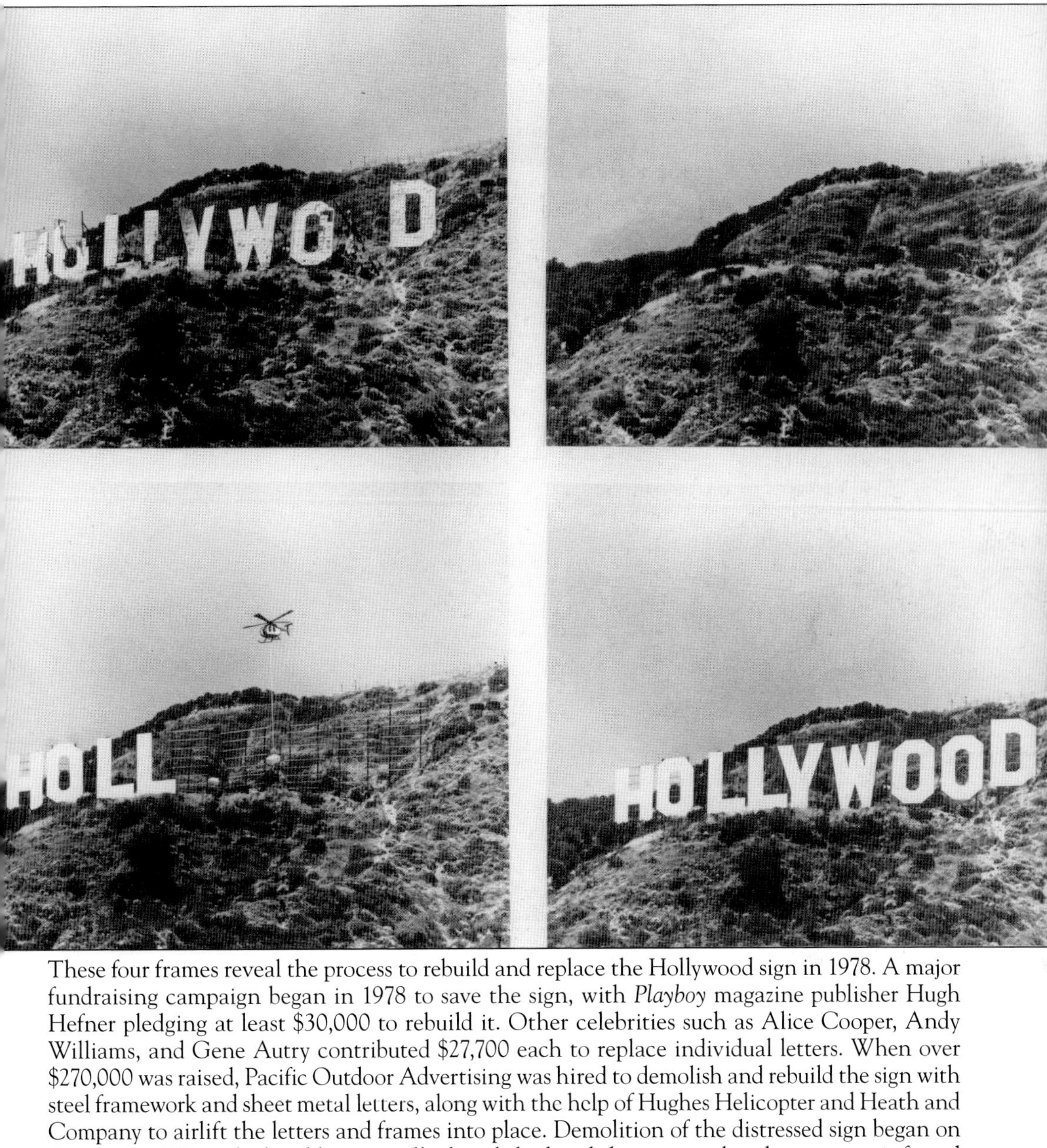

These four frames reveal the process to rebuild and replace the Hollywood sign in 1978. A major fundraising campaign began in 1978 to save the sign, with *Playboy* magazine publisher Hugh Hefner pledging at least $30,000 to rebuild it. Other celebrities such as Alice Cooper, Andy Williams, and Gene Autry contributed $27,700 each to replace individual letters. When over $270,000 was raised, Pacific Outdoor Advertising was hired to demolish and rebuild the sign with steel framework and sheet metal letters, along with thc hclp of Hughes Helicopter and Heath and Company to airlift the letters and frames into place. Demolition of the distressed sign began on August 8, 1978, with the old sign totally demolished and the new steel and concrete reinforced one finished in six weeks. The new sign was formally unveiled on a nationally televised CBS-TV special on November 14, 1978, Hollywood's official 75th anniversary. (Bison.)

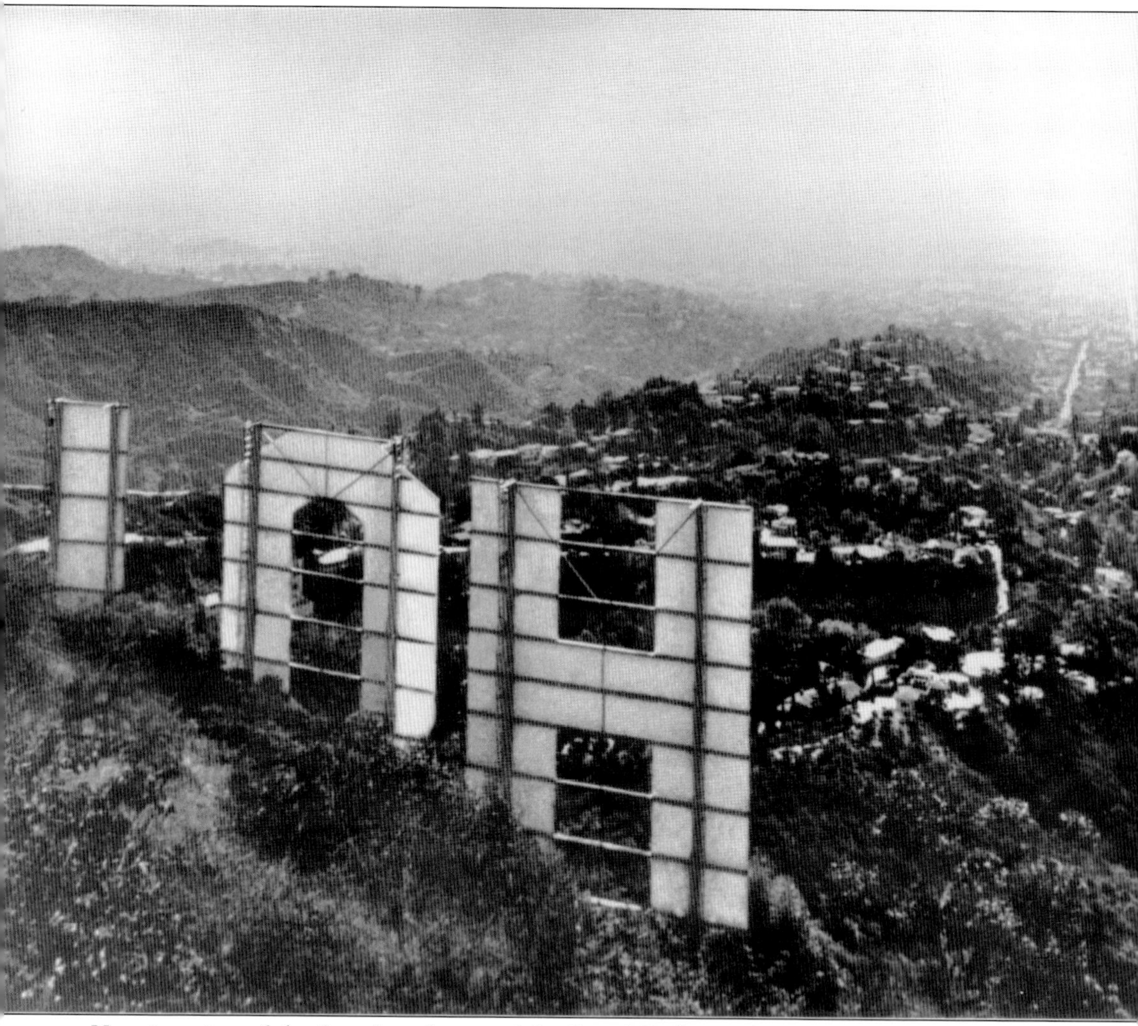

Here is a view of the first three letters of the "new" Hollywood sign constructed in 1978. The Hollywood Chamber of Commerce awarded the demolition and reconstruction of the sign to Pacific Outdoor Advertising in the summer of 1978. They subcontracted parts of the construction work to Heath and Company and Hughes Helicopter. Heath and Company manufactured and installed the new enamelized sheet metal face, while Hughes Helicopter transported and put in place the steel columns. One hundred ninety-four tons of concrete were poured to surround the 20 steel footings, which were sunk at least 14 feet into the hillside. Steel columns, girders, and beams were airlifted by Hughes into location, bolted into place by construction crews onto which corrugated sheet metal was then fastened. The new letters in the sign were only 45 feet high, with the total weight of the sign totaling 480,000 pounds. (Bison.)

Five

For Persons of Discriminating Taste

Hollywoodland developers promoted the neighborhood's elegant layout, closeness to nature, and proximity to business and cultural centers as sales hooks to potential buyers. Brochures touted the stone retaining walls, graceful stairs, and almost fairy tale–like atmosphere of the community. Creative types could fashion storybook castles to live like the cinematic royalty they were or aspired to be. As described in one of the promotional booklets, "Where every home-site is a thing of beauty unto itself and every home surveys a domain of its own."

Artists also appreciated the bohemian, European style of the beautiful area, reminiscent of secluded little mountain towns in Italy or France, with sprawling houses climbing the hills. Raymond Chandler made note of the homes' "clinging vine effect" in one of his short stories. Author and resident James M. Cain referred to this type of upscale house in his novel *Double Indemnity*. He locates the home of Phyllis Nirdlinger, the female protagonist, in Hollywoodland and states, "It was just a Spanish house, like all the rest of them in California, with white walls, red tile roof, and a patio out to one side. It was built cockeyed. The garage was under the house, the first floor was over that, and the rest of it was piled uphill anyway they could get it in."

Hollywoodland has attracted a wide range of residents, including writers James M. Cain, Aldous Huxley, Felix Adler, and Herbert F. Biberman; artists Erté and Einar Petersen; production designer Ben Carré; painter Edward S. Biberman; cartoonist Robert Clampett; sculptor Salvadore Scarpitta; musicians Max Steiner, Constantine Bakaleinikoff, Stan Kenton, Benny Carter, Peter Tork, Alice Cooper, Ray Manzarek, Brian Setzer, Anthony Kiedis, Madonna, and Moby; and actors and movie industry workers Crane Wilbur, Mary Carr, Miriam Seegar, William Perlberg, Esther Ralston, Robert Montgomery, J. Stuart Blackton, Bela Lugosi, Busby Berkeley, Grace Bradley, Eleanore Whitney, Gale Sondergaard, Norman Z. McLeod, Efrem Zimbalist Jr., Spring Byington, Ned Beatty, David Naughton, Kathy Bates, Jon Cryer, and Forest Whitaker.

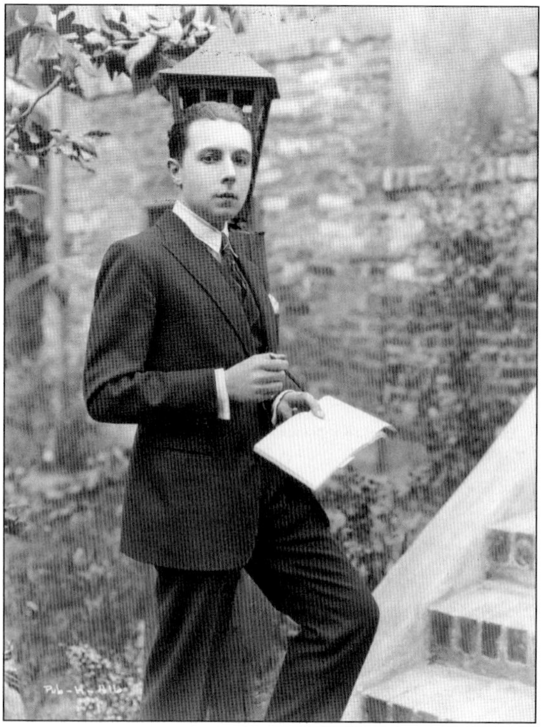

Hired in 1925 by Metro-Goldwyn-Mayer chief Louis B. Mayer as special design consultant, world-renowned fashion and graphic arts designer Romain di Tirtoff, also known as Erté, lived at the top of Beachwood Canyon at 3020 North Beachwood Drive, in this house, during most of his short stay in Hollywood. He designed himself a special studio from which to work at home, as well as having an elegant office on the MGM lot outfitted for him. He worked on films as well as stage shows, assisting Sid Grauman with designing and producing the special prologue that opened before the screening of *The Big Parade* at the Egyptian Theatre on Hollywood Boulevard. (Bison.)

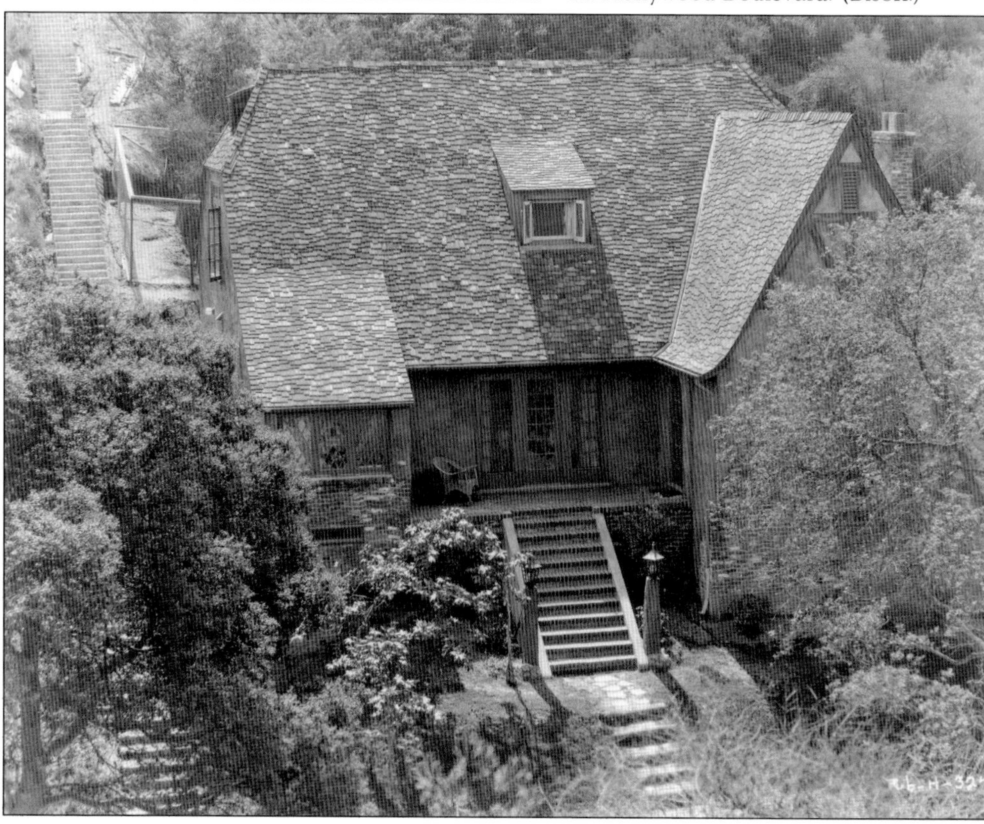

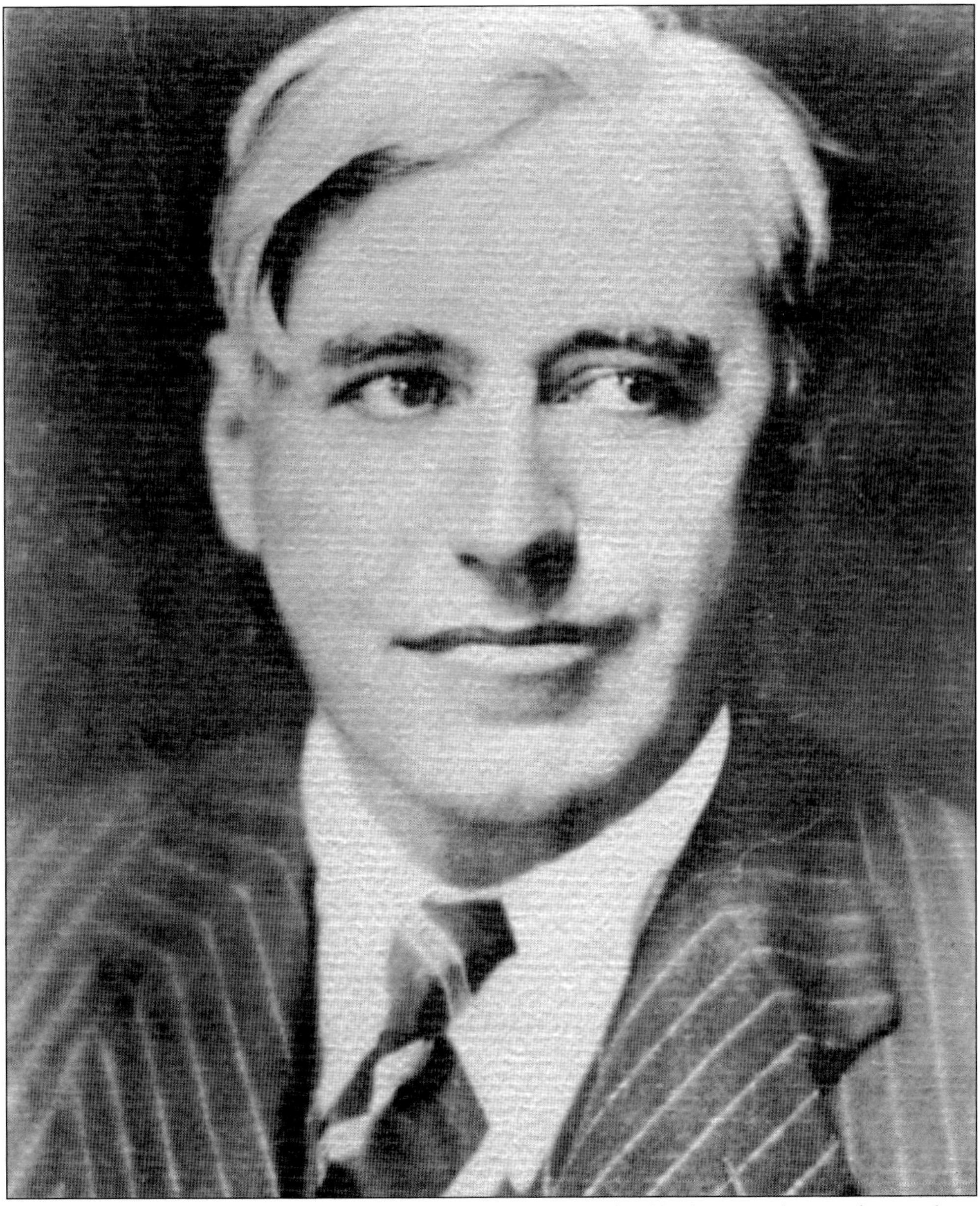

Canadian Mack Sennett, born Michael Sinnott, loved vaudeville shows and aspired to perform on stage. He traveled to New York City in the early 1900s, where he soon joined Biograph, a motion picture company, for which he acted, danced, sang, designed sets, and even directed films. He performed with Mary Pickford under the direction of legendary D.W. Griffith during this period. Sennett moved to Edendale, California, in 1912 and formed Keystone Studios with the financial help of Adam Kessel and Charles O. Bauman. It was here that he innovated and popularized slapstick comedy with his Keystone Kops. Sennett introduced such comedic performers as Roscoe "Fatty" Arbuckle, Charles Chaplin, Harry Langdon, and Ford Sterling to the screen before financial problems forced him into bankruptcy in 1933. He proposed to erect a palatial, Spanish-style home rivaling Greenacres and Pickfair on land above the Hollywoodland sign in 1926, unfortunately never built. (MM.)

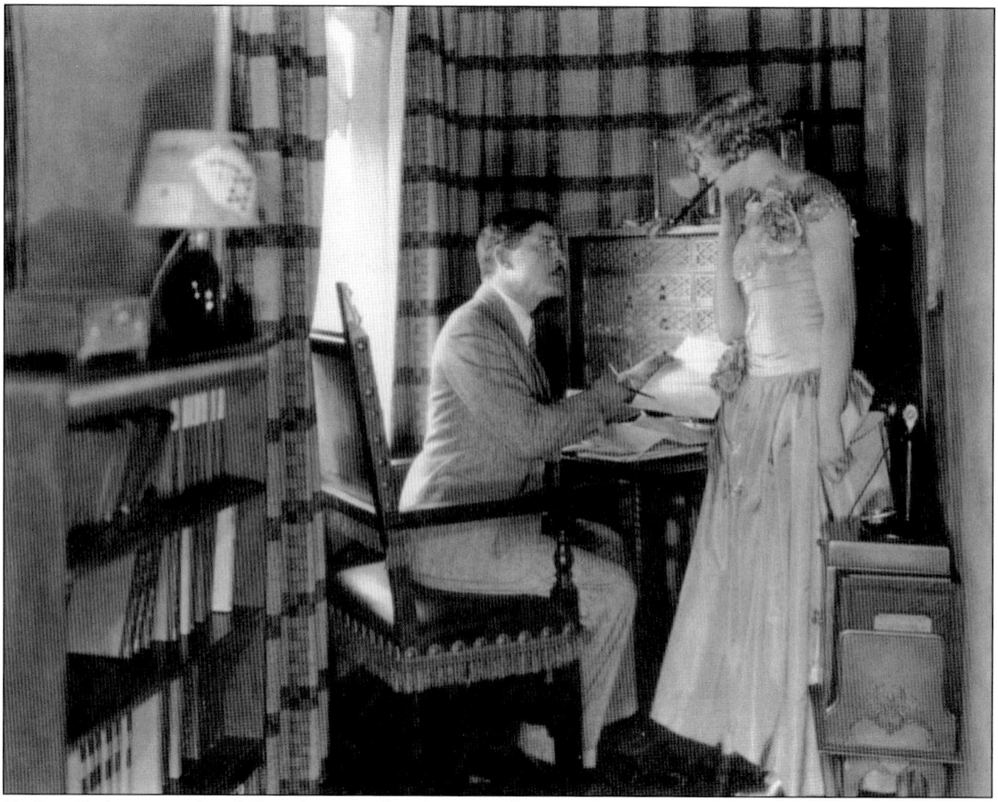

Esther Ralston, right, fell in love with a beautiful Spanish home she toured at 2022 Hollyridge Drive in 1927 and bought it with her husband, George Webb (left). Ralston, a great beauty, starred in films from the 1920s through the 1930s, mostly under contract to Paramount Pictures, appearing in the 1924 film *Peter Pan*. (AMPAS.)

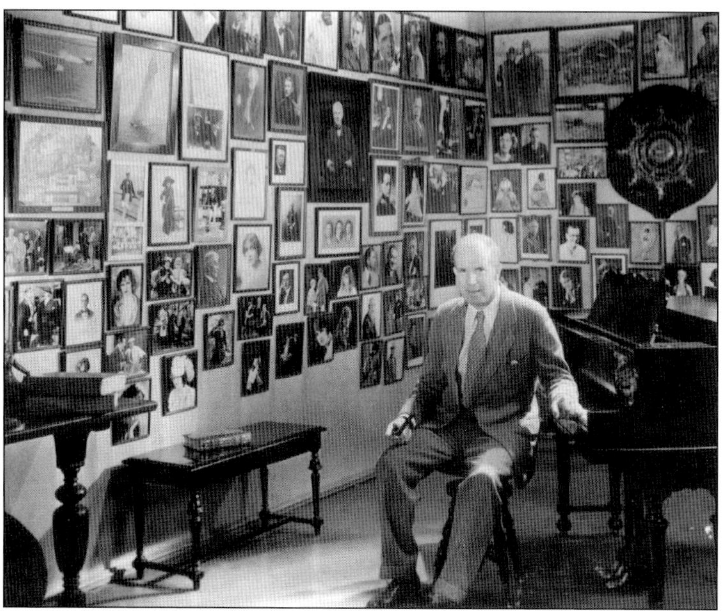

J. Stuart Blackton cofounded Vitagraph Films with Alfred E. Smith in 1896, turning it into one of the world's largest silent film production companies before selling to Warner Bros. in 1925. Blackton is recognized as one of stop-motion animation's pioneers. After the stock market crash in 1929, he lectured on film and rented the home at 2746 Belden Drive for $125 a month in the early 1930s. (AMPAS.)

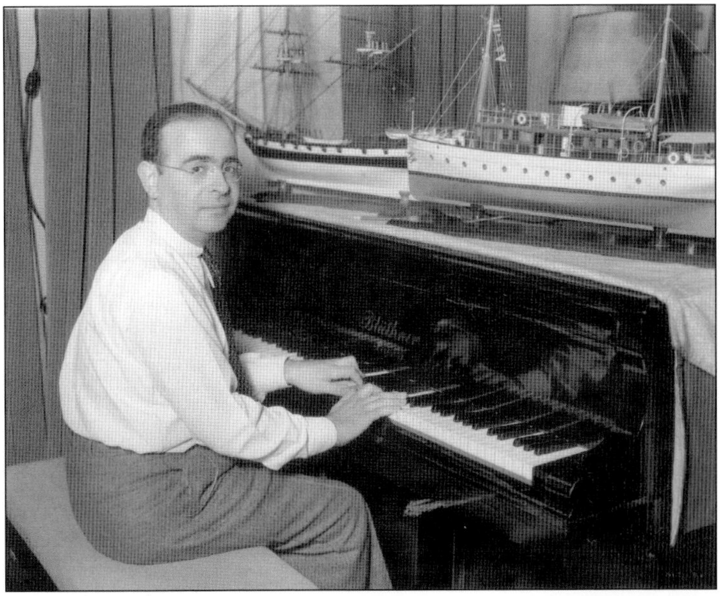

RKO brought Max Steiner to Hollywood in 1929 to score films after a successful career conducting and orchestrating on Broadway. He and his wife, Aubrey, rented 3078 Belden Drive for $175 a month during their first years in California. Steiner would go on to score such classic films as *King Kong* (1933), *Gone with the Wind* (1939), and *Casablanca* (1943). (AMPAS.)

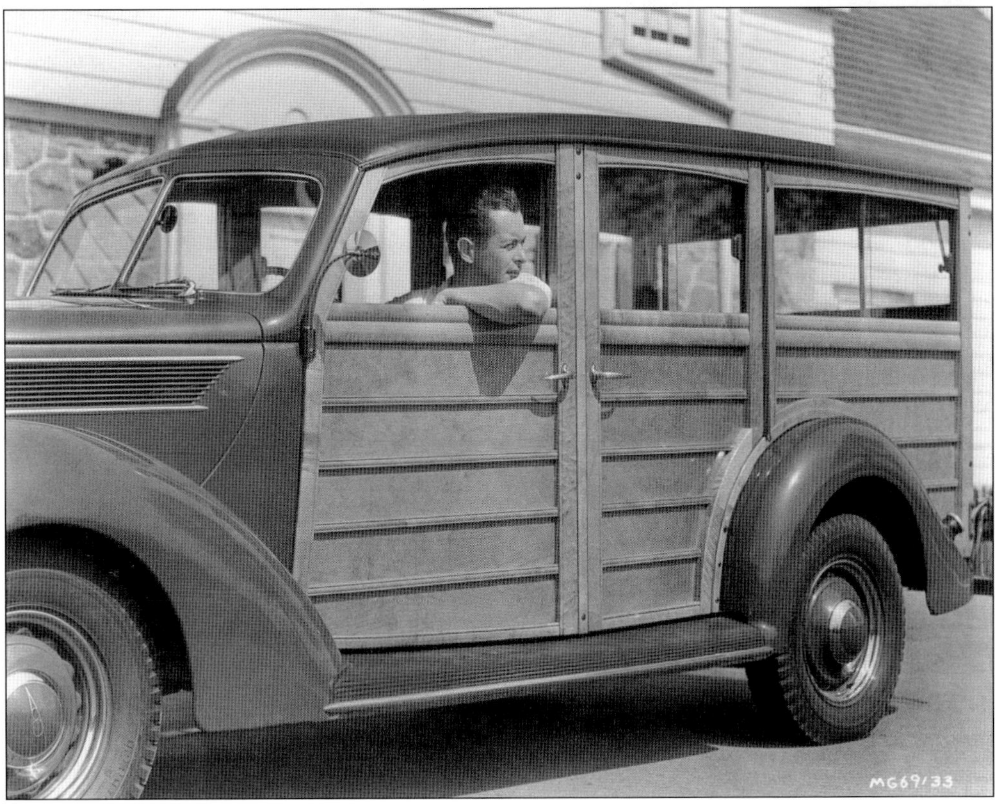

Robert J. Montgomery, one of MGM's top male stars in the early 1930s, costarred with such beauties as Norma Shearer and Joan Crawford during his years at the studio. Montgomery is pictured in his 1937 Ford Woody station wagon near his residence at 2815 Beachwood Drive in Hollywoodland. He would go on to direct himself in films, as well as serve as Screen Actors Guild president in 1935. (AMPAS.)

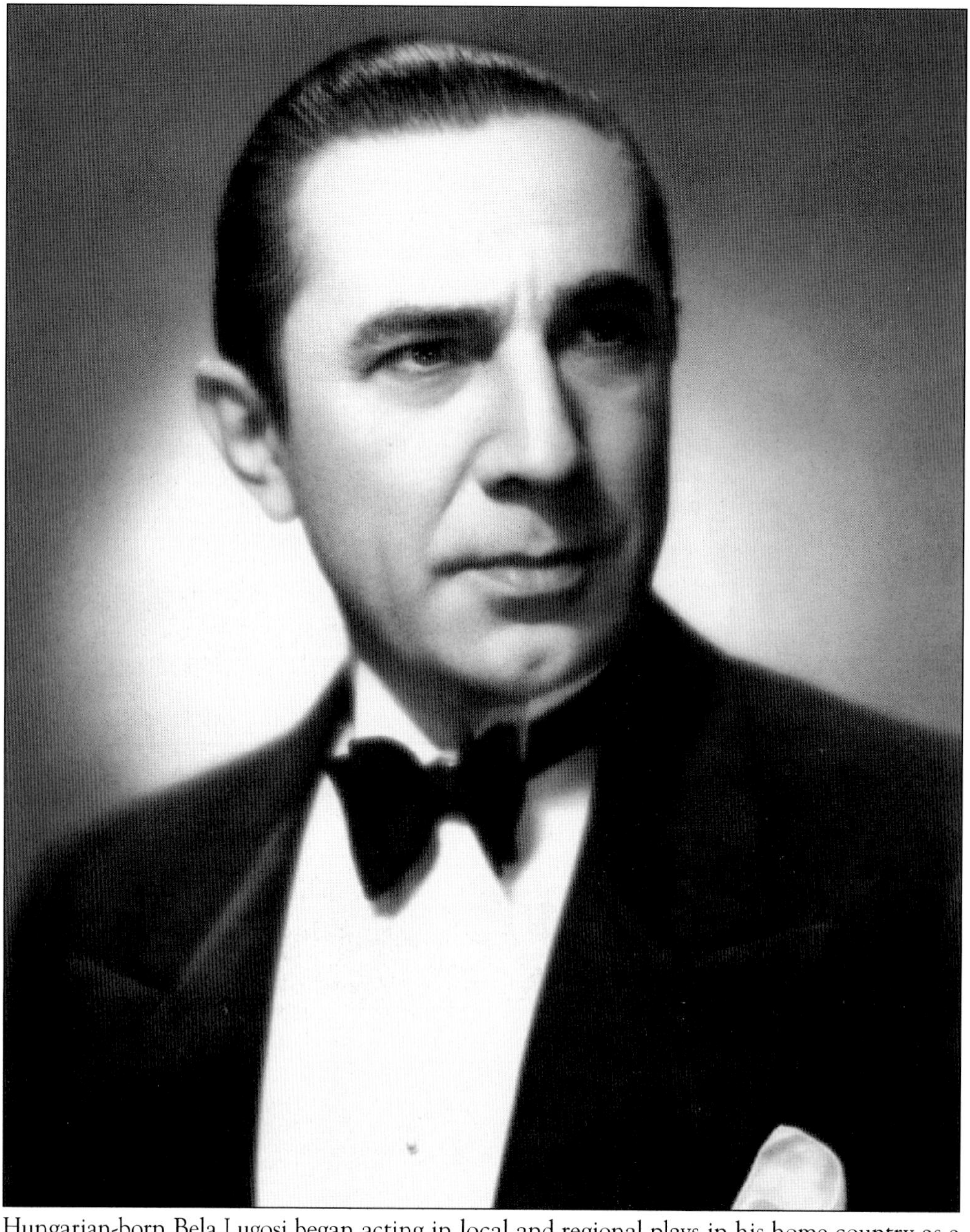

Hungarian-born Bela Lugosi began acting in local and regional plays in his home country as a young man. He moved to Budapest in 1912 and performed with the National Theater and in movies before serving in World War I. Lugosi fled the country during the Hungarian Revolution of 1919, eventually landing in Germany. He appeared in films there before arriving in the United States in 1920. He soon appeared in Hungarian plays before playing on Broadway and in films. Lugosi starred in the Broadway production of *Dracula* before appearing in the legendary 1931 Universal film *Dracula*. It soon typecast him as a horror villain. In the early 1930s, Lugosi lived at 2835 Westshire Drive, an understated English Tudor home. Beset by health and financial worries, his career later faltered, and by the 1950s he was reduced to appearing in such low budget films as *Plan 9 from Outer Space*. (AMPAS.)

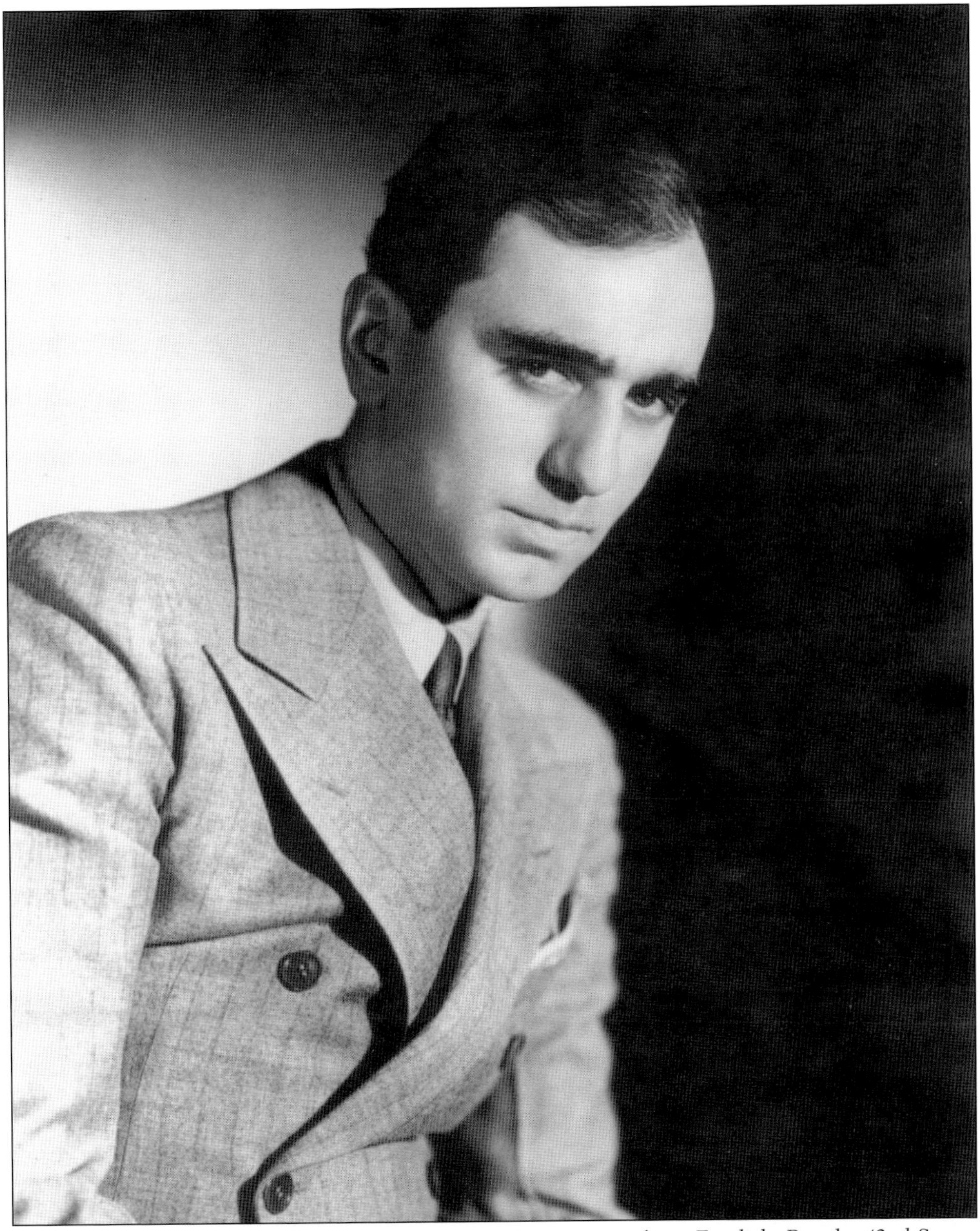

The choreographer of such lavish 1930s Warner Bros. musicals as *Footlight Parade*, *42nd Street*, and *Dames*, Busby Berkeley helmed over 25 films in his renowned career. During World War I, he put on shows for American troops. In the 1920s, Berkeley danced and performed on Broadway before choreographing productions. He began choreographing Eddie Cantor movie musicals in the late 1920s, introducing such concepts as highlighting each chorus girl with a close-up and creating dynamic, geometric patterns of performers shot from overhead. Warner Bros. soon hired him to direct their big budget musicals at the heyday of the Depression. Difficult and demanding, he ventured into directing straight films in the late 1930s before bouncing around between film studios. He later directed the Carmen Miranda film *The Gang's All Here* in 1943. He acquired the home at 2706 North Beachwood Drive in the early 1930s. (AMPAS.)

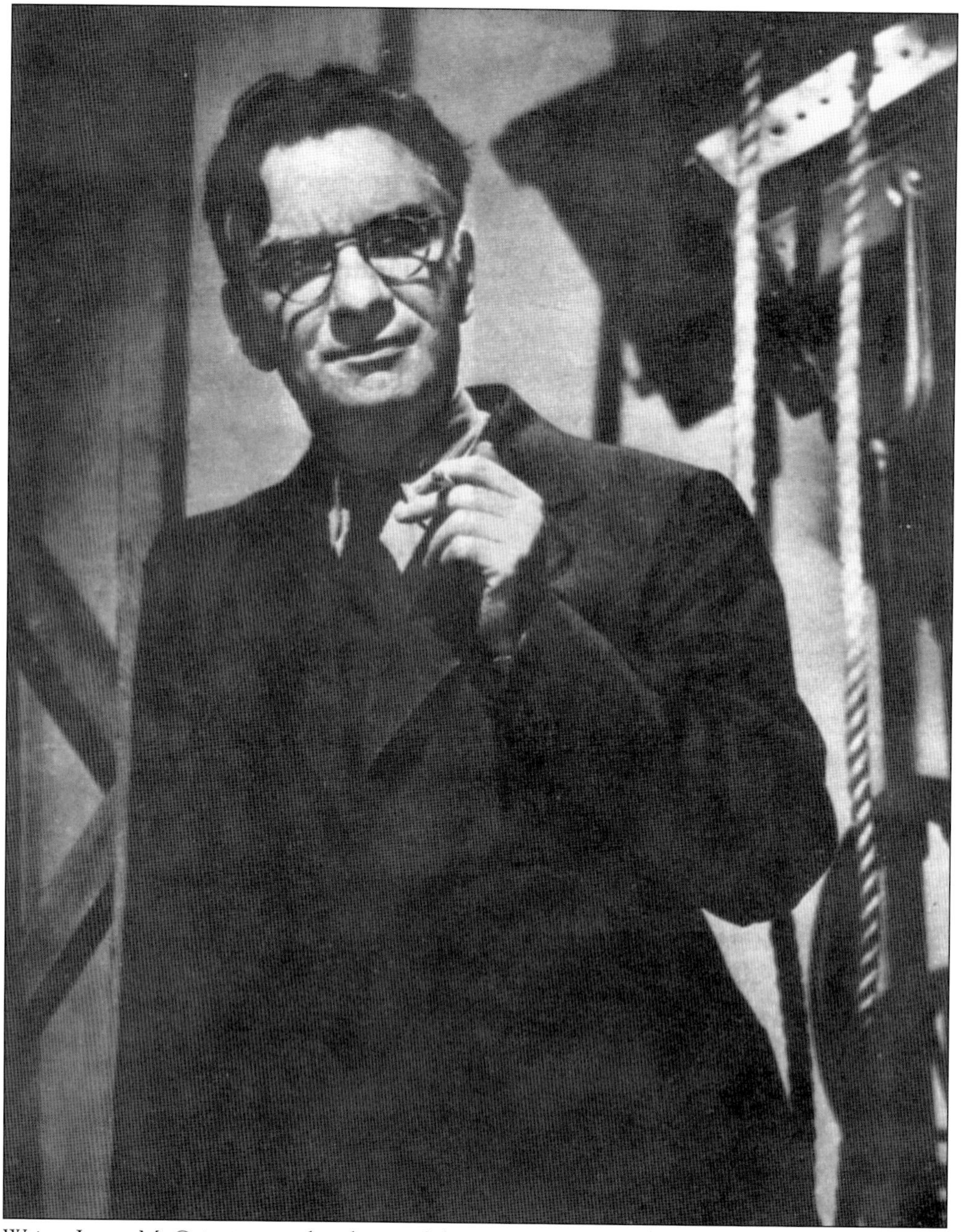

Writer James M. Cain is considered one of the greatest 20th century mystery novelists, thanks to such classic works as *Double Indemnity*, *Mildred Pierce*, and *The Postman Always Rings Twice* written in the mid-1930s. After college, he worked for the *Baltimore Sun* newspaper before writing editorials and articles and working as an editor. Cain turned to writing pulp fiction in 1934, releasing *The Postman Always Rings Twice* as his first novel, earning high praise. The success of these three important works led Hollywood to hire him as a screenwriter, but not on any of the films adapted from his works. Cain received credit for only three screenplays, *Algiers*, *Stand Up and Fight*, and *Gypsy Wildcat*. He moved into 2966 Belden Drive in 1934, where he wrote *Mildred Pierce*. Cain employed Hollywoodland as a location in several of his works. (Richard Adkins.)

Paramount Pictures brought dancer Eleanore Whitney to Hollywood in 1935 to appear in their movies. Whitney, a protégé of dancer Bill "Bojangles" Robinson, appeared in only 13 films while under contract to the studio, before returning to the New York stage. She is pictured outside her home at 3099 Durand Drive. (AMPAS.)

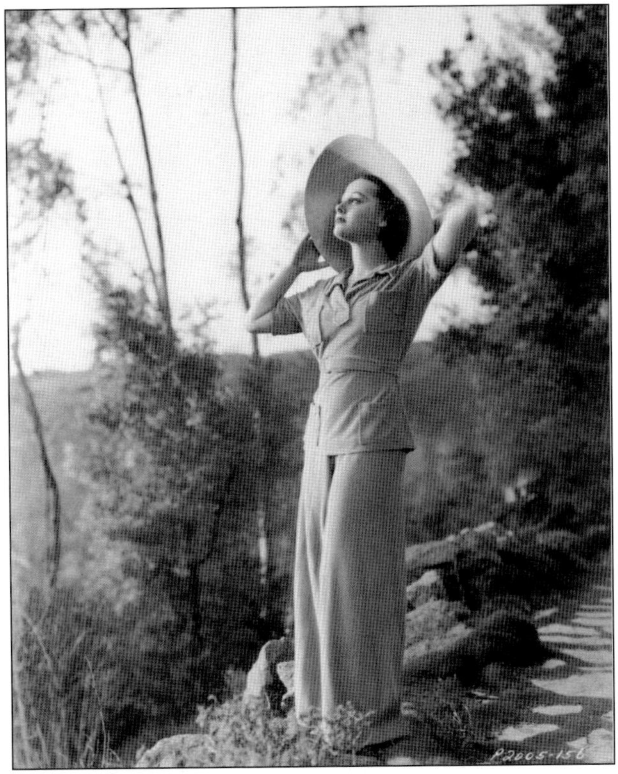

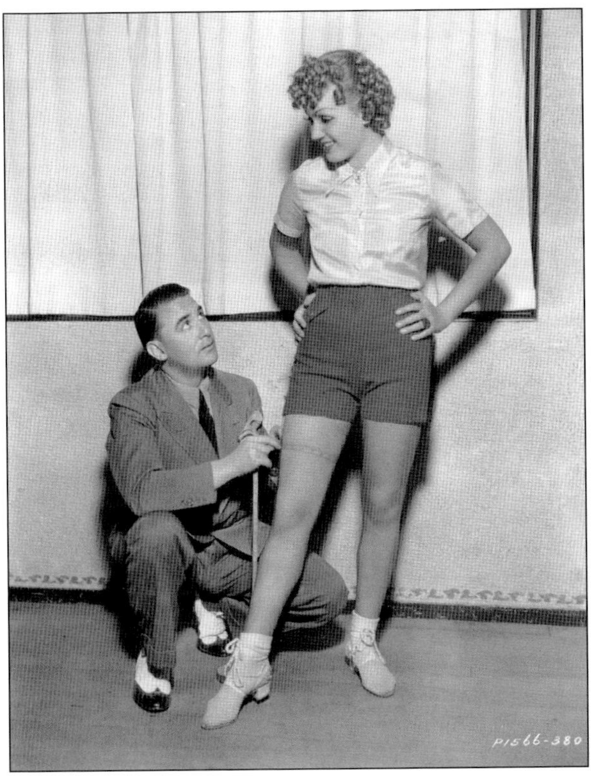

Grace Bradley, right, pictured with LeRoy Prinz, left, worked as a Paramount ingénue and rented 6310 Rodgerton Drive with her mother in 1935. Bradley married William "Hopalong Cassidy" Boyd within three weeks of meeting him in 1937. She retired from the screen soon after her marriage but spent her later life promoting Boyd and his "Hoppy" character. (MM.)

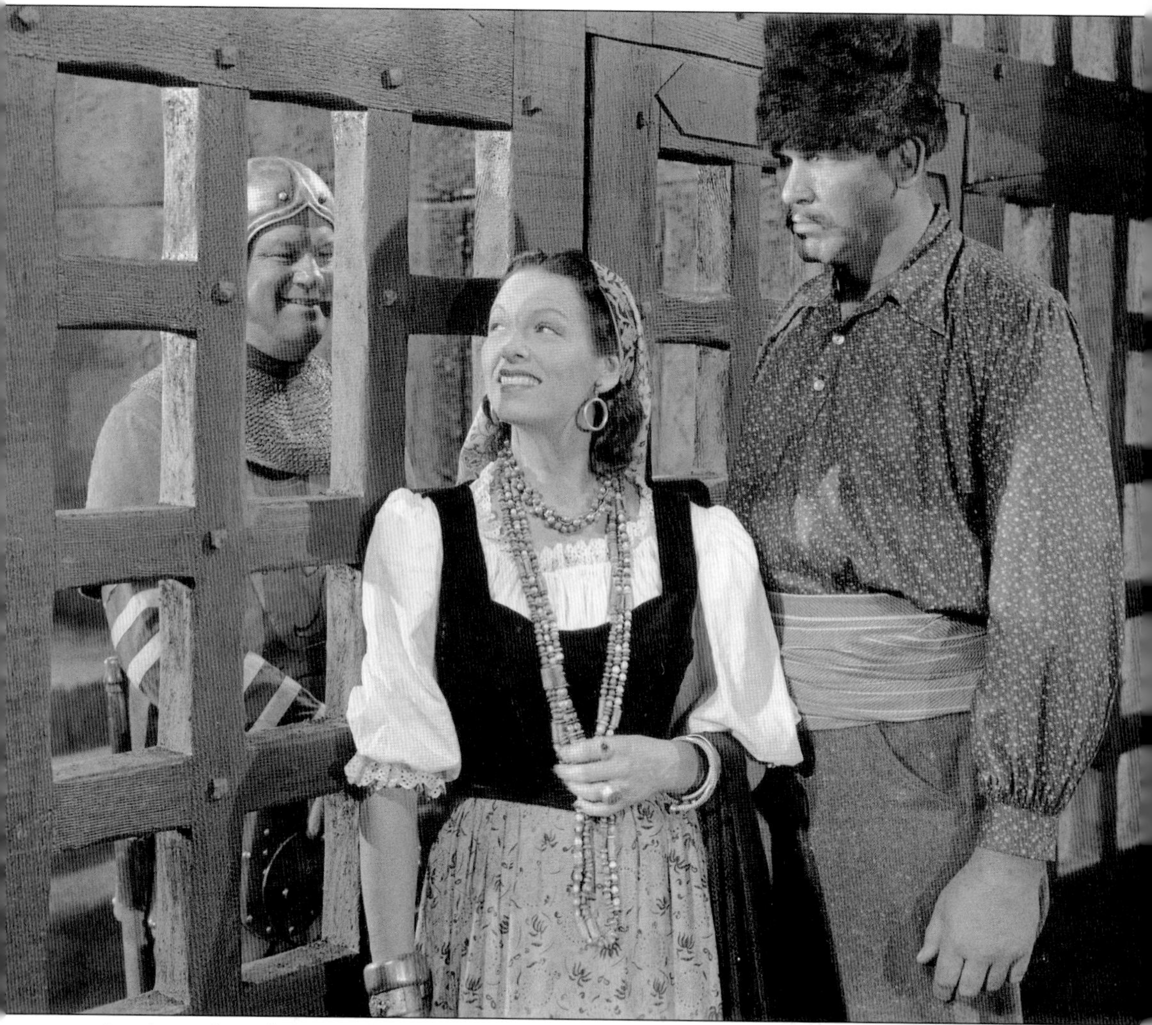

Academy Award–winning actress Gale Sondergaard and her husband, screenwriter Herbert Biberman, bought 3259 Deronda Drive in the 1940s. Sondergaard won the first Best Supporting Actress Academy Award for her first film, *Anthony Adverse*, in 1936. Biberman was a screenwriter later imprisoned for six months for refusing to testify before the House Un-American Activities Committee in 1948 regarding Communists in the motion picture industry. After his imprisonment, he was blacklisted, along with his wife. In 1954, he wrote and directed *Salt of the Earth*, a pro-union film about a zinc miners' strike. Biberman and Sondergaard were married for 41 years. His brother, painter Edward Biberman, lived at 3332 Deronda Drive. A muralist and portrait painter, Biberman was blacklisted in the 1950s because of his leftist politics. Sondergaard starred in the film *Gypsy Wildcat*, written by Hollywoodland resident James M. Cain. (MM.)

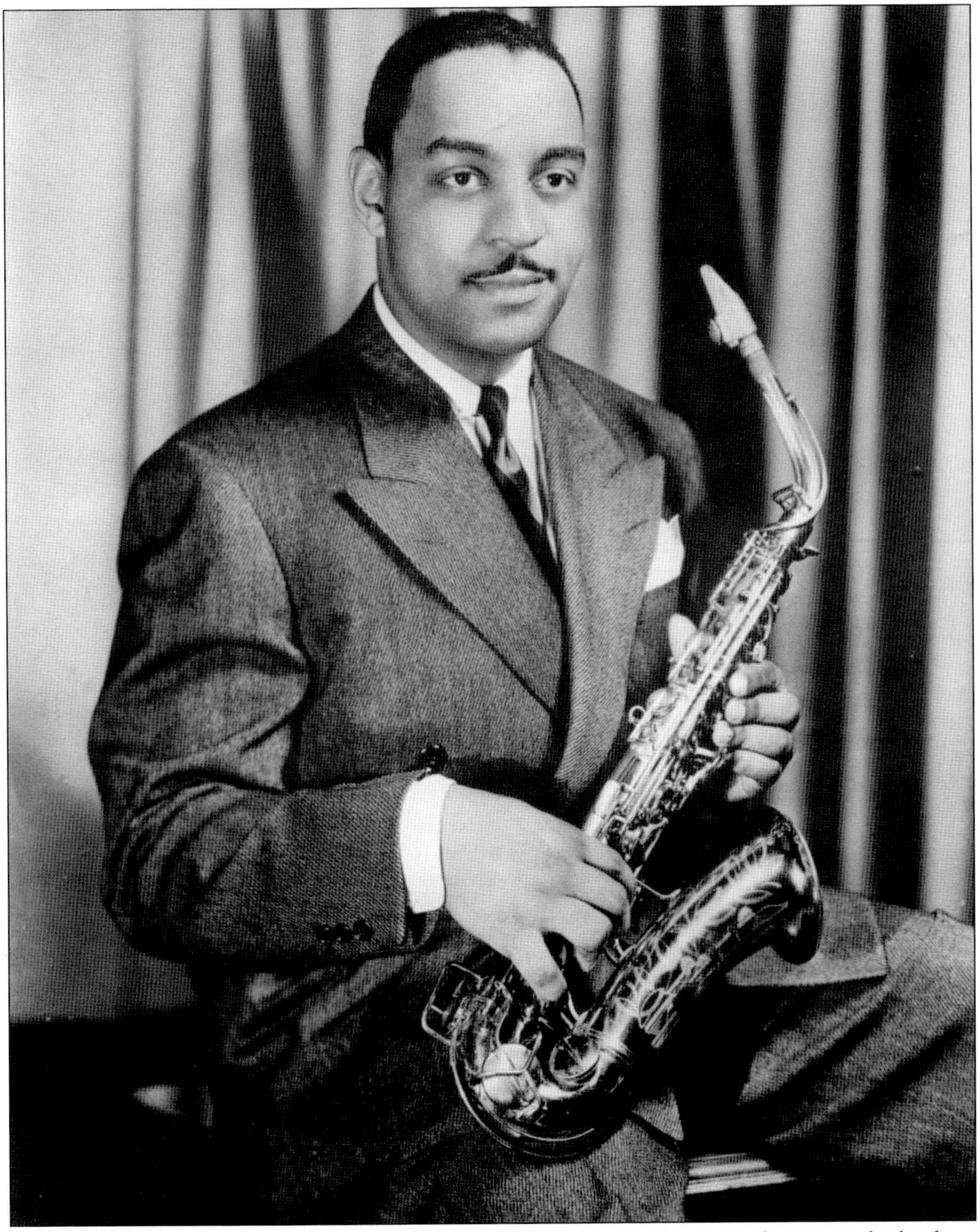

Like most other housing developments at the time, Hollywoodland restricted persons of color from residing within its boundaries. Jazz musician Benny Carter bought a home at 2752 Hollyridge Drive in 1945, ignoring residents' complaints and court attempts to get him thrown out in the 1940s. Trumpeter and saxophonist Carter played in bands with Duke Ellington, Fats Waller, Fletcher Henderson, and Earl Hines before establishing his own band in 1932 and recording albums. Carter moved to the West Coast in 1943, arranging for films and television as well as for such performers as Billie Holiday, Sarah Vaughan, Ray Charles, Peggy Lee, Louis Armstrong, and Mel Torme. Carter also mentored such artists as Miles Davis and Quincy Jones. He won the Grammy Lifetime Achievement Award in 1987, was honored with a star on the Hollywood Walk of Fame that same year, and was saluted as a Kennedy Center honoree in 1996. (MM.)

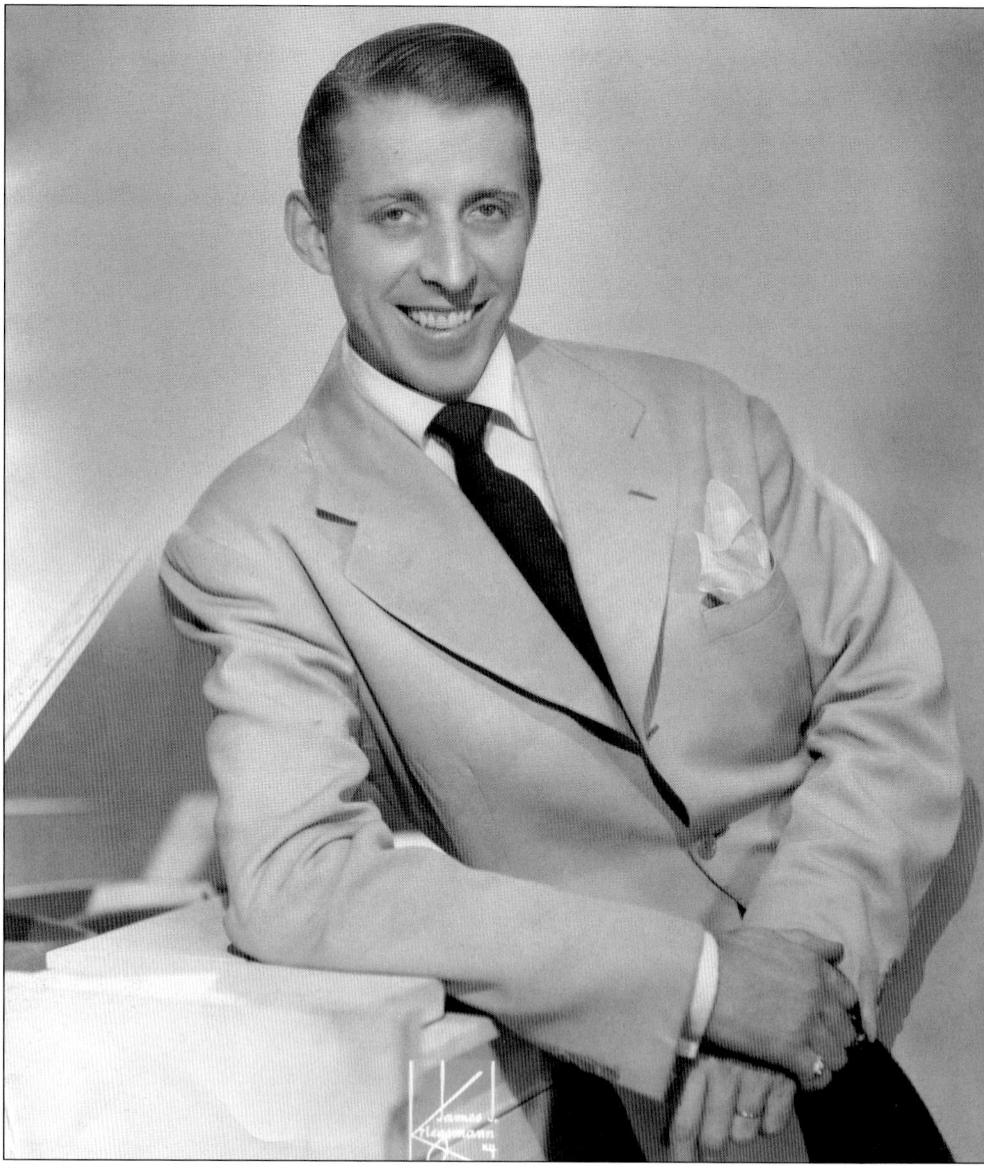

Stan Kenton recorded progressive jazz for the Capitol Records label while performing with his band in the 1940s through the 1950s. He began his career as a sideman in various bands, performed for Earl Carroll, and arranged for other performers as well as performing on the radio in the 1920s. Kenton formed his own orchestra in 1941. Such musicians and singers as Stan Getz and Anita O'Day performed with his group, which was recognized for its "Wall of Sound." During the 1940s through the 1950s, he performed in short musical films and a few motion pictures before pioneering what he called "progressive jazz," featuring a concert orchestra rather than a big band. In the 1960s, Kenton began promoting jazz education and big bands in high schools. He soon traveled the country lecturing and performing. He lived at 2720 Hollyridge Drive with his family. (MM.)

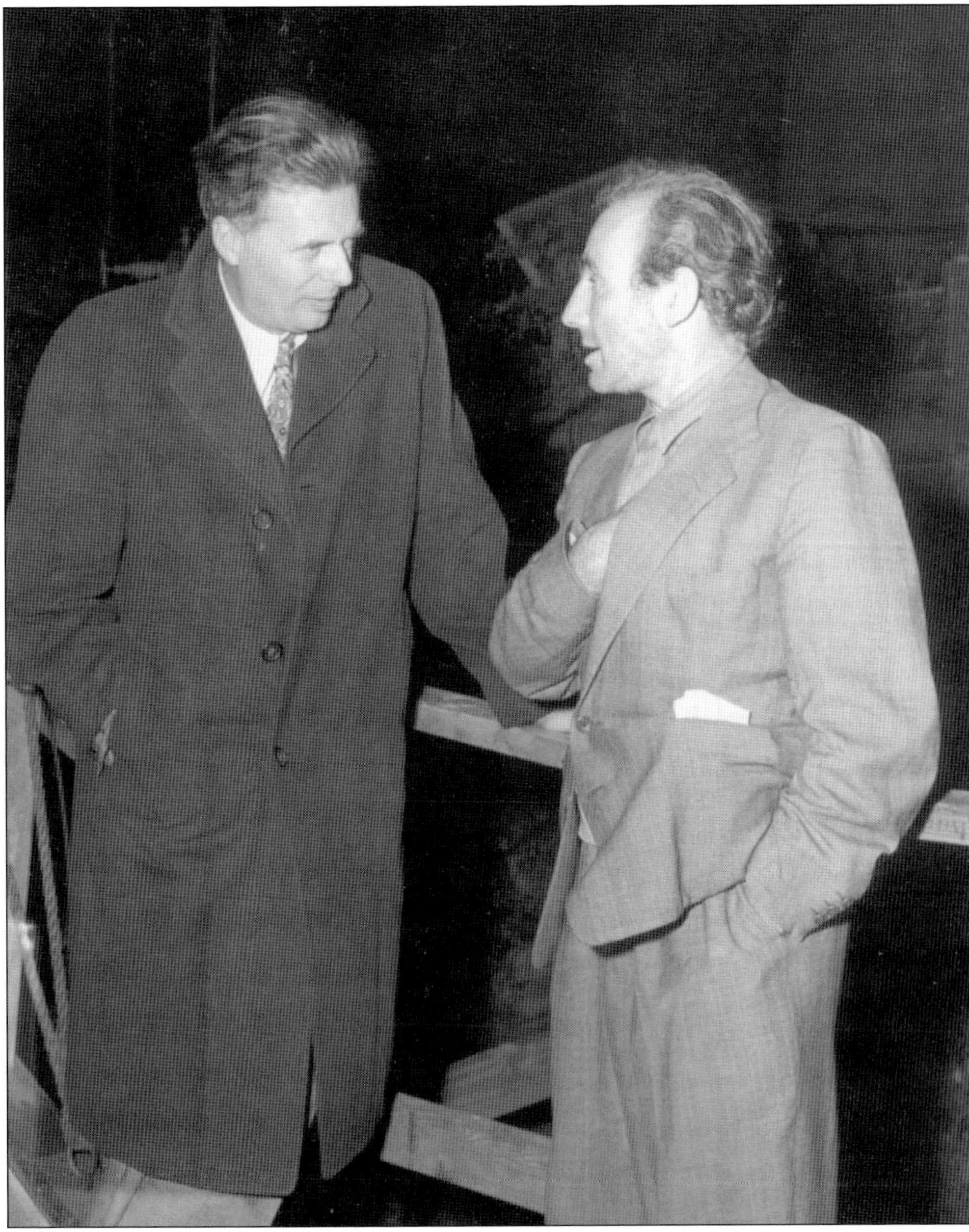

English novelist Aldous Huxley, writer of *Brave New World* and *Point Counterpoint*, and his second wife, Laura, bought a home at 3276 Deronda Drive in Hollywoodland in the 1950s that later burned down. After gaining fame as a novelist in the 1920s, Huxley wrote essays, short stories, articles, poems, and screenplays for such films as *Pride and Prejudice*, *Madame Curie*, and *Jane Eyre*. Huxley was known as a pacifist and supporter of the Vedanta spiritual movement, and he experimented with psychedelic drugs in the 1950s, influencing such people as Cary Grant and Timothy Leary to participate with these drugs as well. Jim Morrison and Ray Manzarek of The Doors named their rock group in honor of his 1954 essay "The Doors of Perception." Huxley (left) and director Zoltan Korda are pictured off-camera on the 1948 film *A Woman's Vengeance*, on which they collaborated. (AMPAS.)

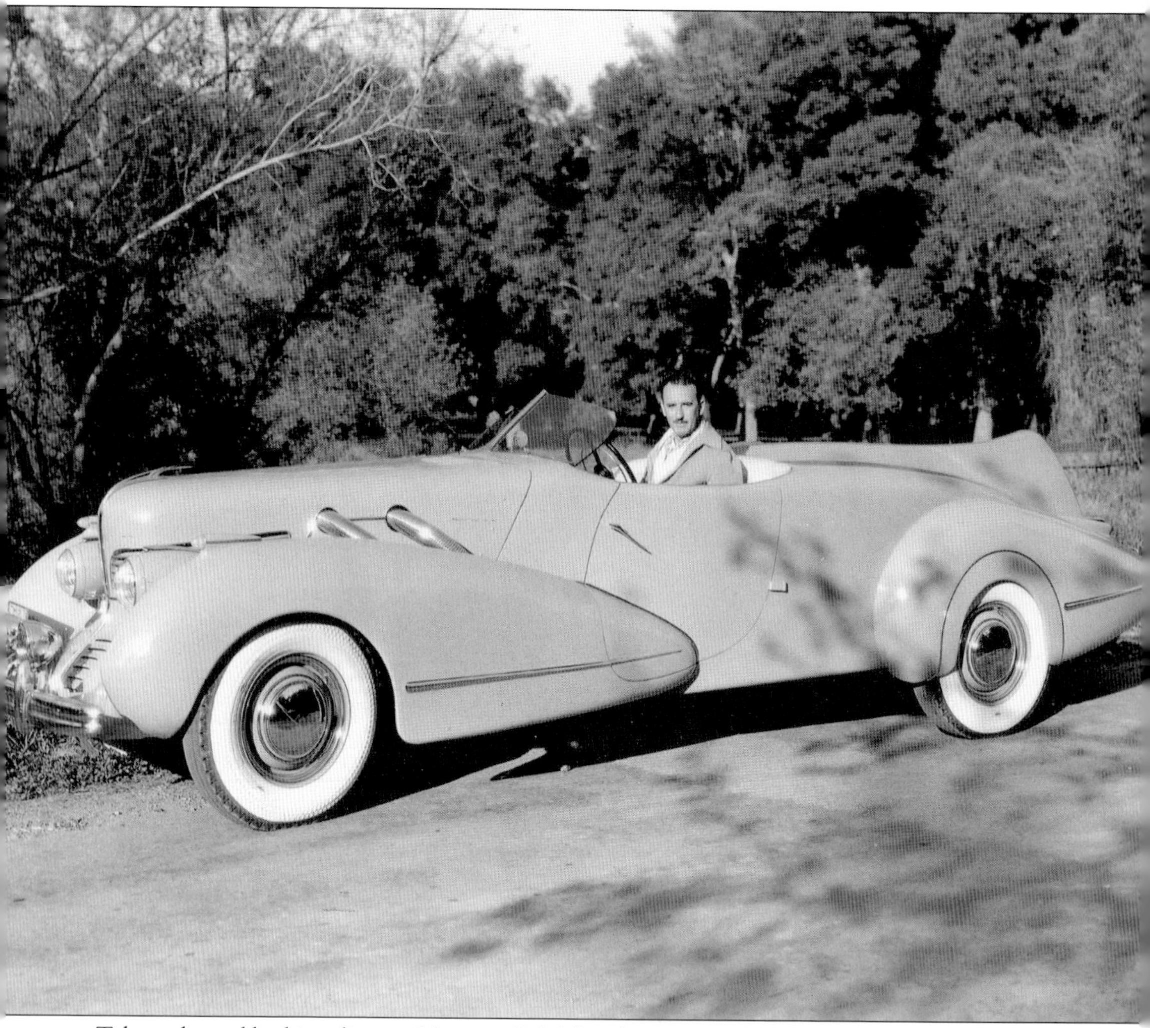

Talented, good looking director Norman Z. McLeod, sitting in the *Topper* car, began his career in Hollywood drawing cartoons and helming comedy shorts. After spending two years as a fighter pilot in World War I, McLeod entered the film business attempting to draw cartoons. He soon switched over to filmmaking, with a knack for comedy timing, sophistication, and visual gags. McLeod later directed the Marx Brothers in *Monkey Business* and *Horse Feathers*. He directed the inimitable W.C. Fields in *It's a Gift*, the story of a henpecked, East Coast grocer who decides to move to California and grow oranges on his inherited property. The car pictured is a customized 1937 Buick Model 80, designed by Anthony Garity and built by Maurice Schwartz of Pasadena, California, for the 1937 movie *Topper*, which McLeod directed. *Topper* stars young couple Cary Grant and Constance Bennett, who discover they are ghosts and decide to loosen up a stuffy friend. McLeod moved into 6220 Rodgerton Drive in the 1950s. (AMPAS.)

Peter Tork achieved stardom as a cast member of the 1960s television show *The Monkees*, about an up-and-coming rock band that also became a short-lived phenomenon spawning several rock hits. He continued to record and make appearances as a solo performer after parting with the Monkees. Tork lived at 6414 Rodgerton Drive in the Hollywoodland community for several years. (MM.)

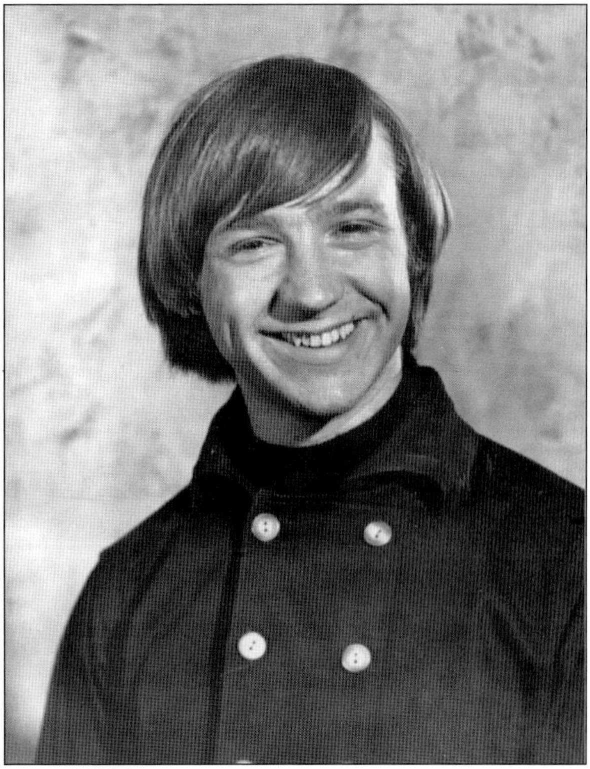

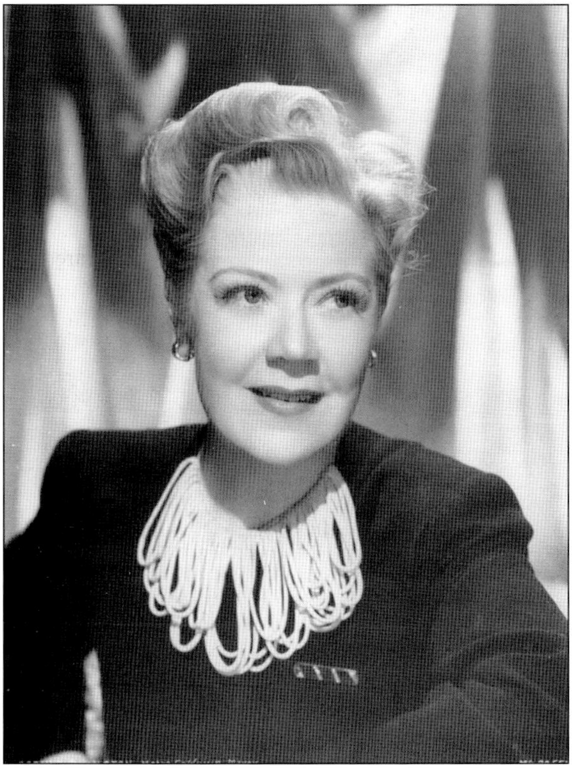

Character actress Spring Byington performed on the stage and in vaudeville in the 1920s after her divorce from her husband. Recognized for her mother and good wife roles in such films as *Little Women* (1932) and *Dodsworth* (1936), Byington also starred on television. She lived at 2946 North Beachwood Drive in the 1960s and 1970s. (MM.)

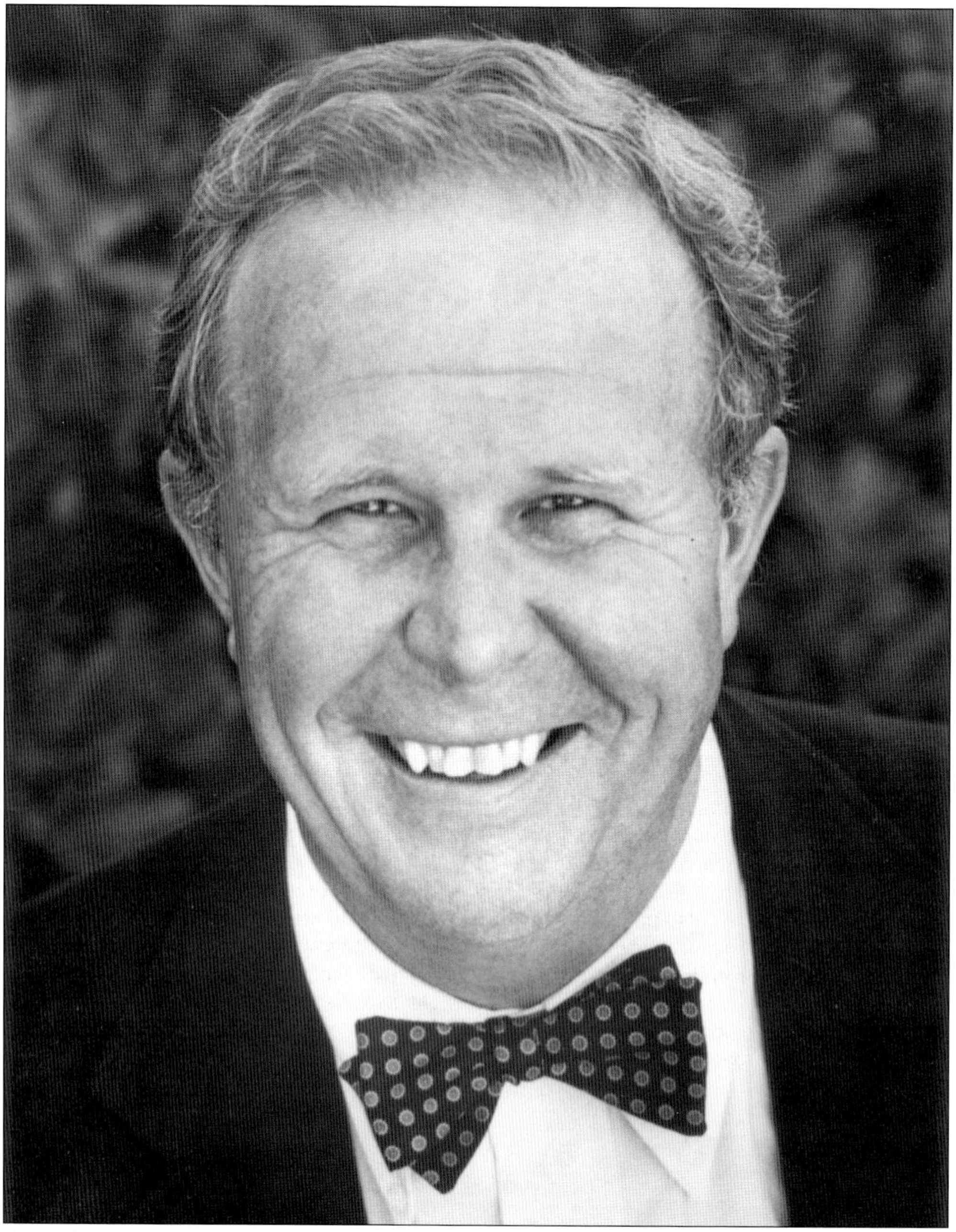

Versatile character actor Ned Beatty has performed in over 159 television and film roles during his almost 40-year career. During the early to mid-1970s, Beatty appeared in his first movie, *Deliverance,* in 1972; won an Academy Award nomination for his role in the 1976 film *Network*; and appearing in the motion picture *The Life and Times of Judge Roy Bean*. Over the years, Beatty has appeared in such other films as *1941*, *Nashville*, and *Superman*, and voiced the character Lotso in Disney-Pixar's 2010 film *Toy Story 3*. In 1979, he starred in the television movie *Friendly Fire*, about a couple dealing with the death of their son by American firepower, appeared in the television show *Roseanne* in the 1990s, and performed on the television show *Homicide* for three years. He lived at 2706 North Beachwood Drive in the 1980s. (AMPAS.)

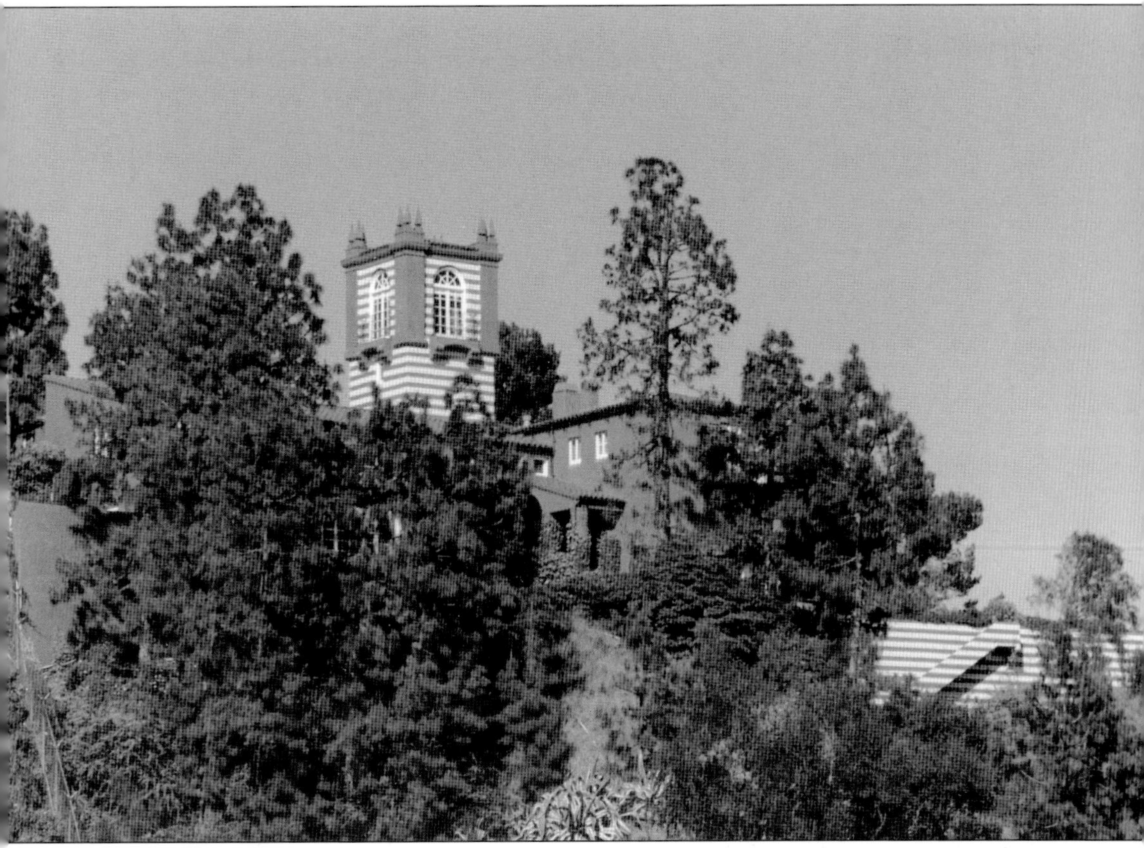

Music superstar Madonna has sold millions of records, performed in controversial music videos, and spawned countless fashion trends. She has acted onstage in the play *Speed the Plow*, as well as starred in such films as *Desperately Seeking Susan*, *Dick Tracy*, *A League of Their Own*, and *Evita*. Over the years, she has also published a photography book as well as several children's books. Madonna acquired the magnificent, nine-level Castillo del Lago at 6342 Mulholland Highway in 1993 and hired her brother, interior decorator Christopher Ciccone, to reimagine it as an Italian and Mediterranean home. He painted it in striped colors as shown. Madonna sold the house in 2001, and later in the decade, commercial director Joe Pytka owned it. The house is rumored to have served as an illegal gambling joint for notorious gangster Benjamin "Bugsy" Siegel in the 1930s. (Bison.)

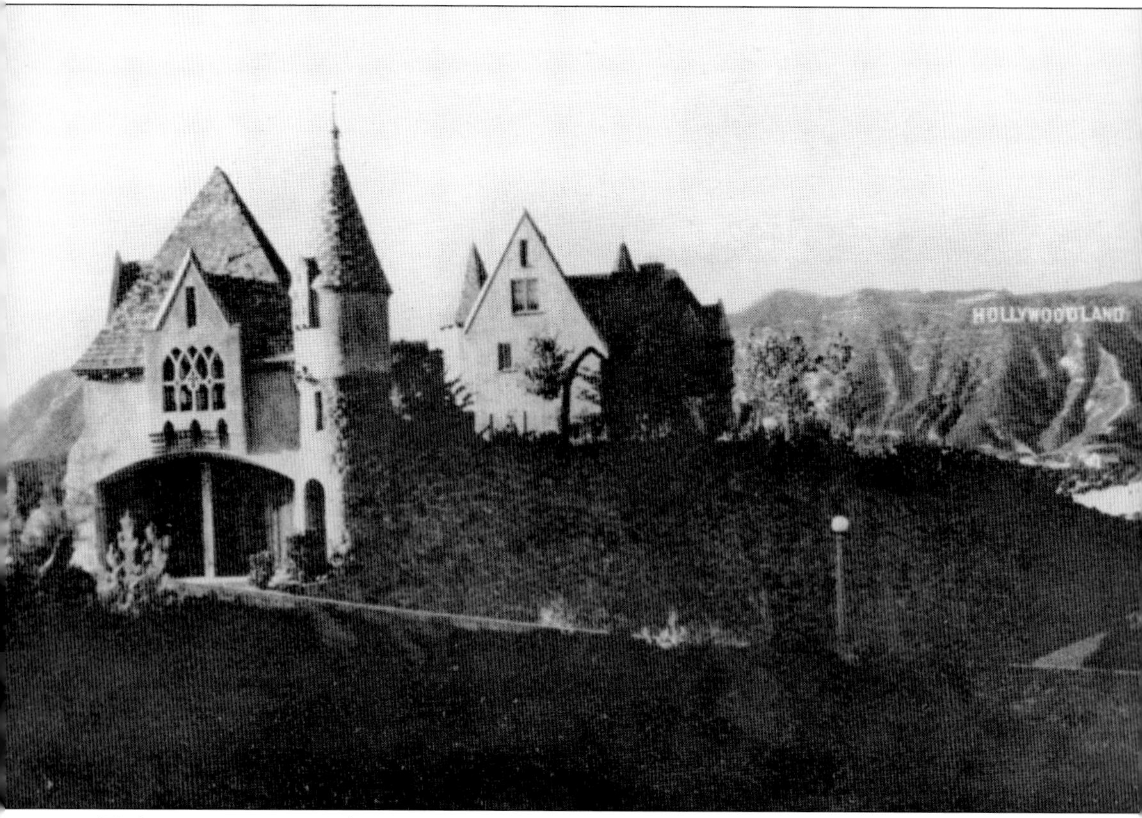

Techno music artist Moby promotes vegan, animal rights, and liberal causes while maintaining a busy composing and recording career both for motion pictures and solo albums. Many of his tracks are often featured in movies, television shows, and video games, and often include such things as collectible art cards designed by Moby himself as bonus extras. He has also composed songs for movies, as well as documentaries, television shows, and shorts. Moby owns a vegan restaurant in New York and is an active support of the animal rights group PETA. In 2010, he acquired the storybook castle Wolf's Lair at 2869 Durand Drive with the goal of restoring the house, pictured in a 1920s photograph, and using it as a recording studio. Moby is actively involved in social media, sending tweets about purchasing the home, as well as e-mailing photographs of the home's speakeasy to the blog CurbedLA. (Bison.)

Six

Hooray for Hollywoodland

Developers S.H. Woodruff and Tracy S. Shoults summoned newsreel cameramen to capture the "dislodging of more than 20,000 tons of rock and dirt" during the June 1923 demolition. The dirt was used in filling and the rocks were later utilized for structural material and neighboring retaining walls.

In June 1924, Hollywoodland publicity director L.J. Burrud displayed a film revealing the construction of a nine-room French Normandy hillside home designed by architect John L. DeLario to the National Association of Real Estate Boards in Washington, DC.

The Mack Sennett Company shot scenes for the 1926 short film *Hoboken to Hollywood* starring Billy Bevan and Vernon Dent, the first movie shot on location in Hollywoodland, as well as shooting stock footage in 1925.

The iconic Hollywood sign either establishes location, serves as a visual punch line, or foreshadows disaster in film appearances. The Hollywoodland sign first appeared on film in the opening montage for the 1935 feature film *Hollywood Boulevard.* The sign first appeared in a short film in 1939, as background for a scene in the Three Stooges' romp *A-Ducking They Did Go.* The 1947 Walt Disney cartoon *Fun and Fancy Free* is the first animated film to feature the landmark. *Under the Hollywood Sign* is the first documentary to record the history of the Hollywoodland community and the sign.

The first feature lensed in the neighborhood and at the Hollywood sign was the gritty 1954 film noir *Down Three Dark Streets*, followed by *Invasion of the Body Snatchers, It Conquered the World, House of the Damned*, and *Return From Witch Mountain.*

Films and TV shows as diverse as *The Rocketeer, Superman, Hollywood Knights, Pretty Woman, Bugsy, Chaplin, Lost Highway, Mighty Joe Young, Mulholland Drive, The Black Dahlia, Hollywoodland, The Runaways, Hollywood Boulevard, Beyond the Valley of the Dolls, 1941, Valley Girls, Ed Wood, Bean, The Truman Show, Austin Powers in Goldmember, Percy Jackson & the Olympians: The Lightening Thief, Earthquake, Death Wish II, Escape From L.A., Independence Day, Volcano, The Day After Tomorrow, Terminator Salvation, Resident Evil: Afterlife, Columbo, The Rockford Files, The Carol Burnett Show, Hollywood Beat, The Bold and the Beautiful, RKO 281, 10.5, Beverly Hills 90210, The Big One: the Great Los Angeles Earthquake, Monk*, and *Joey* have filmed here.

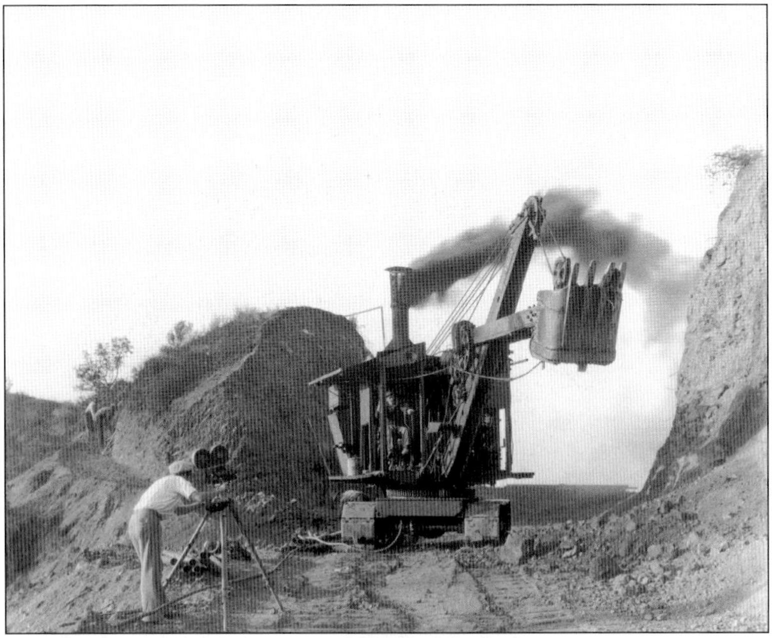

In 1925, an unknown Mack Sennett Studios cameraman records the giant crane as it cuts away the rocky hillside to create a road to the proposed home of Sennett at the tract's summit. The home was never built. It is unknown whether this roll of film still exists. (AMPAS.)

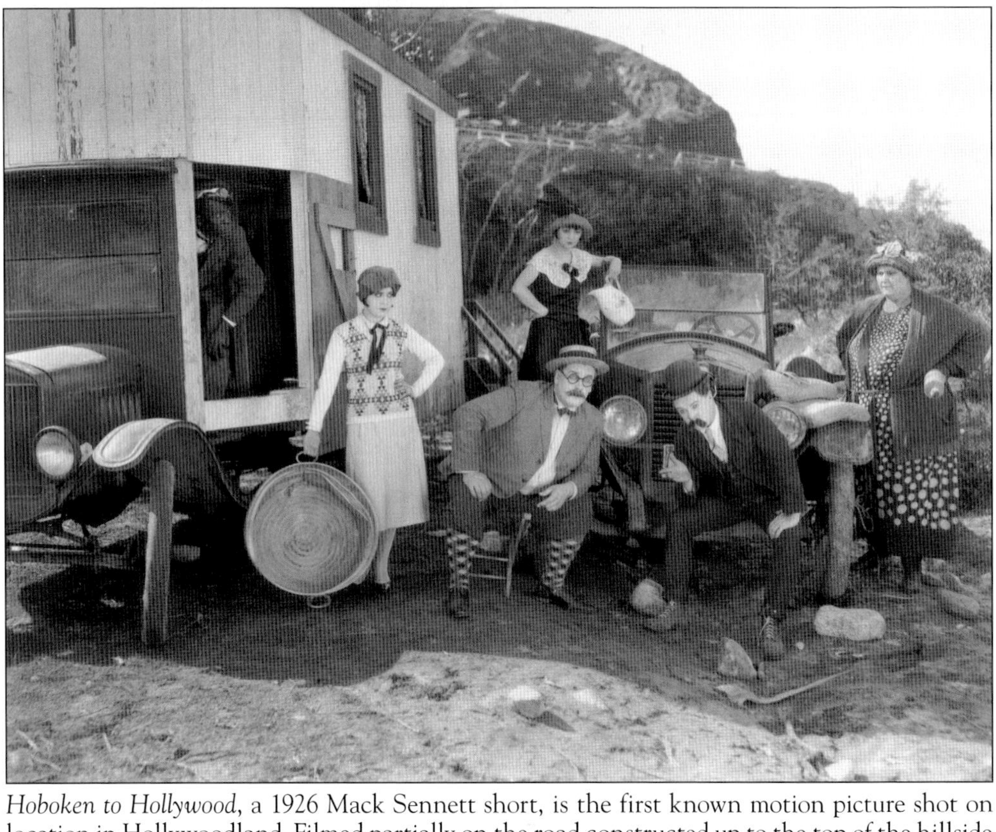

Hoboken to Hollywood, a 1926 Mack Sennett short, is the first known motion picture shot on location in Hollywoodland. Filmed partially on the road constructed up to the top of the hillside for the proposed Mack Sennett estate, the photograph features, from left to right, unidentified, Thelma Hill, Vernon Dent, Lenore Summers, Billy Bevan, and Anna Magruder. (AMPAS.)

The Three Stooges—Moe Howard, Larry Fine, and Curly Howard—appear in the first sound short that contains an appearance of the Hollywoodland sign, the 1939 short *A-Ducking They Did Go*. The sign is briefly visible behind a policeman on Gower Street just outside Columbia Studios. (MM.)

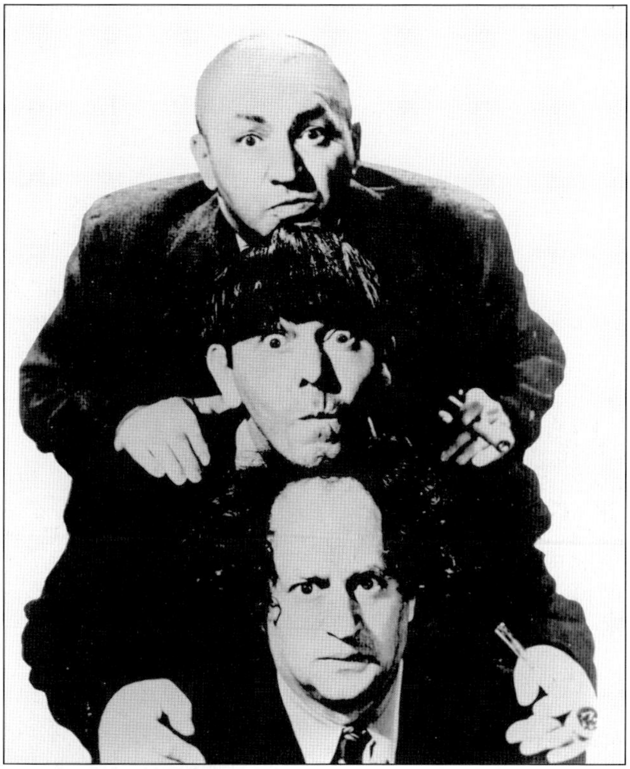

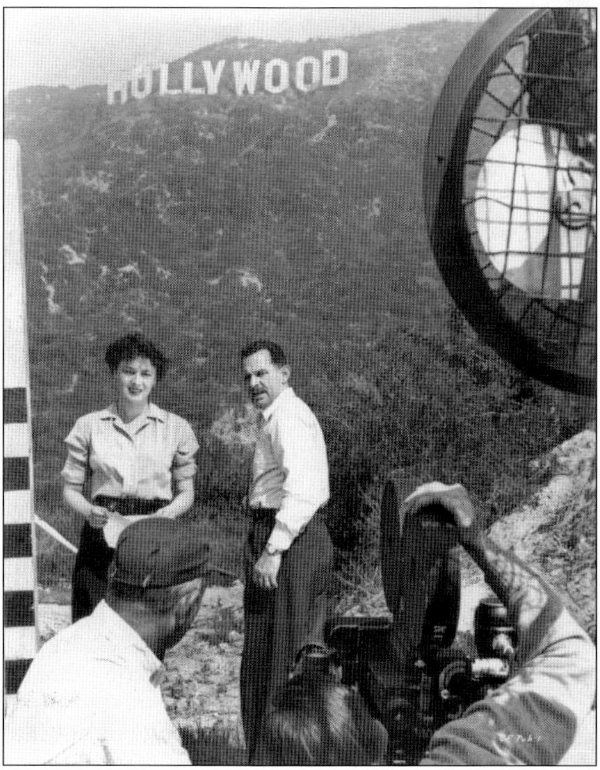

Actress Ruth Roman waits while cinematographer Joseph Biroc lines up a shot for the 1954 film noir *Down Three Dark Streets*. This photograph is probably one of the first film production stills displaying the Hollywood sign that was employed in advertising. This movie is the first known feature film to showcase the Hollywood sign onscreen. (Bison.)

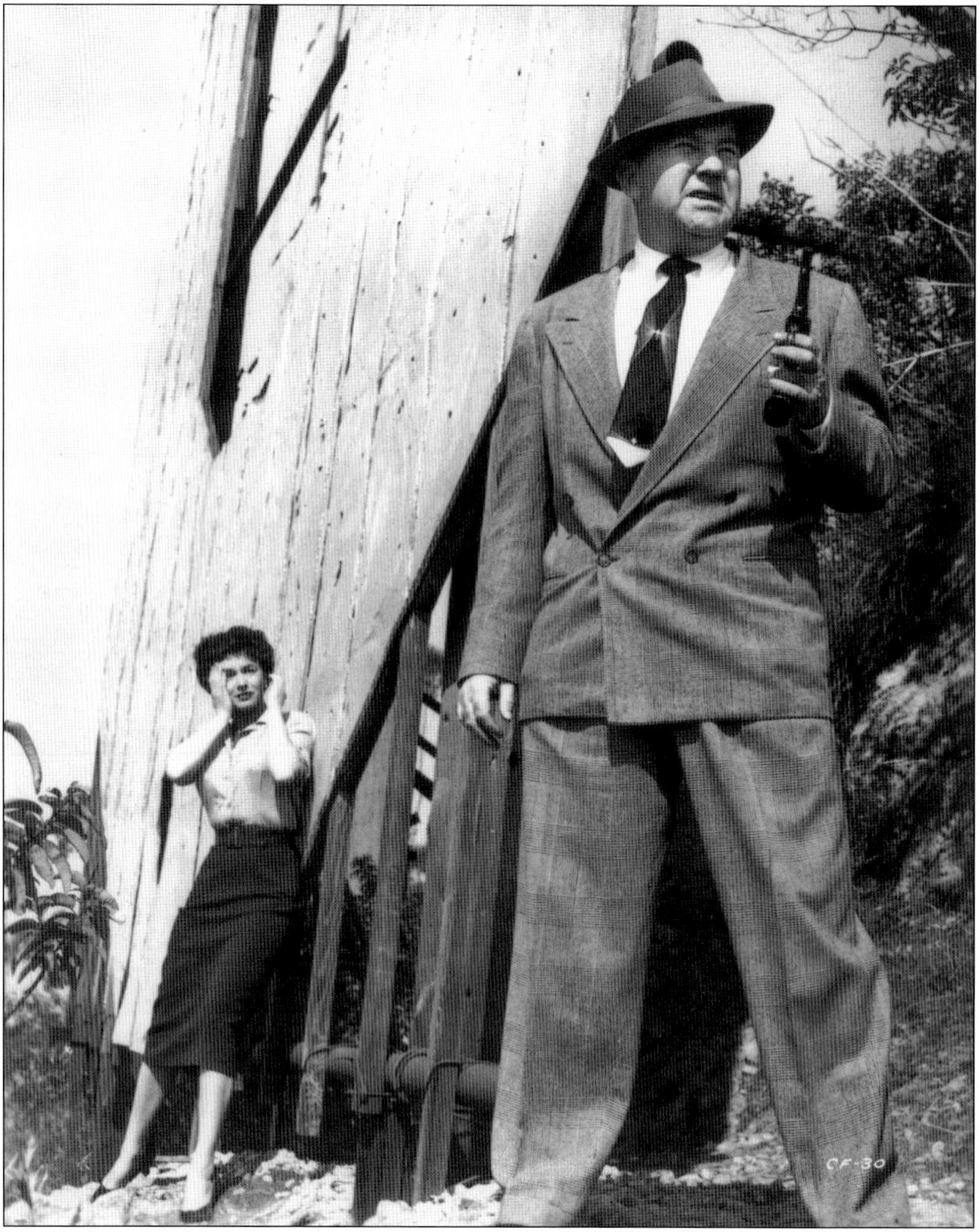

Ruth Roman and Broderick Crawford battle an assailant in front of the letter "D" in the Hollywood sign for the 1954 crime noir *Down Three Dark Streets*. As visible in the background, the sign has been graffitied and presents a false sense of security, as its framework consists of telephone poles, wires, and sheet metal. *Down Three Dark Streets* features Broderick Crawford as FBI agent John Ripley, who must investigate the three cases agent Zack Stewart (Kenneth Tobey) was working on to discover who might have killed him. The film was produced by Jules Levy, Arthur Gardner, and Edward Small and directed by Arnold Laven. It was based on a book titled *Case File: FBI*. None of the film's reviews mention the sign's appearance, though the *Hollywood Citizen News* commented that Los Angeles residents would appreciate the locales. Reviews also complimented the acting and Joseph Biroc's cinematography. (Bison.)

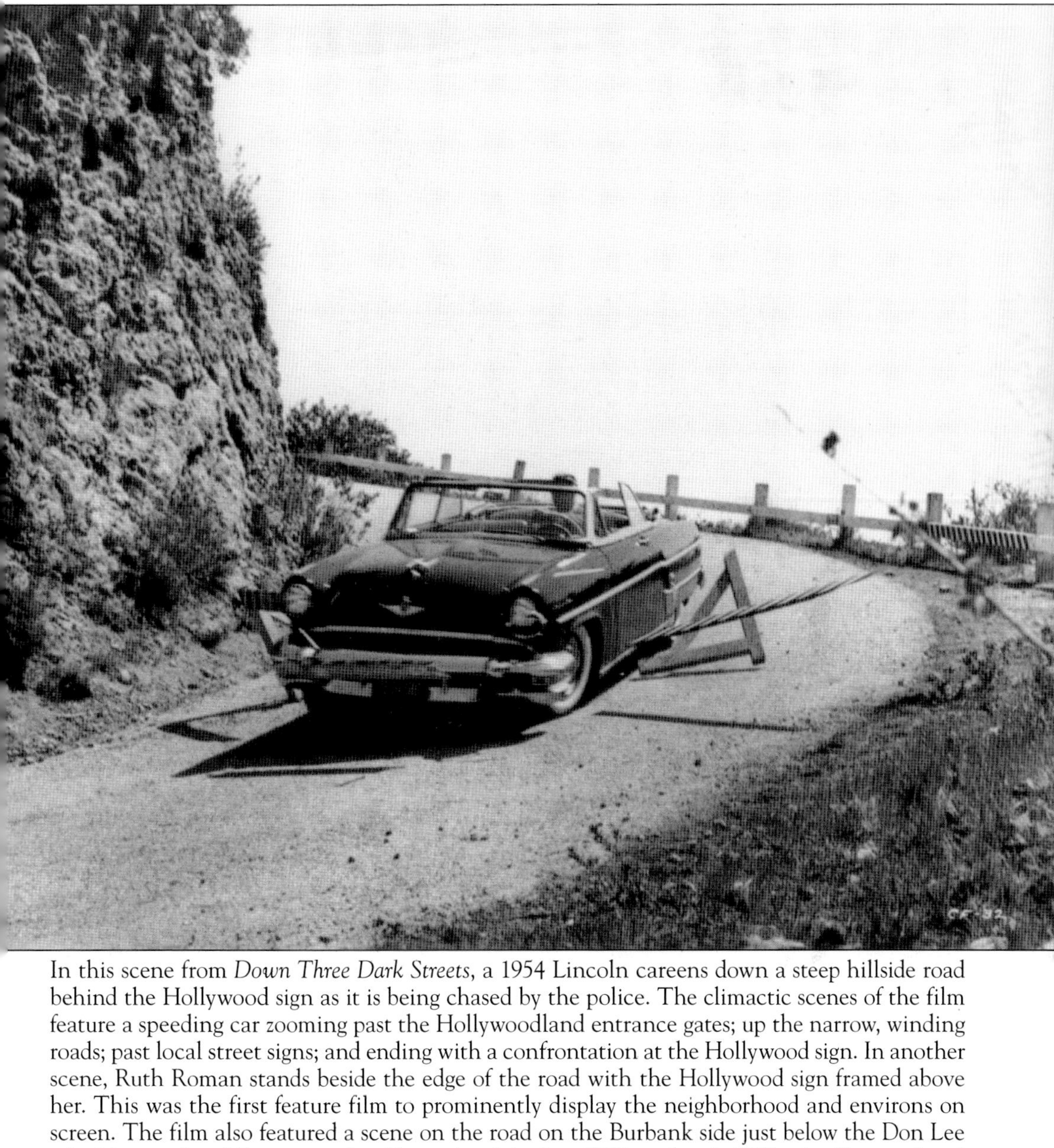

In this scene from *Down Three Dark Streets*, a 1954 Lincoln careens down a steep hillside road behind the Hollywood sign as it is being chased by the police. The climactic scenes of the film feature a speeding car zooming past the Hollywoodland entrance gates; up the narrow, winding roads; past local street signs; and ending with a confrontation at the Hollywood sign. In another scene, Ruth Roman stands beside the edge of the road with the Hollywood sign framed above her. This was the first feature film to prominently display the neighborhood and environs on screen. The film also featured a scene on the road on the Burbank side just below the Don Lee television station. Like many other film noirs of the late 1940s and early 1950s, the film employed recognizable Los Angeles locations, including Los Angeles City Hall, a Pacific Electric train tunnel, and various office buildings. (Bison.)

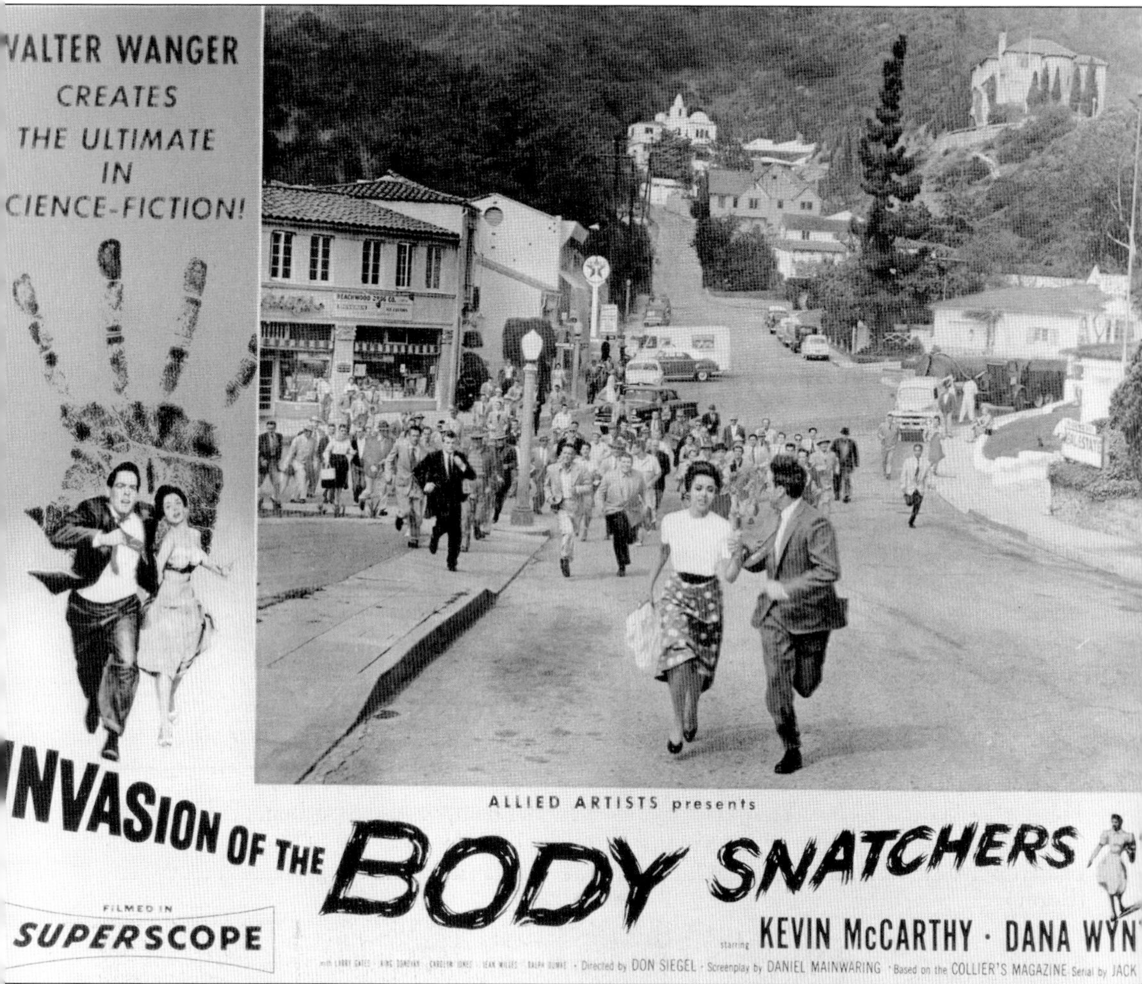

Invasion of the Body Snatchers tells the story of Dr. Bennell (Kevin McCarthy), a friendly small-town doctor who discovers strange goings-on occurring in his hometown. Once-normal people begin acting strangely and coldly, and soon the doctor finds himself and his girlfriend (Dana Wynter) threatened and pursued by emotionless replicants through the community streets. One of the first films of director Don Siegel, *Invasion of the Body Snatchers* is a creepy and compelling thriller, full of paranoia and hysteria. Many critics find it to be a metaphor for the Red Scare of the 1950s, in which mindless hordes blindly followed leaders like Sen. Joseph McCarthy, destroying the lives and careers of people who supported liberal causes or promoted better opportunities for all. The pod people determinedly chase frightened Kevin McCarthy and Dana Wynter up Westshire Drive, with the drugstore visible behind them. (Bison.)

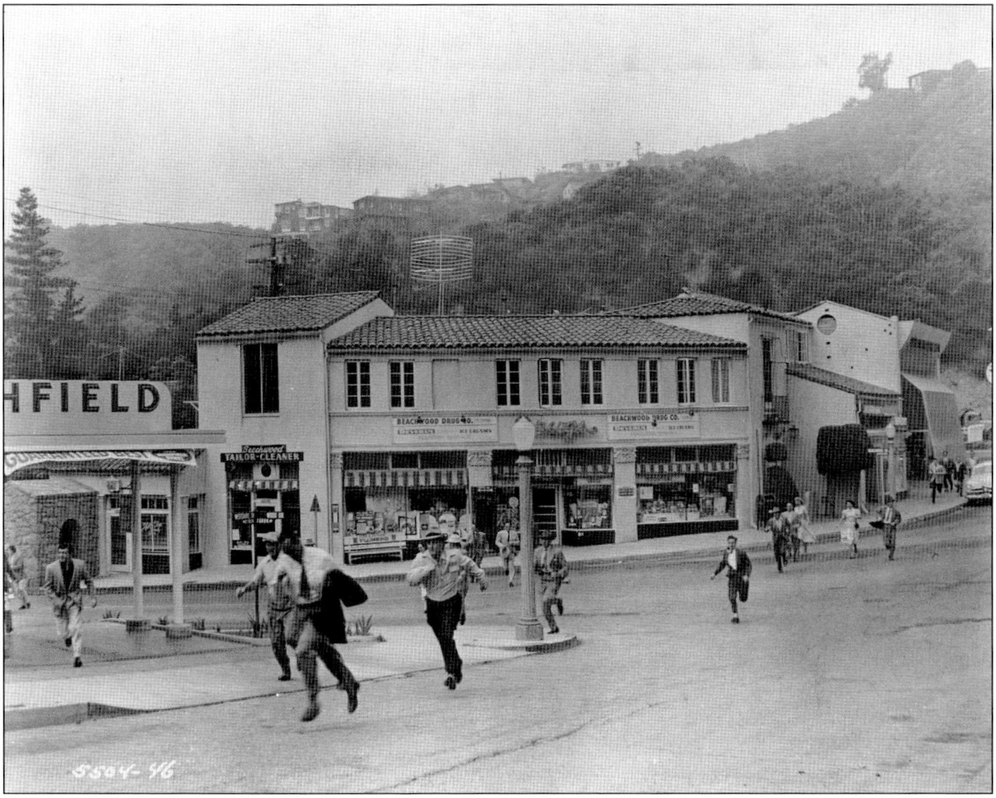

The science fiction film *Invasion of the Body Snatchers* shot many scenes throughout Hollywoodland in 1956. In this scene, zombie-like pod people pursue Dana Wynter and Kevin McCarthy from Belden Drive up Westshire Drive, past Beachwood Village shops and the gas station on the left. (Bison.)

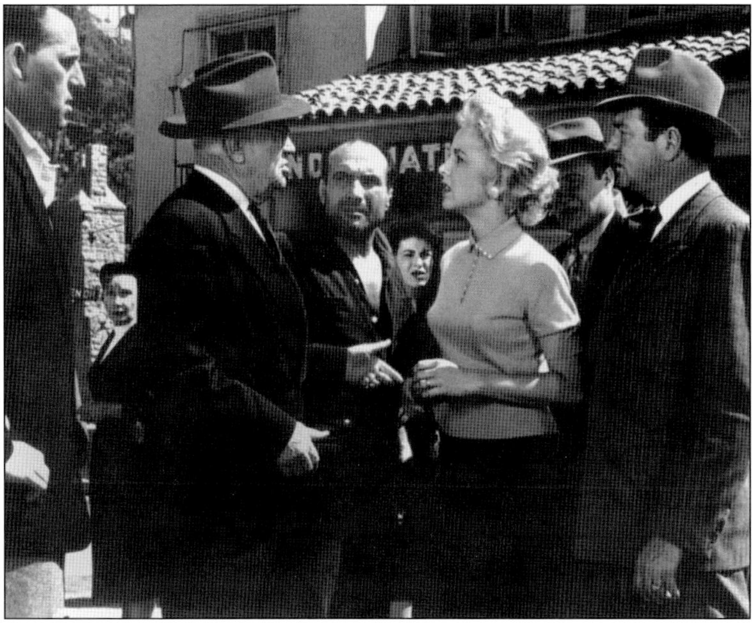

Beverly Garland and some unidentified cast members are pictured in the 1956 sci-fi film *It Conquered the World*, filming in front of the Beachwood Village Market at 2710 North Beachwood Drive. One of the Hollywoodland entrance gates can be glimpsed to the left of frame, as well as part of the Belden Drive street sign. (MM.)

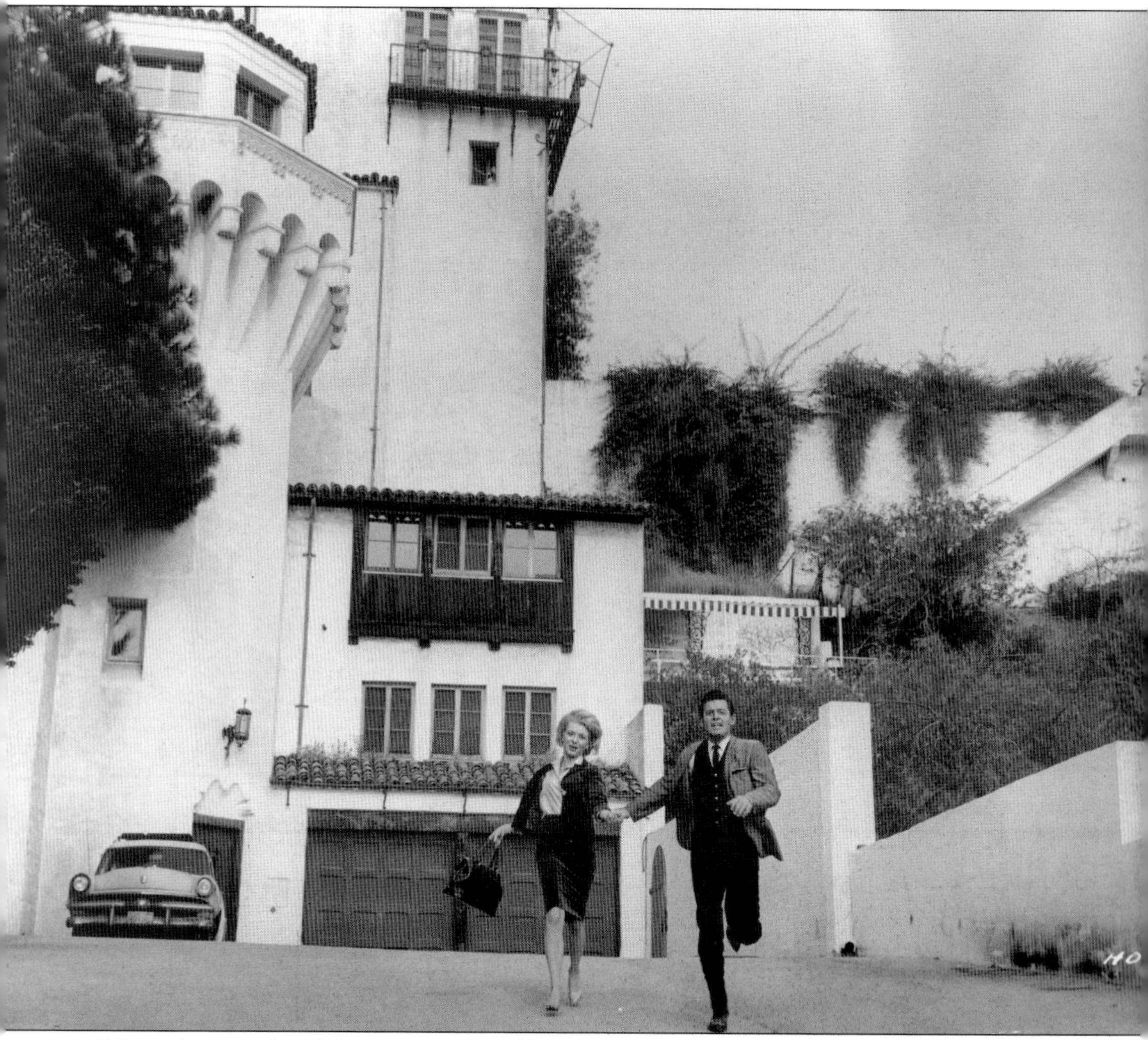

Filmmakers employed the towering Castillo del Lago as a location for the 1963 horror film *House of the Damned*. In this photograph, Merry Anders and Ronald Foster run for their lives away from the luxurious mansion. The movie tells the story of a young architect and his wife attempting to perform an architectural survey in an abandoned and notorious house in which they must spend the night. Another couple joins them, and weird and unexpected events interrupt their stay. The film was not well reviewed, with many critics calling it shockless and predictable. It was not widely released in theaters but mostly seen on television. None of the critics recognized the home or where it was located, but the journal *Films and Filming* did print, "The house, an ornate mansion in a secluded spot on the California coast, is aptly described as 'Hollywood Spanish.'" (Bison.)

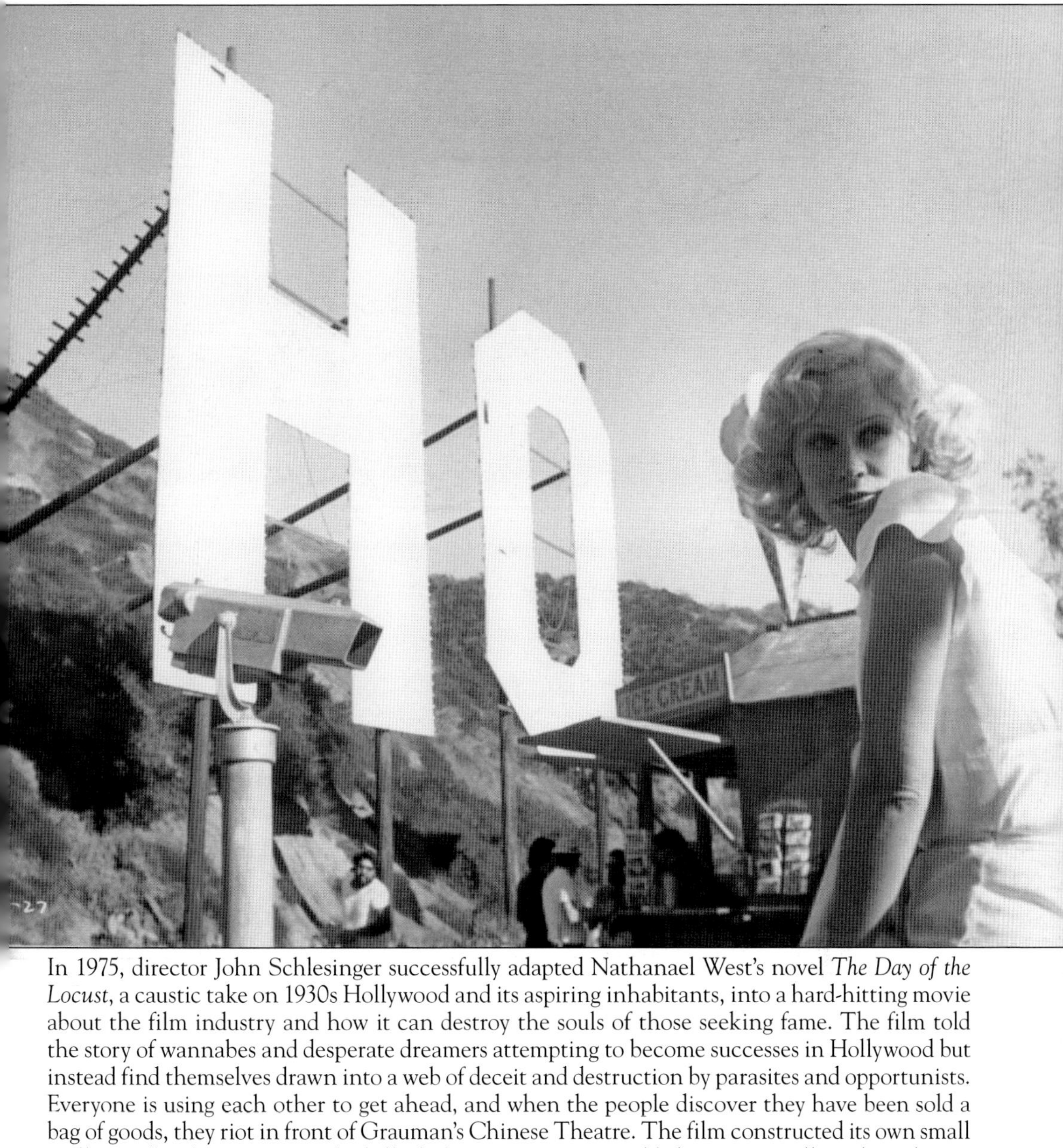

In 1975, director John Schlesinger successfully adapted Nathanael West's novel *The Day of the Locust*, a caustic take on 1930s Hollywood and its aspiring inhabitants, into a hard-hitting movie about the film industry and how it can destroy the souls of those seeking fame. The film told the story of wannabes and desperate dreamers attempting to become successes in Hollywood but instead find themselves drawn into a web of deceit and destruction by parasites and opportunists. Everyone is using each other to get ahead, and when the people discover they have been sold a bag of goods, they riot in front of Grauman's Chinese Theatre. The film constructed its own small Hollywoodland sign on a nearby hillside for an important establishing scene telling the sad story of a suicide victim similar to that of Peg Entwistle. Karen Black poses beside the sign. (Bison.)

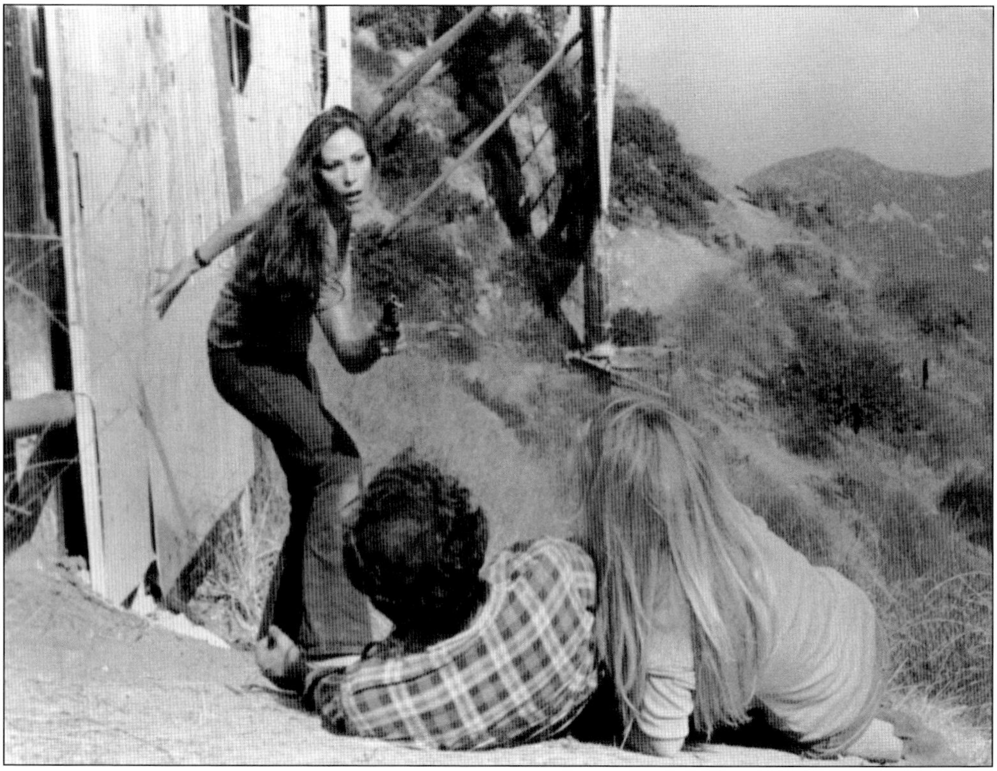

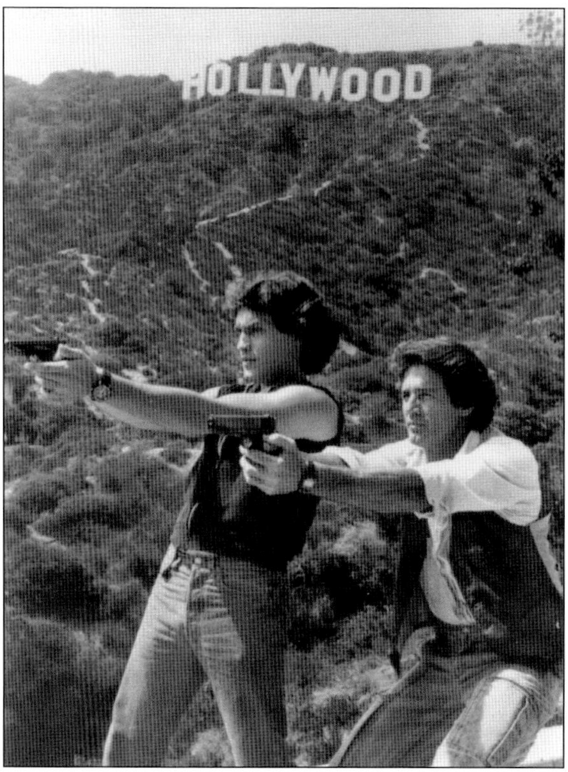

The Hollywood sign is featured in a scene with the actress Mary Woronov and two unidentified people in Joe Dante's 1976 *Hollywood Boulevard*, a hilarious homage to B filmmakers who grind out films for the struggling Miracle Pictures. In the feature, the studio ironically employs the tagline, "If it's a good picture, it's a Miracle" to sell its films. (MM.)

One of many cop shows set in Los Angeles that have shot scenes with the Hollywood sign, the Aaron Spelling television series *Hollywood Beat* filmed a dramatic shootout below it. Jack Scalia and Jay Acovone starred as detectives in the show, which lasted only 14 episodes during the 1985 season. (MM.)

BIBLIOGRAPHY

Fleming, E.J. *The Movieland Directory*. Jefferson, NC: McFarland & Company, Inc., 2004.

Lennig, Arthur. *Count: The Life and Films of Bela "Dracula" Lugosi*. New York: Putnam, 1974.

The Los Angeles Times. 1895–1978.

Palmer, E.O. *History of Hollywood*. Hollywood, CA: A.H. Cawston, 1937.

Pitt, Leonard and Dale. *Los Angeles A to Z: An Encyclopedia of the City and County*. Berkeley: University of California Press, 1997.

Ralston, Esther. *Some Day We'll Laugh: An Autobiography*. Metuchen, NY: Scarecrow Press, 1985.

Spencer, Charles. *Erté*. New York: C.N. Potter, 1970.

Torrence, Bruce T. *Hollywood: The First 100 Years*. Hollywood, CA: Hollywood Chamber of Commerce, 1979.

Walker, Brent E. *Mack Sennett's Fun Factory: A History and Filmography of His Studio and His Keystone Personnel*. Jefferson, NC: McFarland & Company, Inc., 2010.

Watters, Sam. *Houses of Los Angeles*. New York: Acanthus Press, 2007.

Williams, Gregory Paul. *The Story of Hollywood: An Illustrated History*. Los Angeles: BL Press, LLC, 2005.

Williams, Greg. *The Story of Hollywoodland, Established 1923*. CA: Papavasilopoulos Press, 1992.

Discover Thousands of Local History Books Featuring Millions of Vintage Images

Arcadia Publishing, the leading local history publisher in the United States, is committed to making history accessible and meaningful through publishing books that celebrate and preserve the heritage of America's people and places.

Find more books like this at
www.arcadiapublishing.com

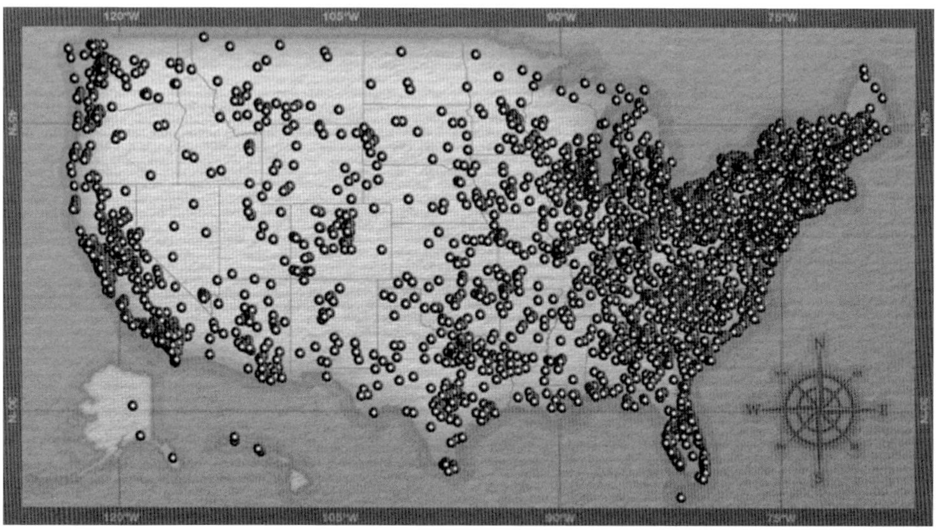

Search for your hometown history, your old stomping grounds, and even your favorite sports team.

Consistent with our mission to preserve history on a local level, this book was printed in South Carolina on American-made paper and manufactured entirely in the United States. Products carrying the accredited Forest Stewardship Council (FSC) label are printed on 100 percent FSC-certified paper.

MADE IN THE USA